Rhodes
&
More Rhodes Around Britain

Special omnibus edition of
Rhodes Around Britain
and
More Rhodes Around Britain

Rhodes
Around Britain

Gary Rhodes

Photographs by Anthony Blake

To my wife Jenny
and my sons
Samuel and George

Acknowledgements

Thank you to everyone who has supported me during the writing of this book,
and in particular: David Levin, my boss; Sue Fleming for all her advice;
Anthony Blake and Joy Skipper for making the photography fun; Nicky
Copeland for putting up with me; Clare Adkins for all her typing; and my
sous-chefs and all the team. And finally, a very special thank you to my parents
for their help and encouragement over the years.

Family and friends in the photographs: Stuart, Elinor and Louella Busby; Alan
and Diane Jefford; Gary, Babette and Amy Oliver; Jenny, Samuel and George
Rhodes; Christopher and Susan Rhodes; Keith Wyatt.

This edition produced for
The Book People Ltd
Guardian House
Borough Road
Godalming
Surrey GU7 2AE
by BBC Books,
an imprint of BBC Worldwide Publishing,
BBC Worldwide Ltd, Woodlands, 80 Wood Lane,
London W12 0TT

First published 1994

© Gary Rhodes 1994

Designed by Tim Higgins
Illustrations by Kate Simunek
Photographs © Anthony Blake
Styling by Anthony Blake and Joy Skipper
Food prepared by Gary Rhodes
Cutlery and crockery provided by Villeroy and Boch

Set in Monotype Ehrhardt and Ellington
by Selwood Systems, Midsomer Norton
Printed and bound in Great Britain by Butler & Tanner Ltd, Frome and London
Colour separation by Radstock Reproductions Ltd, Midsomer Norton
Jacket printed by Lawrence Allen Ltd, Weston-super-Mare
Cover printed by Clays Ltd, St Ives plc

Contents

Introduction

O, scent of the daubes [stews] of my childhood!

During the holidays, at Gémeaux, in the month of August, when we arrived in my grandmother's dark kitchen on Sunday after Vespers, it was lit by a ray of sunshine in which the dust and the flies were dancing, and there was a sound like a little bubbling spring. It was a daube, which since midday had been murmuring gently on the stove, giving out sweet smells which brought tears to your eyes. Thyme, rosemary, bay leaves, spices, the wine of the marinade, and the fumet [bouquet] of the meat were becoming transformed under the magic wand which is the fire, into a delicious whole, which was served about seven o'clock in the evening, so well cooked and so tender that it was carved with a spoon.

Don't you feel inspired by those words? You can see the bubbling pot, smell the richness of the sauce, and 'taste' the texture of it. Every time I read this I start to feel hungry and want to cook something. I think the late and great Elizabeth David must have felt the same, for she quoted it in her wonderful book, *French Provincial Cooking*. That was first published in 1960, and the book from which she took the quote – *Les Meilleures Recettes de ma Pauvre Mère*, by Pierre Huguenin – was published in 1936. Those words, written two generations before my own, characterize to me everything that cooking should be – full of honesty and simplicity, and using one of the finest, possibly *the* finest, techniques of cookery, good old-fashioned stewing. I'm sure somewhere in France today there are still *daubes* bubbling in pots until the meat is so tender it can be carved with a spoon. And that's the difference between the French and the British: the French have never forgotten their traditions.

So what happened to us? Was it that the traditions weren't strong or numerous enough? Or that we just didn't have the passion for food and cooking that we associate with the French and Italians? Probably, on reflection, a combination of all these.

OPPOSITE
I've always enjoyed creating a stir with my cooking.

British cookery had always been simple – with wonderful ingredients like our own beef, which didn't need anything more fancy than just roasting. The British always wanted everything to taste of exactly what it was, so there were no rich complementary sauces, or tricksy combinations of foods. It was a question of featuring the main ingredient and achieving the very best taste with it. Perhaps when nothing much had changed for hundreds of years, the passion for the dish and for the art was lost.

Our cooking by the early to mid 1970s consisted of well-done roast beef, soggy Yorkshire puddings, mostly served with over-cooked cabbage and thick, floury gravy. It was when *nouvelle cuisine* hit these shores that I believe we finally lost the confidence in our own traditions and techniques, and dropped them in favour of the new ideas. The principles of the new cooking (the literal translation of *nouvelle cuisine*) had already existed in France for many years. The most renowned of modern French chefs, Fernand Point, had led a whole brigade of famous chefs – Paul Bocuse and Alain Chapel among them – away from the heavy and tyrannical traditions of classical French cookery as characterized by Escoffier. Point believed – as we in Britain once did – that flavour was of prime importance, that chicken should taste of chicken, and needn't be disguised.

However, we first encountered *nouvelle cuisine* in the form of *cuisine minceur*, food for slimmers and for health introduced by Michel Guérard, the three-Michelin-starred chef of Eugénie les Bains. We made a mistake yet again. Instead of embracing the true principles of the new French cooking, we thought the Guérard alternative was what it was all about – light, pretty, and not very much of it. We dropped everything that was British and combined all sorts of new flavours and ingredients to make small pictures on large plates, to make a riot of colour rather than big tastes. (The roast beef, stews and dumplings became foods to feed the staff!)

British chefs copied the Troisgros brothers' modern classics, such as duck breasts with blackcurrants. Fish would be served with two or three different sauces, and decorated with half a dozen sprigs of chervil or chives. Looking back at that *nouvelle* period, I can remember that, for most chefs, cooking consisted of pan-fried medallions of pork, veal or beef, or chicken breasts, served with kiwi fruit or raspberries.

Sadly, a lot of this still exists now, but I think we needed something new. We needed to think again about the flavours and textures of foods, and to reconsider our presentation – never one of our strong points. I certainly passed through this phase, believing I was a culinary artist, and that tiny crayfish garnishing each fish dish was the ultimate in modern cookery.

However, we'd missed the boat in more than one way. Even in the Troisgros' books and restaurant, the old dishes still existed alongside the new. They still cooked their boiled bacons and hams, and beef and lamb stews, whereas we had foolishly left all that behind. They still cherished their traditions. And it is those basic methods of classic cookery – whether French or British – that I believe are the essence of good cooking, and they are the backbone of my cooking today. Many other chefs in Britain have been re-assessing their own basic skills and their own heritage, but too many are still over-elaborating. Good food doesn't need elaboration. Good tastes simply need loving care.

Early Days

So how did I come to cooking? Well, as a young boy, I'd never thought of becoming a chef. I'd always wanted either to play for Manchester United (who doesn't?) or be a policeman. They say that most things start in the home. Well, that's exactly where it all started for me.

I must have been about fourteen or fifteen at the time. Because my mother and older brother, Christopher, were at work all day, someone had to look after my younger sister, Cheryl, during the school holidays, and it was up to me. And so the cooking started: something simple for lunch, a sandwich perhaps (I was hooked on cheese, tomato and pickle for years!), and something more filling for tea, or vice versa.

We'd always been brought up on good home cooking – home-made pies, roasts, stews and even a lovely corned beef hash. In fact, I think most people were then; there certainly wasn't the variety of ready-prepared foods we have now. My mother always insisted on fresh meat and vegetables, and her stews were the ones I remembered when reading the quote at the beginning, to be followed by her *pièce de résistance*, sherry trifle.

My cooking was a lot more basic – every now and again it would even be a tinned steak and kidney pie. My first real dish was shepherd's pie: cooked mince with carrots, onions and gravy topped with mashed potatoes – a complete meal. It became a regular favourite, with a few additions – baked beans or peas, and the potatoes topped with sliced tomatoes and glazed with grated Cheddar until golden brown. It was delicious; a very ordinary, everyday meal, but it gave me the inspiration to want to cook.

Another early passion was for my Uncle George's toasted cheese sandwiches. We've been trying for years to get the exact recipe out of him, but he's guarding the secret closely. Basically, it was grated onion and cheese, some mayonnaise to bind, with black pepper and mustard, I think, spread on toast and grilled. The taste was sensational, and very much another part of my culinary childhood. I would always try to re-create the sandwich at home; it was never quite the same, but those memories probably led me on to using a Welsh rarebit topping with smoked haddock. (I'm still very keen on toasted sandwiches as well.)

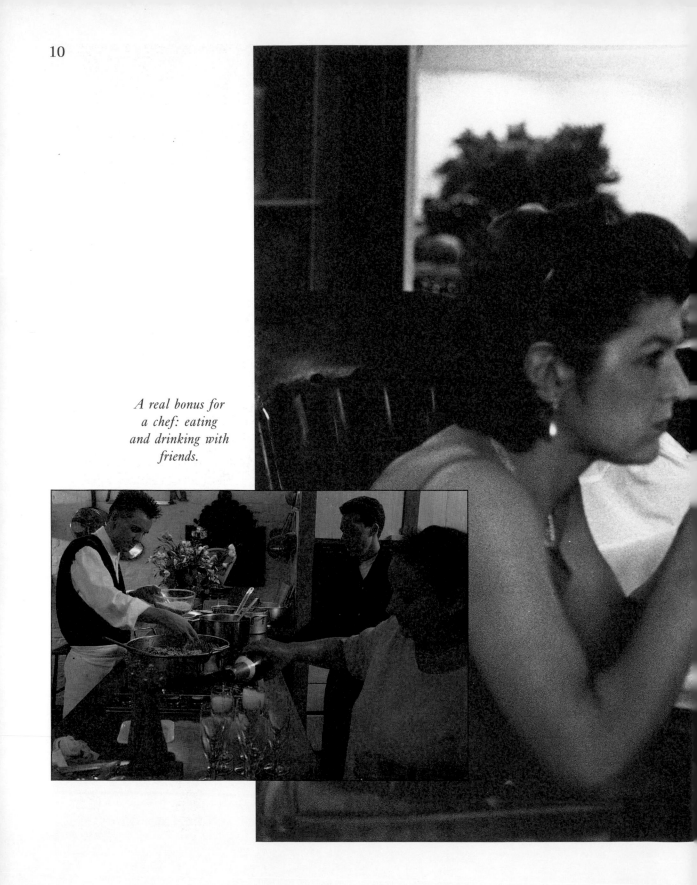

A real bonus for a chef: eating and drinking with friends.

So the next move was to cook for the whole family, and what could have been better than the traditional Sunday lunch? Roast beef, lamb or pork with roast potatoes and fresh vegetables: this was quite a tall order – and on top of that a pudding! The first pudding I made was a steamed lemon sponge with lemon sauce. I'd taken the recipe from one of my mother's cookery books and followed it step by step: weighing everything, stirring, folding, re-stirring, tasting, checking all the time. In one of today's modern food processors it would probably be all mixed and made in two or three minutes, but I doubt I would have been so proud and happy with the result.

The pudding was a huge success: a light sponge with a sharp lemon taste, and a warm, rich sauce. When you make a dish for the first time and it works, it never seems to work or taste as well on the second, third or any other attempt. We all think that the first one is in a league of its own.

I'm sure that lemon sponge changed my mind about being a policeman and I was certainly never going to make it as a footballer! It was cooking that I wanted to do. But how was I to go about it?

The First Steps

I didn't have the remotest idea. So my mother and I investigated over a few weeks and we heard about Thanet Technical College in Broadstairs, which was about three-quarters of an hour by train from our home in Gillingham. I applied for a general catering course which would teach me about kitchens, restaurants and management, giving me a lot more choices in the industry.

I was interviewed and accepted. It was 1976, I was sixteen years old, and ready to go. The new students were easy to spot – floppy chef's hats, trousers three inches too long and aprons so crisp they could stand up on their own! It really was quite frightening; you know nobody and virtually nothing. In one of my first lessons, we were asked what a béchamel sauce was. Well, I didn't have a clue, but quite a few hands went up. One in particular belonged to Martin, who seemed to know a lot more than most of us, and he soon became the natural leader of the class.

As time went by, I realized that cooking was all I wanted to do, and as I learned more, my confidence grew. Towards the end of my first year, I wanted to lead the class and was determined to get there. Second best wasn't going to be good enough.

The style of cooking taught at Thanet was very traditional, very Escoffier, but I shall always value those three years. It was there that I learned all the basics that are so important to good, creative cooking – the stocks, sauces, the braising, pot-roasting and stewing, etc. – and I don't think I could have had a better training. It was there, too, that I learned how to make ingredients work together to create the flavours and smells that are the foundation of delicious dishes.

To boost my confidence during that first year, I took over virtually all the cooking at home, and I still remember cooking my first Christmas lunch for the family. It was all very traditional – turkey, chestnut stuffing, bread sauce, gravy and vegetables. I was a little more adventurous with some of the potatoes, mashing them and piping them into little nests filled with Provençale tomatoes. I made my own Christmas pudding as well, and it was all a huge success. I felt such a great sense of achievement.

After a couple of terms at college, the class was divided up into groups, each to have a speciality and each to have a leader (a *chef de partie* in the professional kitchen). I was put on to the sauce section, and I was the leader. There I was, full of myself, telling everyone what to do, and my course was set.

Things were looking up in other directions, too. My mother had happily re-married (I later gained another sister, Anna), and in my second year I began cooking dinner parties for them and their friends. I'd got a little more ambitious by then, and my favourite dish was pheasant *à la Souvaroff*. The bird was stuffed with pâté instead of the foie gras and truffles, then pot-roasted in brandy and Madeira in an earthenware dish sealed with a flour and water paste. When that seal was broken, the smell was immense, very rich and absolutely delicious. I would follow that with *omelette à la norvégienne* (baked Alaska) or *crêpes Suzette* – nothing simple! I liked the first especially – sponge, fruit and ice-cream topped with meringue and baked only until the meringue had become golden and set. I would put a little dish on top filled with cherries in Kirsch and flambée them. The tastes were there, and so were the flames, so it was re-christened omelette Vesuvius!

My parents' friends must have been impressed because soon I was cooking for them. I loved the pressure – the food had to be right, the timing had to be right. Best of all, I was learning and gaining confidence, achieving a sense of self-worth. This reflected in my work in college, and I started to do a lot better – so much so that at the end of my second year I was the student of the year, and one of my ambitions was already fulfilled.

My next ambition was to be selected for the third-year advanced cookery course, and I was. For the first time I used things like beef fillet and *foie gras*. I was taught how to recognize textures, tastes, seasonings and the richness of finished flavours. The tutors were really passionate about their cooking, and if you showed enthusiasm you were given all the help you needed. I learned a bit about sugar work, too, and how to bake bread, and widened my repertoire considerably. We all entered cookery competitions (a sort of culinary olympics), and did well, and we thought we were the *crème de la crème*. I was even more convinced of my starry future when I'd finished the course. Not only did I pick up the chef of the year award, but also the student of the year award. Perhaps the most important acquisition from college was my wife, Jenny. She couldn't bear me for the first couple of years, then eventually came to her senses! We've been together since 1979, but only married in 1989 – we had to be sure . . . .

To sum up, those years at Thanet gave me all the basic knowledge I needed to enable me to pursue my career successfully. It was because of those years that I'm cooking what I'm cooking today. I've since been through all the trends and fashions – been there, seen it and done it – but I've only 'come home' again, in a way.

My First Job

I left college with all those awards under my belt, feeling the world was my oyster. In my very first job, I was to discover that I had a lot more to learn!

All the lecturers had suggested we go to the Savoy, the Berkeley, Claridges and all the other top London hotels. However, I was determined to go abroad. The really famous names at the time were Bocuse, Guérard, Troisgros, Chapel etc., and the cookery world had begun to be dominated by *cuisines nouvelle*, *minceur*, *gourmande* etc., all coming from France. I wrote off to many famous chefs, hotels and restaurants throughout France, and I've still got all the 'thanks but no thanks' letters.

I decided that working for a hotel group might be one way of getting myself to foreign parts, so I wrote to many Hiltons throughout Europe. Amsterdam was the first to say yes, and although Paris and Zurich also offered me places, I'd already accepted the Dutch offer. So off I went to Amsterdam, leaving behind Jenny and my friends, and thought to myself – here I am, ready to show them all.

Working in a top-class hotel restaurant kitchen was a revelation. On my second day there, I found produce that I'd never seen or even heard of – kiwi fruit, finger bananas, yellow, black and white peppers, and all the varieties of wild mushrooms – and although I'd never seen a fresh truffle before, now they were arriving in virtual lorry-loads daily. I was learning all over again. Should I have ever *been* to college, or just started from scratch in a kitchen such as this? It's only now that I've realized that if I hadn't been to college, I would have a very limited range of skills. I would know how to grill, pan-fry, poach perhaps – all methods of the modern *nouvelle* kitchen – but I doubt I would have seen all the basics which are so important to me now.

The Amsterdam Hilton's newest *commis* (chef's assistant) really thought that he should be a *chef de partie* (he *had* been chef of the year at college, after all), but he soon realized why he wasn't. I was put in the larder, on the starter section for the first few days, and then it was on to the coffee shop. This was busy all day. On my own, I turned out mixed salads galore, *croques-monsieurs* by the dozen, untold numbers of club sandwiches as well as all the Dutch specialities – smoked eel salad, soused herrings and *uitsmijters* (buttered slices of bread topped with cheese, ham or beef, and finished with fried eggs). You are always under pressure on this section. The orders keep coming and you've got to keep running. But I would never accept any help; I had to do it on my own. A club sandwich wasn't going to beat me. However, the chef seemed happy, and so was I.

Things were going well, I was moving from section to section, and the hotel was almost Thanet College all over again. Jenny had joined me, Martin had arrived, and eventually there were five of us there.

After about a year, we had a new head chef, Graham Cadman, who was to be a great influence on me. I told him I wanted to be a *chef de partie* instead of a *commis*. He listened, but he made me work for it. I was put in charge of the sauce section, but still with the rank and pay of a *commis*, and 'tested' for three months. I got the job, and happily stayed on for another year.

Nouvelle cuisine was at its height then, and we would get quite carried away, often making dishes up as we went along. We garnished everything in sight, and painted as many pictures on plates as there were Dutch masters in the Rijksmuseum. We thought we were sensational.

After two and a half years, a move seemed in order, so both Jenny and I approached and were accepted by the new Hilton Hotel in Strasbourg. We were due to start there in March 1982, but when a friend asked me to join him at a new restaurant opening in Bournemouth, I changed my mind. All I could see was superstardom at home. (I *was* still only twenty-one or so, after all!)

Back in Britain

After a couple of months in this new restaurant, I started to wish I'd listened to Graham Cadman's warnings. Things weren't going to work, so it was time to move on again.

Where was I going to go? What was I going to do? My mother came up with a suggestion.

OVERLEAF
The working kitchen.

'The Connaught's the place to be,' she said, so I wrote to Michel Bourdin. It worked. He offered me the job as *demi-chef de partie*. I was delighted. My brother then told me of a job at the Reform Club in Pall Mall. At twenty-one, I knew I wasn't ready for a *sous-chef*'s job, but I thought I'd take a look anyway. I got it, and turned down the Connaught (silly boy). I was far too young, but I liked the challenge. Jenny started with me, and we stayed there for about a year.

For the first couple of months there was no head chef, so I was cooking squab pigeons with wild strawberries and chervil, all kinds of mousses and fruit plates. They looked lovely, but didn't really eat well at all. I constantly sought out those sweetnesses which every English chef seemed to think characterized *nouvelle*. A new head chef arrived, Mark Streeter, and he brought us back to real cooking. I was reminded of asparagus, tripe and onions, braised chump chops and all those basic skills which I'd neglected over the previous few years. Even though it might have seemed mad to have turned down the Connaught, the Reform Club got me thinking again.

My next step was brief, but had its effect. One of the vegetable suppliers at the Reform told me about a job going in a restaurant in Coptic Street called Winston's Eating House. I went there as head chef. The food was very English – steak and kidney puddings, sausages and mash etc. – but I was still playing with nouvelle salads with mangetouts and beans, or crayfish and artichokes, and other tricksy dishes. It was a mixture of many things. It was good, too, to make steak and oyster pies, summer puddings and beef stews. Jenny was with me and Martin joined us. There were five of us ultimately, with me running the show. It was all very exciting.

Another of the vegetable suppliers at Winston's told me he was coming to eat, and was bringing as his guest Brian Turner, chef at the Capital Hotel in Knightsbridge. I didn't have a clue who he was, but after a few ventures into food guides, I was on cloud nine. The Capital had a Michelin star, one of the few restaurants in Britain with that accolade, and Brian Turner became an instant hero. When he came, he obviously enjoyed his meal, but I must admit he looked a little suspicious when I appeared in earrings and Duran Duran haircut.

A few days later Brian Turner asked me to go and meet him. He said his *sous-chef* was leaving and that he would like me to think about taking the job. An answer in a couple of days would be fine. Two days later I accepted the job.

From Capital to Country

Things were really looking up, and I think it was then that everything began to change for me. It was all still full of surprises, too. The first person I met in the Capital kitchen was Mark Clayton, a *sous-chef* who had been at Thanet. I didn't know him then, but we recognized each other instantly, and have since become the closest of friends.

It was 1983, *nouvelle* was still flourishing, and here I was joining a Michelin-starred restaurant. I expected to find pretty pictures on plates, but it was good, honest French cooking – best end of lamb roasted with a herb crust, and *dauphinoise* potatoes: the lamb was cooked to perfection, with a crisp crust, and the potatoes had just the right texture. This was real cooking, and that people wanted to eat it was proved by the numbers of diners who returned again and again to enjoy the same things.

I stayed at the Capital for about eighteen months, and that, too, was an extremely valuable time. Brian Turner's cooking was probably the most reliable and real cooking around then, and he taught me that the simplest of foods and techniques can result in classy flavours. I also learned from him how to *run* a kitchen, and that it could be a happy place, not one ruled purely by temperament.

I then ventured into a new restaurant opening in Essex, and tried to bring the Capital to the country. I stayed about a year, but began to feel out of touch, so I returned to Brian. While there, I was told of a head chef's job in Taunton, at the Castle Hotel. I was put in touch with Kit Chapman and he asked me to meet him one day at the Inn on the Park in London. He owned the Castle and his head chef, Chris Oakes, was leaving. We met at three one Saturday afternoon, and were still talking enthusiastically about food and the future at seven in the evening – is this a record for an interview? The first question was the testing one: 'How would you feel, Gary, about putting Lancashire Hot-pot on the menu at the Castle?' To be honest, I was a little shocked – a hot-pot in a Michelin-starred restaurant? It didn't sound quite right, but I thought quickly, and said, 'Yes, of course, I would, it's a great classic dish.' It was the right answer, and I got the job. By the early evening, we'd virtually got the whole lunchtime and dinner menus planned.

Before starting in Taunton, Kit organized for me to work with Peter Kromberg at the Inter-Continental Hotel in London. It was only for a couple of weeks, but gave me an insight into the running of a large hotel. I'm convinced he is the master of executive chefs in hotels, the whole operation ran so smoothly.

It was June 1986 when I started. There were already a few Great British Classics on the menu, and I was there to take over and keep them going. It wasn't easy, but as time went on, I became convinced this was the direction in which to be moving. These dishes were so exciting, and for me the revival of braising, stewing and pot-roasting had truly begun.

That Michelin star was quite a responsibility. I feel you are obliged to produce what *they* want, not necessarily what you or the customer want. So we kept lobster, venison, sea bass and fillet of beef dishes on the *à la carte* dinner menus, and ventured wholeheartedly into the British dishes at lunchtimes. We had a different roast every day, and plenty of daily British specials – calves' liver and bacon, salmon fish cakes, steak and kidney pudding and, of course, bread and butter pudding.

I loved it all, and it wasn't just the dishes that changed. This was my first real head chef post, and so I was able to take a look at the very essence of all our cooking, the making of the stocks and sauces. It's something I learned then, and I now always teach it to the keen young cooks coming into my kitchen. A good stock is not made just by throwing bones and vegetables into a pan and boiling in water for a couple of hours; that will have some flavour, but will probably be cloudy and lack texture and the real depth of flavour necessary. I slow-roasted halves of unpeeled onions until their juices and sugars caramelized, and used these as the basis for the stock. The idea wasn't new, but I'd improved on the quick searing of an onion, which can lead to bitter flavours. My basic stock was born, and it soon became a three-day event, and still is.

I thought in Taunton that I had achieved everything I'd wanted. I was a Michelin-starred chef (I'd retained the star), and I had Jenny and our first son, Samuel (later to be joined by George). I'd also enjoyed the trip of a lifetime, arranged by Graham Cadman, my old chef from Amsterdam. I cooked braised oxtail and mashed potato in the searing heat of Singapore for two weeks as a promotion – and they loved it!

On my return to England, it was still the British Revival that interested me. Once again outside circumstances were to lead to my next move. The Chapman family were looking to sell the hotel, and I wasn't going to stay after they'd gone. At a function in London I met David Levin, who owned and had been my boss at the Capital. He knew about the Castle plans, and asked what I was going to do. I wasn't sure, and he replied, 'You never know, Gary, it may lead you straight back to me.' With Phillip Britten running the Capital, that left the Greenhouse restaurant in Mayfair, where Jenny had been *sous-chef* while I was at the Capital. It had been open for some fourteen or fifteen years, and was very busy, and I was offered the position of head chef. I was a little dubious at first – did I really want to come back to London? Did I want to be cooking for so many people each day? However, what really sealed the whole arrangement for me was that the boss wanted exactly what I wanted to do, to return to honest, basic food – the revival of the Great British Classics.

Back in London

With completely new kitchens and a new menu, we opened. The Great British Classics – faggots, fish cakes, boiled bacon, cod and parsley, oxtails – were back in town. We have enjoyed an amazing success. In 1991, we were voted *The Times'* Restaurant of the Year by one of my favourite food writers, Jonathan Meades. He always writes about what he finds and feels, which is exactly the way that I cook. He had already eaten my food at the Castle, and I just knew, when I saw the order in the Greenhouse kitchen for faggots as a starter, followed by braised oxtail and bread and butter pudding, that it had to be him! The fact that he was testing my faggots again confirmed to me that, once having achieved a high standard, that standard has to be maintained and developed.

And that's what I've been striving for ever since. The core of my menu will aways be the same five or so of my dishes, my signature dishes. I always want people to come back time and time again to eat those dishes because they like them, and because they are so consistent. The pressed duck at Le Tour d'Argent in Paris is probably the most famous dish in France, so why shouldn't my faggots or oxtails be the talk of London? Consistency, I truly believe, is the real key to success.

These dishes are mostly British in origin, and I'm proud of the part I've played in reviving them. There's a huge tradition out there, from north to south, and east to west, and the ingredients to match it. The dishes are honest and simple, with real and delicious flavours – much more satisfying to cook than a pan-fried chicken breast or veal medallion. They're also economical, because I believe you don't have to save or spend a fortune to eat good food. That's another one of my 'rules': along with simple dishes and honest flavours, you must offer value for money.

Neither does good eating involve constantly dreaming up new ideas. You should cook what you believe in, and what you enjoy. This will surprise a few other chefs, but I'm not afraid of putting baked beans on toast on the menu, or hamburgers and onions. They're all home-made, of course, and I believe that's what people want – something simple, something they know they like, something they know their *children* will like. I've even made the infamous knickerbocker glory, but all I've really done is arrange what

OVERLEAF
*My two young chefs, Samuel, right,
and George, left.*

other chefs might call *Assiette de sorbet de framboises et glace de vanille au coulis de fruits rouges* in a glass instead of like a picture on a plate. And it's much more fun to eat!

I don't just stop at British dishes. A lot of my favourite recipes are French, Italian and Eastern in origin, as most of them are just too good to ignore. There's the French *confit* of duck and *crème brûlée* (although some food historians would insist that the latter was originally Britain's 'burnt cream'), Italian *carpaccio* of beef, *risotto* and *gnocchi*, and Mediterranean cod *brandade* and *tapenade*. These, I think, are part of the same national culinary traditions as British dishes.

Cooking has been a passion for me ever since my teens, and I do believe that to do it well you have to do it from the heart. You have to look at what's available – the produce – and be inspired by it. In Britain, everybody should be so inspired, because there are so many delicious ingredients: the fish from Scotland, the puddings and sausages of the north, the cheeses and pasties from the west, the fruits of the east and the lamb of the south. I think we should revive scrumping for fruits! Well, perhaps not, but when we've bought a couple of pounds of damsons, apples or cherries, instead of eating them just as fruits, why not save some and make them into a home-made pie, and serve it with thick double cream. It's going to be a lot tastier than buying a ready-made pie – and so much cheaper as well.

Over 90 per cent of the recipes in this book are perfectly easy to prepare at home and they use ingredients which are readily available. I hope that they will help inspire you to cook, and that they will make producing delicious dishes much less hard work. I've explored many avenues during my career, but I'm now wedded to the many interesting culinary roads that are our heritage in Britain. Bread and butter pudding, for instance, has become a classic of today, but it was always made from the waste of yesterday. So remember, let's not lose what has been achieved, let's revive what has been lost.

Good luck.

GARY RHODES

Notes on the Recipes

1 Follow one set of measurements only, do not mix metric and imperial.

2 Eggs are size 2.

3 Wash fresh produce before preparation.

4 Spoon measurements are level.

5 A tablespoon is 15 ml; a teaspoon is 5 ml.

6 If you substitute dried for fresh herbs, use only half the amount specified.

7 Mixed herb tea bags are readily available and can be used as an alternative to bouquet garni.

8 Unless otherwise stated, 'season' or 'seasoning' simply means seasoning with salt and pepper.

9 For information on alternative recipes for Veal *Jus* and stocks, see page 225.

10 If shallots are not available, substitute with double the quantity of onions.

Soups, Starters and Snacks

This first chapter contains a wide variety of dishes, several of which could even be served as main courses for lunch or supper. Many of the soups, for instance, are quite filling and, eaten with some chunky bread, would make good and satisfying meals on their own.

ABOVE *The Rhodes 'Open' Club Sandwich (see p. 64).*
LEFT *Tomato Soup served with croûtons (see p. 30), Cabbage Soup with Dumplings (see p. 31), and the ingredients for Ham and Vegetable Soup (see p. 32).*

Perhaps the first thing you'll notice about my recipes is that the titles are very basic and simple. This continues throughout the book because far too often, I think, recipes are described as if they were a book. My Chicken Liver Parfait would probably read elsewhere as 'A mousse of light chicken livers spiked with garlic and brandy, bound with cream, on crisp bread with wilted green leaves and a compote of grapes, apples and onions.' If I read that, my imagination would probably run riot, visualising a towering dish with every item perfectly placed and looking as if a food Meccano set was used to build it! The reality might be a little disappointing.

None of the recipes are engraved in stone, and you can easily adapt them to your own taste. The Tomato Soup is simple enough already, but if you don't like bacon, then just leave it out. I like using the bacon because, when cooking it with the onion and vegetables, it gives a wonderful smoky flavour and yet another taste to the soup. The croûtons are an optional extra as well, adding a crunchy texture. The usual way of making these is to fry them in oil, but they're delicious and much healthier if you bake them with a little olive oil in a moderate oven for about ten minutes, turning every so often. They become golden all over and much crisper. For a little extra taste, roll them in grated Parmesan while still hot.

You can use ordinary tomatoes, but do try to find the plum tomatoes that are becoming more available in greengrocers and supermarkets. Most come from Italy, Spain or America, and are much better for cooking and eating. They have a lot lower water content than most tomatoes; squeeze one in your hand (make sure you've bought it first!), and you'll be left with a thick tomato pulp. If you did that to an ordinary tomato, you'd be left with virtually nothing. Plum tomatoes, when cooked, are packed with flavour, but if you can only find ordinary tomatoes, add a little tomato purée to compensate – the soup will still be good.

Tomatoes, in fact, are a bit of a passion of mine, and I use them a lot in these recipes. If they're good and tasty, they can add a wonderful Continental flavour to our own classic ingredients. For instance, I love buying our British mackerel and herring – so great to look at in fishmongers, piled high on crushed ice – and mackerel can take on some wonderful tastes with stewed tomatoes, onions and pesto. Grilled sardines on toast with tomatoes are just as good. The tomatoes just lift the dishes to new heights with new tastes.

I usually choose my starter after I've picked my main course to help balance the meal, but sometimes I don't worry at all and just eat whatever I fancy. I think you'll find quite enough to choose from here, most of which are French or Italian, certainly Mediterranean, in influence. These can balance the very British main courses, but there are, of course, a few of our own ideas as well.

After all, you can't get much more British than Cabbage Soup with Dumplings. The inspiration for this particular version was my stepfather John, who loves cooking, and influenced us quite a lot at home. Most Sundays we would have cabbage as a vegetable, simply boiled, seasoned and tossed in butter. Well, there's nothing wrong with that, but John decided it needed a boost. He first tossed some onions and bacon in butter, then added a little chicken stock and threw in the cabbage. It cooked very quickly and had so much more flavour, so I just added more stock and created a soup! The dumplings finish it all off. The dumpling recipe I've given is fairly basic, but can be given a lot more variety by adding garlic, bacon or mixed herbs.

Perhaps the most British dish here is the Great British Breakfast offered as a starter salad. Well, why not? Lots of delicious tastes together: the sautéed potatoes, black pudding, bacon and poached eggs with some fresh green leaves. Now that really is variety.

Tomato Soup

This soup stands up as both a starter or a main course (see pp. 26–7). It has a chunky texture and draws on all the flavours of the ingredients. The real beauty, of course, is how simple it is to make. I always like to serve it with bread croûtons cut from a loaf of crusty or olive bread and then fried or baked in olive oil. Also, fresh Parmesan flakes (done with a potato peeler) sprinkled over the soup are really delicious, but of course all these bextras are really up to you. This soup can make a great vegetarian dish – simply leave out the bacon and replace the chicken stock with a vegetable stock.

SERVES 6–8

3 onions, chopped
3 carrots, cut into 6 mm (¼ in) dice
3 celery sticks, cut into 6 mm (¼ in) dice
50 ml (2 fl oz) olive oil
25 g (1 oz) unsalted butter
½ bunch of fresh basil, chopped
½ bunch of fresh tarragon, chopped
1 bay leaf
1 large garlic clove, crushed

6 smoked back bacon rashers, rinded and chopped
900 g (2 lb) ripe tomatoes, preferably plum
600–900 ml (1–1½ pints) Chicken Stock (see p. 228)
Salt and freshly ground white pepper
Tomato purée (optional, to taste)

Sweat the chopped onions, carrots and celery in the olive oil and butter for a few minutes, then add the herbs, bay leaf and garlic and cook for a few more minutes. Add the bacon and continue to cook for about 5 minutes until the vegetables are slightly softened.

Cut the tomatoes into quarters and then cut again into eight pieces. Add them to the vegetables, cover the pan and cook gently for about 15 minutes. The cooking will create its own steam and slowly cook the tomatoes. The mixture must be stirred occasionally, which will help the tomatoes to break down and start to create the soup.

When the tomatoes have softened, start to add the chicken stock, just a ladle at a time, until you have a looser consistency. This brings us to personal choice. The soup can be as thick or as thin as you like. Leave it to cook for a further 20 minutes. Check for seasoning, and you may find that a little tomato purée will help the strength of taste. The soup is now ready to serve.

Cabbage Soup with Dumplings

Good food does not have to be made with fancy, unusual ingredients. Everyday produce will cook and taste just as delicious. This recipe is easy to prepare, simple to cook and cheap to make – and it can be served as a starter or a complete meal (see pp. 26–7). The dish itself came together purely by accident. I was braising some cabbage for one dish and making dumplings for a beef stew. The cabbage and dumplings became an instant success, as it has plenty of textures, tastes and flavours from just a few ingredients.

Both the cabbage soup and dumpling recipes are very basic and can, of course, be varied – a little garlic in the soup, or different herbs and spices in the dumplings. Even the Spinach Dumplings on page 150 could be rolled smaller and used as a garnish.

SERVES 4–6

1 Savoy cabbage, finely shredded
50 g (2 oz) unsalted butter
1.2 litres (2 pints) Chicken Stock (see p. 228) or Vegetable Stock (see p. 229)

2 onions, finely shredded
6 smoked bacon rashers, rinded and cut into thin strips
Salt and freshly ground white pepper

For the Dumplings

225 g (8 oz) plain flour
15 g (½ oz) baking powder
100 g (4 oz) dried shredded suet
½ teaspoon chopped fresh thyme
1 teaspoon chopped fresh basil

About 150 ml (5 fl oz) water
450 ml (15 fl oz) Chicken Stock (see p. 228) or Vegetable Stock (see p. 229), warmed

If you are baking the dumplings (see below), pre-heat the oven to 200°C/400°F/gas 6.

To make the dumplings, mix together the flour, baking powder, suet and herbs and season with salt and pepper. Gradually add just enough water until the mixture forms a dough. Leave to rest for 20 minutes then roll into 2 cm (¾ in) balls. These can be placed in the warm stock and either cooked in the pre-heated oven or on top of the stove, allowing them to bake or simmer slowly for about 20 minutes.

While the dumplings are cooking, cook the cabbage. Place the butter in a warm pan, add the onions and cook for 5 minutes without allowing them to colour. Add the bacon and cook for a further 5 minutes. Pour in the stock, bring to the simmer and simmer for 5–10 minutes. Bring to the boil, add the cabbage and simmer for about 4–5 minutes until tender. Check the seasoning and add the dumplings. The dish is now complete.

Ham and Vegetable Soup

To achieve the maximum taste from this soup it is best to buy some fresh ham or bacon, to soak it in cold water for 24 hours to remove any saltiness, and then cook it in some stock. This will create a good ham stock, and you can cut up the meat to go in the soup. If this all sounds a bit too much, then you can make a vegetable broth and I would suggest you add some diced smoked ham to give a more pronounced flavour. Anyway, here is my recipe for the original idea.

The soup can be served as a starter, main course or a supper dish. It looks lovely in a bowl with all the colours and tastes there. You can make it with your own favourite vegetables and serve it with garlic toasts and Parmesan, fried croûtons or just good old-fashioned bread and butter!

SERVES 8 as a starter,
4–6 as a supper or main course

For the Ham or Bacon

900 g (2 lb) raw bacon or ham collar,
     soaked in cold water for 24 hours
1 onion
2 carrots
1 leek
2 celery sticks

1 sprig of fresh thyme
1 bay leaf
25 g (1 oz) unsalted butter
2.25 litres (4 pints) Chicken Stock
     (see p. 228) or water

For the Soup

450 g (1 lb) carrots
2 onions
6 celery sticks
450 g (1 lb) swede
450 g (1 lb) parsnips

100 g (4 oz) unsalted butter
50 ml (2 fl oz) olive oil
1 large garlic clove, crushed
50 g (2 oz) pearl barley (optional)
Salt and freshly ground white pepper

To cook the ham or bacon, roughly chop all the vegetables into 1 cm (½ in) dice and cook in the butter for about 5 minutes without allowing them to colour. Add the herbs, cover and continue to cook until slightly softened. Keeping a lid on the vegetables will create steam within the pan; this prevents them from colouring and cooks them at the same time.

Pour on the chicken stock and bring to the simmer. Add the bacon or ham and bring back to the simmer. Cover the pan and cook for about 45 minutes. Leave the meat to stand in its own cooking liquor until cold. This part of the job can be done the day before or in the morning. It keeps the meat moist and helps the stock take on the maximum taste.

Remove the bacon or ham from the stock and cut it into 1 cm (½ in) cubes. Strain the stock through a sieve.

To prepare the soup, roughly chop all the vegetables into 1 cm (½ in) dice, keeping the swede and parsnip separate from the others. Melt the butter in a large pan with the olive oil. Add the carrots, onions, celery and garlic, cover and cook for 2–3 minutes. Add the pearl barley, if using, and cook for a further 2–3 minutes, stirring from time to time. Pour on the reserved stock and bring to the simmer. Allow the soup to simmer gently until the diced carrots are softened, about 20 minutes.

Add the diced swede and parsnips and continue to cook for a further 10 minutes until all the vegetables are cooked. Add the diced bacon or ham and season with salt and pepper.

66 *We've all heard of moules marinières, but this is my variation on how to eat mussels – it's nutty, garlicky and buttery.* **99**

Mussels with Garlic, Almonds and Parsley (see p. 37).

Mussel and Macaroni Soup

This soup is very wholesome, and I like to eat it as a supper dish with toasted French bread in the bowl – this soaks up all the juices and is lovely to eat.

SERVES 4

For the Mussels

450 g (1 lb) fresh mussels
225 g (8 oz) mixed vegetables (carrot, onion, celery and leek), cut into 6 mm (¼ in) dice
1 sprig of fresh thyme
1 bay leaf

6 black peppercorns
1 star anise (optional)
50 g (2 oz) unsalted butter
300 ml (10 fl oz) dry white wine
1.2 litres (2 pints) Fish Stock (see p. 227)

For the Soup

2 carrots, cut into 6 mm (¼ in) dice
2 onions, cut into 6 mm (¼ in) dice
4 celery sticks, cut into 6 mm (¼ in) dice
1 garlic clove, crushed
50 ml (2 fl oz) olive oil
100 g (4 oz) unsalted butter
1 bouquet garni (1 bay leaf, 1 star anise, a few fresh basil leaves, 1 sprig each of fresh thyme and tarragon tied in

a square of muslin) or bouquet garni sachet
300 ml (10 fl oz) dry white wine
100 g (4 oz) dried or fresh macaroni, cooked
6 tomatoes, skinned, seeded and diced
1½ tablespoons Pesto Sauce (see p. 243)
A few knobs of unsalted butter
Salt and freshly ground white pepper

Scrape and wash the mussels well. Remove the beards (the threads that hang out of the shells). Discard any mussels that gape and do not close when tapped sharply with a knife.

To cook the mussels, sweat all the diced vegetables, herbs and spices in the butter for a few minutes, then add the white wine and boil to reduce until almost dry. Add the fish stock, bring to the simmer and cook for 10 minutes. Bring the liquor to the boil and add the mussels. Cover with a lid and shake carefully. The mussels will start to open after a few minutes. Drain the mussels and pass the stock through a fine sieve. Discard the vegetables and spices. Remove the mussels from their shells and keep them moist in a little of the stock. Discard any that have remained closed.

To make the soup, sweat the diced vegetables and garlic in the olive oil and butter for a few minutes. Add the bouquet garni and continue to cook for about 4–5 minutes until the vegetables have softened. Add the white wine and boil to reduce until almost dry. Pour in the mussel stock and simmer for 15–20 minutes.

To finish the soup, add the cooked macaroni, tomatoes and shelled mussels. Stir in the pesto sauce and a few knobs of butter, remove the bouquet garni and taste for seasoning before serving.

Mussels with Garlic, Almonds and Parsley

This is usually served as a starter, but it also makes a great main course (see p. 34).

SERVES 4

For the Butter

6 shallots, finely chopped
1 large garlic clove, crushed

250 g (9 oz) unsalted butter, softened

For the Mussel Cooking Liquor

½ onion, chopped
1 carrot, chopped
2 celery sticks, chopped
1 small leek, chopped
15 g (½ oz) unsalted butter
1 garlic clove, crushed
1 bay leaf

1 sprig of fresh thyme
½ bottle dry white wine
600 ml (1 pint) Fish Stock
   (see p. 227)
1 kg (2¼ lb) mussels, scrubbed
   and bearded (see previous recipe)

For the Garnish

50 g (2 oz) nibbed almonds, lightly
   toasted
2 tablespoons chopped fresh parsley

4 slices white bread, crusts removed,
   crumbed and toasted until
   golden

Sweat the chopped shallots and garlic in 1 tablespoon of the butter until translucent, then leave to cool. Mix them with most of the remaining butter and keep aside for later.

To start the mussel liquor, sweat the chopped onion, carrot, celery and leek in the butter with the garlic, bay leaf and thyme for a few minutes. Add the white wine and boil to reduce until almost dry. Add the fish stock and bring to the boil, then add the mussels. Stir until the shells begin to open, then remove from the heat.

Strain the cooking liquor through a fine sieve and discard the vegetables. Remove the mussels from their shells, discarding any that have not opened, and remove any sinews from the mussels. Keep them moist in a little of the stock. Rinse the shells.

Boil the liquor to reduce it until a good mussel flavour is achieved, then gradually add the shallot and garlic butter in knobs. Add the mussels, toasted almonds and parsley. Place some of the shells in a circle on large individual bowls or plates. Spoon the mussels into the shells and pour over some of the cooking liquor. To finish the dish, sprinkle with the warm, golden toasted breadcrumbs.

Red Mullet Soup

I love all fish soups, but I find red mullet gives the best taste. For this soup, fresh or frozen red mullet fillets can be used. Garlic toasts with Rouille (see p. 241) are delicious with this soup. Cut a French stick into 1 cm (½ in) slices and spread with some garlic butter (simply mix crushed garlic to taste into softened butter). Toast the slices then top with Rouille.

SERVES 8–10

225 g (8 oz) tomatoes, chopped
1 fennel bulb, chopped
1 large onion, chopped
2 carrots, chopped
1 leek, chopped
2 celery sticks, chopped
1 garlic clove, crushed
½ bunch of fresh basil
½ bunch of fresh tarragon
A pinch of saffron

25 ml (1 fl oz) olive oil
50 g (2 oz) unsalted butter
450 g (1 lb) red mullet fillets, scaled and
    sliced into pieces
300 ml (10 fl oz) Noilly Prat or dry white
    vermouth
300 ml (10 fl oz) dry white wine
1.2 litres (2 pints) Fish Stock (see p. 227)
2 teaspoons tomato purée
Salt and freshly ground white pepper

Sweat all the chopped vegetables, garlic, herbs and saffron in the olive oil and butter for a few minutes. Add the red mullet fillets, the Noilly Prat and white wine and allow to cook and reduce for 5–6 minutes. Pour on the fish stock and tomato purée. Bring the soup to the simmer and cook for 40 minutes.

Purée the soup in a food processor or liquidizer and push through a sieve. Season with salt and pepper. The soup should be a rich, orangey-red colour with a powerful depth of flavour and eats beautifully with the Rouille toasts (see p. 241 and above).

Cod Brandade
with Warm Poached Egg

This dish needs a lot of planning and thinking time, but really is worth every effort. The basic mixture makes more than you need for four, because 75 g (3 oz) will be enough per starter portion. The rest of the mixture can be stored in the fridge for a day or so and can be rolled into balls and coated with breadcrumbs then deep-fried as for the Salmon Fish Cakes (see p. 88).

SERVES 4

900 g (2 lb) cod fillet with skin
Rock salt
8 black peppercorns
1 sprig of fresh thyme
1 bay leaf
200 ml (7 fl oz) olive oil

1 large garlic clove, finely chopped
1–1.5 kg (2–3 lb) Mashed Potatoes
    without cream or butter
    (see p. 142)
2 tablespoons chopped fresh parsley
Freshly ground white pepper

To serve

Milk
4 eggs, poached
    (see p. 56)

300 ml (10 fl oz) Brandade Dressing
    (see p. 40)
Olive oil

Sprinkle the cod liberally with rock salt, cover and place in the fridge for 48 hours, turning it at least once. After the fish has been salted, it needs to be washed to remove the salt, then soaked for 12 hours in cold water.

Drain the fish well and cut it into eight pieces. Place in a pan with the peppercorns, thyme and bay leaf and just cover with cold water. Bring to the boil then remove from the heat and allow to cool. Remove the cod from the liquid, take off the skin and pick out any bones. Flake the flesh.

Warm the olive oil in a large pan then add the cod. While it is cooking for a few minutes, add the garlic and break up the fish with a wooden spoon. Add some mashed potatoes, working on a ratio of two parts potato to one part cod. Add the parsley and season with white pepper. This mixture can now be left to cool, then chilled.

To serve the brandade, place it in a pan with a little milk over a gentle heat until warmed through. While the cod is warming, poach the eggs. Then spoon the cod on to the centre of the plates and sit the warm poached eggs on top. Spoon the dressing generously all around and trickle a little extra olive oil over the eggs.

Brandade Dressing

This may look fairly complex, but in fact is very simple to make. This recipe will make a reasonable amount and will keep very well in the fridge. It's also absolutely delicious to eat with the Cod Brandade or other salads.

Makes about 600 ml (1 pint)

1 onion, finely chopped
½ teaspoon chopped fresh thyme
½ teaspoon chopped fresh rosemary
½ teaspoon chopped fresh basil
½ teaspoon chopped fresh parsley
1 garlic clove, crushed
50 g (2 oz) unsalted butter
500 ml (17 fl oz) olive oil
300 ml (10 fl oz) red wine
50 g (2 oz) shelled walnuts, chopped

50 g (2 oz) black olives, stoned and chopped
25 g (1 oz) anchovy fillets, drained and chopped
25 g (1 oz) capers, drained and chopped
1 fennel bulb, cooked (see p. 84), and cut into 6 mm (¼ in) dice
8 tomatoes, skinned, seeded and diced
Salt and freshly ground white pepper

In a large pan, sweat the chopped onion, herbs and garlic in the butter and 3 tablespoons of olive oil for a few minutes. Add the red wine and boil to reduce until almost dry. Add the remaining olive oil and all the remaining ingredients except the tomatoes, bring to the simmer and simmer for a few minutes. Add the diced tomatoes, season with salt and pepper and remove from the heat. The sauce is now ready.

Soused Mackerel
with Warm Potatoes

Sousing or pickling is usually associated with raw fish. This recipe is slightly different. The mackerel is heated briefly in its spicy liquor, then served warm with the potatoes. This makes the liquor a sauce, and the addition of potato makes the mackerel a complete dish (see overleaf).

SERVES 4

1 small fennel bulb, very thinly sliced
2 carrots, thinly sliced
2 celery sticks, thinly sliced
1 leek, thinly sliced
2 shallots or 1 onion, thinly sliced
1 bouquet garni (1 bay leaf, 1 star anise, a few fresh basil leaves, 2 sprigs each of fresh thyme and tarragon tied in a square of muslin or a strip of leek leaves) or bouquet garni sachet

6 black peppercorns
50 ml (2 fl oz) olive oil
100 g (4 oz) unsalted butter
150 ml (5 fl oz) dry white wine
150 ml (5 fl oz) white wine vinegar
600 ml (1 pint) water
4 mackerel fillets, all bones removed
Salt and freshly ground white pepper
1 quantity Mashed Potatoes with lemon and shallots (see p. 142)
1 tablespoon chopped fresh parsley

Cook all the sliced vegetables in a pan with the bouquet garni, peppercorns, olive oil and half the butter for a few minutes. Add the white wine, wine vinegar and water and simmer for about 10–12 minutes until the vegetables are cooked. This is your sousing liquor. Allow to cool and remove the bouquet garni.

Place the fillets in a lightly buttered flameproof dish and cover with the liquor and vegetables. Season with salt and pepper. Bring slowly to the simmer then remove from the heat. The fish is now ready.

Spoon some of the hot mashed potatoes into serving bowls and sit the mackerel on top. Stir the remaining butter and the parsley into the cooking liquor. Spoon the vegetables and sauce around the fish and serve.

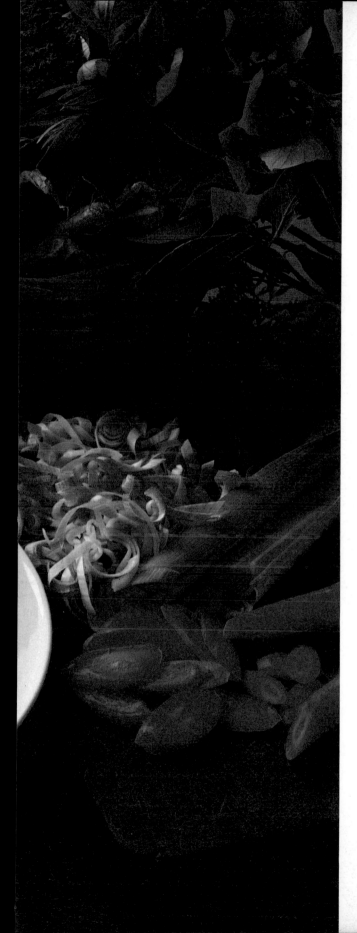

43

*Soused Mackerel
with Warm Potatoes
(see p. 41).*

Grilled Mackerel
with Stewed Tomatoes, Pesto
and Onions

Here we are looking at simple ingredients, and we all know that tomatoes, onions, garlic and basil work well together (see pp. 222–3). I have added the slight Italian influence, using pesto sauce. This has so many uses: as a seasoning, a sauce on its own, or to flavour cream sauces or tomatoes. It can be made at home, but good pesto can be found in almost any supermarket or delicatessen.

I use the mackerel as a starter and so only serve one fillet a portion, but like most dishes this would also make a good main course for two.

SERVES 4

For the Tomatoes, Pesto and Onions

2–3 tablespoons olive oil
3 onions, thinly sliced

12 tomatoes, preferably plum, skinned
     and quartered
1 tablespoon Pesto Sauce (see p. 243)

For the Mackerel

Salt and freshly ground white pepper
Oil for deep-frying (preferably
     ground-nut)
25 g (1 oz) unsalted butter
4 mackerel fillets, all bones removed

1 tablespoon plain flour
Curly endive leaves
1–2 tablespoons Basic Vinaigrette
     (see p. 245)

Pour the olive oil into a pan and add one-third of the sliced onions. Allow to cook gently for about 10 minutes until the onions are soft but not coloured. Add the quartered tomatoes and continue to cook for 15–20 minutes until the tomatoes have stewed with the onions, creating their own sauce. Add the pesto sauce to taste (approximately a tablespoon will be enough) and season with salt and pepper.

Pre-heat the grill to moderate and heat the oil for deep-frying. Brush a tray with a little of the butter and season it with salt and pepper. Lay the mackerel fillets on top and brush with butter. Cook the fillets under the grill for about 5–6 minutes until the skin is crisp. Meanwhile, lightly dust the remaining onions with flour. Fry in the deep hot fat until golden and crisp. Drain well and season with a little salt.

Spoon some of the warm tomato mixture on to individual plates. Dress the curly endive with a little vinaigrette and place a few leaves on to each tomato mound. Lay the mackerel fillets on top and finish the dish with the crispy onions.

Grilled Sardine Fillets on Tomato Toasts

This is a similar dish to the mackerel recipe (p. 44) but with this we've created different tastes and textures. It's not just an alternative, therefore, but a dish quite rightly out on its own (see pp. 234–5). It may sound a little complicated but believe me, it's simple and tasty, so try it!

SERVES 4

8 fresh sardines, scaled and filleted
4 tablespoons olive oil
Juice of ½ lemon
Salt and freshly ground white pepper
4 × 1 cm (½ in) slices crusty or onion
    bread
1 quantity Stewed Tomatoes, Pesto and
    Onions (see p. 44)
300 ml (10 fl oz) Hollandaise Sauce (see
    p. 244) (optional)

In a dish large enough to hold the sardines in one layer, mix the olive oil with the lemon juice and season with salt and pepper. Lay the sardine fillets into the oil and leave for 1–2 hours to take on the taste.

Brush the bread slices with a little of the marinade oil. These slices can now be toasted on both sides until golden. Warm the stewed tomatoes with pesto.

Pre-heat the grill to hot. Season the sardine fillets with salt and pepper and lay them on a tray or grill rack and place under the hot grill. Just cook until slightly coloured. Providing the grill is hot this will only take 2–3 minutes.

To serve, spoon some hollandaise sauce, if using, on to four plates or into bowls, spreading it a little into a circle. Sit the toasts on top, and spoon the tomatoes with pesto on to them. Sit the sardines overlapping on top and just pour a little of the excess oil from the tray over the fish.

Smoked Eel Kedgeree

This dish could also be called a smoked eel risotto because it's made by the risotto method, but it holds all the flavours of a good old-fashioned kedgeree. I serve it as a starter, but it can be a total meal in itself. Hard-boiled eggs are traditionally used, but having a warm poached egg sitting on top of the rice and just breaking the yolk over it is a dream. The recipe for the Curry Cream Sauce is on page 237, but you can buy a ready-made one just to make the dish a little easier. If you really cannot find smoked eel, you can make the dish with smoked haddock.

Serves 4

900 g (2 lb) smoked eel

For the Eel Stock

1 onion, chopped	2 sprigs of fresh tarragon
1 leek, chopped	A few black peppercorns
2 celery sticks, chopped	50 g (2 oz) unsalted butter
6 mushrooms or 50 g (2 oz) mushroom	300 ml (10 fl oz) dry white wine
trimmings	1.2 litres (2 pints) Fish Stock (see p. 227)
1 bay leaf	or water
1 sprig of fresh thyme	

For the Kedgeree

2 onions, finely chopped	1 garlic clove, crushed
100 g (4 oz) unsalted butter	225 g (8 oz) arborio or long-grain rice
50 g (2 oz) bone marrow, chopped	½ quantity Curry Cream Sauce
(optional)	(see p. 237)

To serve

4 eggs, poached (see p. 66)
3 tablespoons olive oil
2 teaspoons snipped fresh chives

Smoked eel is one of my favourite smoked fish. Firstly it has to be filleted and skinned. Hopefully your fishmonger will do this for you, but if not, simply cut off the head and position the knife against the top half of the central bone. Carefully cut along the bone, removing the fillet of fish. Turn the fish over and repeat the same process. Now the skin can be removed: slide your finger or thumb under the skin at the head end and it should tear off all the way along. The fillets may need a little trimming down the sides to remove any excess skin. Turn the fillets on to their back to show the centre. From the head end to half-way down there will be some bones. Simply position the knife under these bones, and cut away from the flesh. You now have two long, clean fillets of eel. Cut these into 2.5 cm (1 in) pieces and put in the fridge.

To make the eel stock, chop all the bones, skin and trimmings. Place the chopped vegetables, herbs and peppercorns in a large, warmed pan with the butter and cook them gently for 10 minutes without letting them colour. Add the bones and trimmings and continue to cook for a further 5 minutes. Add the white wine and boil to reduce until almost dry. Add the fish stock or water. (Fish stock will give you a stronger and better taste. If you are using water, ask the fishmonger to give you some fish bones as well to cook with the eel.) Bring the stock to the simmer and cook for 20 minutes. Strain through a sieve and the stock is ready.

For the kedgeree, cook the chopped onions in the butter with the bone marrow, if using, and the garlic for 5–6 minutes until softened. Stir in the rice and cook for 2 minutes, then start to add the hot eel stock a few tablespoons at a time, stirring continuously. This will create a steam and help the cooking process. Wait for the stock to be absorbed before adding more, and keep adding the stock and stirring until the rice is just softening – this will take about 15–20 minutes. The rice should be tender and the mixture still moist.

When the rice is cooked, stir in half the curry sauce and taste. At this stage it becomes a matter of personal choice; some more or all of the curry sauce can be added if you want a stronger taste.

Add the pieces of chopped eel to the kedgeree and stir in to warm through. Warm the poached eggs for a few minutes in a bowl of boiling water, then drain well. Spoon the kedgeree into four bowls and sit a poached egg on top of each one. Spoon a little olive oil over the eggs and sprinkle with the snipped chives. The dish is now ready.

Welsh Rarebit

This recipe is really the minimum amount you can make for a successful mixture. It will keep in the fridge for up to ten days, so can be used in plenty of other dishes. My favourite use is with the Smoked Haddock with tomato salad opposite. It's also delicious as a simple cheese on toast.

SERVES 16

700 g (1½ lb) mature Cheddar, grated
150 ml (5 fl oz) milk
25 g (1 oz) plain flour
50 g (2 oz) fresh white breadcrumbs
1 tablespoon English mustard powder
2 shakes of Worcestershire sauce
Salt and freshly ground white pepper
2 eggs
2 egg yolks

Put the Cheddar into a pan and add the milk. Slowly melt them together over a low heat, but do not allow the mix to boil as this will separate the cheese. When the mixture is smooth and just begins to bubble, add the flour, breadcrumbs and mustard and cook for a few minutes, stirring, over a low heat until the mixture comes away from the sides of the pan and begins to form a ball shape. Add the Worcestershire sauce, salt and pepper and leave to cool.

When cold, place the mixture into a food processor, turn on the motor and slowly add the eggs and egg yolks. (If you don't have a processor or mixer, just beat vigorously with a wooden spoon.) When the eggs are mixed in, chill for a few hours before using. After it has rested in the fridge, you will find the rarebit is very easy to handle and has so many uses. The mix also freezes very well. When I make it at home, I divide it into four and freeze three batches for use later!

Smoked Haddock with Welsh Rarebit

This has to be one of my favourites – possibly a signature dish, and hopefully a classic (see overleaf). It's lovely as a starter or main course. Cheese and tomato are a great combination, so placing the haddock on to a tomato salad works really well and, of course, gives us those hot and cold tastes. Choose really good tomatoes – plum are much the best.

I have chosen natural smoked haddock which is quite white in colour. The yellow-dyed haddock is not really needed as the cheese is, of course, already that colour – and you know that I like natural tastes, textures and colours!

SERVES 4

6 ripe plum or salad tomatoes
Salt and freshly ground white pepper
4 × 100 g (4 oz) slices natural smoked
    haddock
175 g (6 oz) Welsh Rarebit mix (see left)
1 tablespoon finely snipped fresh chives
150 ml (5 fl oz) Basic Vinaigrette
    (see p. 245)

Pre-heat the oven to 180°C/350°F/gas 4 and pre-heat the grill to medium.

Firstly remove and discard the eyes from the tomatoes. Blanch the tomatoes in boiling water for 5–6 seconds. Cool them quickly in iced water and the skins should peel off easily. Slice the tomatoes and arrange overlapping on to the centre of individual plates. You'll need about 1½ tomatoes per portion, and this should make a nice circle. Sprinkle with a little salt and a twist of pepper.

Arrange the haddock portions in a buttered flameproof dish. Split the rarebit into four pieces, pat out on your hands to about 2–3 mm (⅛ in) thick and lay on top of the haddock (the mix should be quite pliable and easy to use). Colour under the grill until golden then finish the haddock in the pre-heated oven for 3–4 minutes.

Add the chives to the vinaigrette and spoon over the tomatoes. When the haddock is cooked, just sit on top of the tomatoes and serve.

Smoked Haddock with
Welsh Rarebit served on
a tomato salad
(see p. 49)

Gruyère Cheese Flan

This is my basic flan recipe, but of course you can add any other ingredients you like. One of my favourites is to make this into a leek, mushroom and Gruyère flan by simply omitting one of the onions and replacing it with a shredded leek and 50 g (2 oz) of sliced mushrooms, both lightly cooked in butter. It then eats very well with a Spicy Tomato Sauce (see p. 24).

If you don't have the time to make your own pastry, both shortcrust and puff are easily found in most food stores, although they're not quite as good as home-made! I prefer to use puff pastry for this recipe as it cooks much more lightly and suits the flan. It eats very well as a starter or main course with salad.

SERVES 8

2 large onions, sliced
40 g (1½ oz) unsalted butter
1½ tablespoons ground-nut or vegetable oil
2 eggs
1 egg yolk

150 ml (5 fl oz) double cream or milk
100 g (4 oz) Gruyère or Cheddar, grated
Cayenne pepper (optional)
175 g (6 oz) Puff or Savoury Pastry (see pp. 216 or 219)
Salt and freshly ground white pepper

To start the filling, cook the sliced onions in 1 tablespoon of the butter and ½ tablespoon of the oil until soft and transparent. Leave to cool. In a basin, beat the eggs and egg yolk together, then add the cream or milk and leave to one side. Melt the remaining butter and oil together until blended, then leave to cool. Mix the grated cheese with the eggs and cream and fold in the onions and the cool butter and oil mixture. Season with salt and pepper and a little cayenne, if you like. The mixture can be made the day before it's needed, as it refrigerates very well.

Pre-heat the oven to 180°C/350°F/gas 4 and prepare a 24-cm (9½-in) flan tin or a flan ring and a baking sheet.

Roll out the pastry and use to line the flan tin or ring. Line the pastry with greaseproof paper and fill with baking beans or dried rice. Bake blind in the pre-heated oven for 15–20 minutes, then allow to cool. Remove the beans and paper.

Reduce the oven temperature to 150–160°C/300–325°F/gas 2–3. Pour the filling mixture into the pastry base and cook in the oven for about 45 minutes until the flan is just set. The tart should colour during cooking. If it starts to over-colour, lightly cover with foil or greaseproof paper. The flan is best left to rest for 20–30 minutes before serving as this will help set the texture of the filling.

Grilled Aubergines
with Tomatoes and Cheddar

This dish is very good as a starter, or it can be served with a salad for a vegetarian main course.

SERVES 4

2 aubergines
300 ml (10 fl oz) Tomato Coulis (see p. 240)
A few drops of Spicing Essence (see p. 242)
Salt and freshly ground white pepper
2 onions, finely chopped

1 garlic clove, crushed
10 fresh basil leaves, chopped
2 tablespoons olive oil
25 g (1 oz) unsalted butter
150 ml (5 fl oz) dry white wine
4 tomatoes, skinned, seeded and diced
175 g (6 oz) Cheddar, thinly sliced

Slice the aubergines into 5 mm (¼ in) rounds, allowing three to four per portion. Lightly salt the slices and place in a colander for about 30 minutes to drain out all the bitterness. Pat dry.

Heat the tomato coulis gently and add a few drops of the spiced essence to give the coulis a slightly spicy taste. Season with salt and pepper.

Sweat the chopped onions, garlic and basil in the olive oil and butter for a few minutes, then add the white wine and boil to reduce until almost dry. Add the spiced tomato coulis and simmer for 15 minutes.

Pre-heat the grill. Grill the aubergines for 5 minutes each side (or they can be pan-fried in some extra butter). Lay the grilled or fried aubergine slices on flameproof plates. Add the diced tomato to the coulis and spoon it on to each portion of aubergines. Cover the sauce with the Cheddar and brown quickly under the grill.

Ricotta and Spinach Gnocchi

Gnocchi is an Italian dish of little dumplings which can be made in three ways: with semolina, potato or flour and eggs. I'm using the latter with ricotta cheese, which is readily available and is probably the cheese most used in cooking in Italy.

SERVES 4

350 g (12 oz) fresh spinach, stalks removed
175 g (6 oz) ricotta, drained and diced
1 egg

50 g (2 oz) plain flour
25 g (1 oz) Parmesan, grated
A pinch of freshly grated nutmeg
Salt and freshly ground white pepper

For the Dressing

150 ml (5 fl oz) olive oil
4 shallots or 1 large onion, finely chopped
1 large garlic clove, crushed

6 tomatoes, skinned, seeded and chopped
Juice of ½ lemon
1 bunch of fresh basil, chopped

To serve

Parmesan flakes

Wash the spinach well to remove any grit then shake off any excess water. Place the spinach into a hot pan and cook in its own water for a few minutes until the leaves begin to wilt. Remove them from the pan and squeeze out any excess liquid. Blitz the spinach in a food processor or chop it very finely. Mix the spinach with the ricotta, egg, flour and Parmesan and season with nutmeg, salt and pepper. Leave the mixture to rest in the fridge for 20 minutes.

To make the dressing, warm the olive oil with the chopped shallots or onion and garlic and cook over a gentle heat for about 15 minutes. Add the chopped tomatoes and continue to cook for a further 5 minutes. Season with salt and pepper and add the lemon juice. Keep the dressing warm while you cook the gnocchi.

Using floured hands, shape the gnocchi into small 2.5 cm (1 in) balls. Bring a large pan of salted water to the boil (or you could use vegetable stock) and drop the gnocchi into the boiling water. When the balls rise to the surface after just a few minutes they are cooked. Remove them from the pan using a slotted spoon and drain well. Add the chopped basil to the dressing at the last minute, just before serving, then roll the gnocchi in the dressing and divide between four bowls. Sprinkle with some Parmesan flakes and serve.

*Ricotta and Spinach Gnocchi
with a tomato and basil
dressing.*

Poached Egg Salad
with Sauté Potatoes, Black Pudding
and Bacon

I have always wanted to do something with the Great British Breakfast, it has so many potential combinations. Here is an idea that acts as a starter for lunch, dinner or a complete meal on its own. The leaves listed below are good for this salad as they have different tastes and colours, but you can use any lettuces available to you. The most exciting part of eating this dish is breaking into the egg yolk and mixing it with the salad and sauce. It's tasty, rich and a delight to eat (see pp. 58–9).

SERVES 4

1 tablespoon white wine or malt vinegar (using white wine vinegar prevents any discolouration)

4 eggs

225 g (8 oz) new potatoes, boiled and sliced

50 g (2 oz) unsalted butter

175 g (6 oz) smoked bacon, rinded and cut into strips

½ black pudding, cut into 1 cm (½ in) pieces

A few lettuce leaves per person (lollo rosso, oak leaf, curly endive, rocket)

150 ml (5 fl oz) Basic Vinaigrette (see p. 245)

150 ml (5 fl oz) Red Wine Sauce (see p. 236) (optional)

Salt and freshly ground white pepper

Bring a large, deep pan of water to a rolling boil, add the wine vinegar, then crack the eggs into the water. Poach for about 4 minutes until the white has set. Remove from the pan with a slotted spoon and place in a bowl of cold water.

Fry the potato slices in the butter until golden and crisp on both sides. Remove from the pan and keep warm. Fry the bacon until crisp and nicely browned. Add to the potatoes. Fry the black pudding for a few minutes on both sides and keep warm with the bacon and potatoes.

Separate the lettuce leaves carefully and wash in a little salted water. Drain and shake off any excess water. Place in a bowl and dress with most of the vinaigrette.

The finishing of the salad is up to you. I like to almost 'build' my salad by firstly placing some potatoes, black pudding and bacon on to the plates or bowls and then the lettuce leaves followed by more potatoes etc. until I have what you might call a designer salad, but still looking quite natural. The simplest way is just to mix your garnishes with the salad leaves and separate on to plates.

While assembling the salad, warm the red wine sauce, if using, and re-heat the poached eggs for 1–2 minutes in a bowl of hot water. Drain the eggs well, place on top of the salad and sprinkle with a little of the remaining vinaigrette and a twist of pepper. Pour the red wine sauce around and serve.

58

*Poached Egg Salad
with Sauté Potatoes,
Black Pudding and Bacon
(see p. 56).*

Spanish Omelette

This must be one of the cheapest dishes to produce, and also one of the simplest to make. A Spanish friend of mine gave me this recipe and it works every time. Most tapas bars serve Spanish omelettes, but I've yet to have one as good as this. It can be served as a starter, snack or main course, and I like to serve it with the Red Pepper and Anchovy Salad which follows.

SERVES 4

2 large potatoes, thinly sliced
1 onion, sliced
Salt and freshly ground white pepper
Ground-nut or vegetable oil for
    deep-frying

4 eggs, beaten
1 teaspoon olive oil
1 quantity Red Pepper and Anchovy
    Salad (see opposite)
A handful of salad leaves

Mix the potatoes with the sliced onions and sprinkle them lightly with salt. Heat the ground-nut oil to about 140–150°C (285–300°F) and blanch the potatoes and onions in batches in a deep-fat fryer for about 4–5 minutes, making sure you cook them without colouring. Make sure the oil is not too hot, and while the potatoes are blanching, turn them with a fork to ensure even cooking. When cooked, drain off all excess oil. Mix the potatoes, onions and eggs and season with salt and pepper.

Heat a 15 cm (6 in) frying-pan with sloping sides and trickle in the olive oil. Pour in the potato and egg mixture and move with the fork as the first side is cooking. It should take a few minutes until it is golden brown. Turn the omelette on to a plate then slide it back into the pan to cook the other side. Leave to rest, as it is best eaten just warm. Serve in wedges with a little of the red pepper and anchovy salad, on plates garnished with salad leaves.

Red Pepper and Anchovy Salad

The only way to serve this is to use the marinated and oiled anchovy fillets. These can be obtained from a delicatessen, usually sold loose over the counter. If the only ones available are tinned, then it would be best just to serve a red pepper salad.

SERVES 4–6

2 red peppers
12 anchovy fillets (not tinned)
2–3 tablespoons Vierge Dressing
  (see p. 249)

Pre-heat the grill to hot. Put the whole red peppers under the hot grill and wait until the skin begins to colour and bubble. Turn the pepper until this has happened all round. While the peppers are still warm, peel off all the skin and leave to cool. When cold, halve the peppers and remove all the seeds. Cut the peppers into thin strips and cover with vierge dressing. It is now best to leave them for 1–2 hours to marinate.

Just before serving, split the anchovy fillets in half lengthways and mix them with the peppers. Serve with the Spanish omelette.

Chicken Liver Parfait

This is a great dish for a starter or a main item on a cold buffet (see pp. 222–3). I like to serve a slice on a plate with some good, thick toast, a few lettuce leaves and home-made Grape Chutney (see p. 251) or Green Tomato Chutney (see p. 251). I always cook this parfait in a loaf tin or porcelain terrine mould, but of course individual 7.5 cm (3 in) moulds can be used.

SERVES 8–10

For the Parfait

750 g (1½ lb) chicken livers, soaked for at least 24 hours in cold milk
1 garlic clove, crushed
Pinch of freshly grated nutmeg
Salt and freshly ground white pepper
3 eggs

900 ml (1½ pints) double cream
3 tablespoons brandy
About 3 tablespoons Veal *Jus* (see p. 232) or bought alternative (see p. 225) (optional)

Pre-heat the oven to 160°C/325°F/gas 3. Butter a 30 × 8 × 8 cm (12 × 3 × 3 in) terrine dish with a lid, a 900 g (2 lb) loaf tin, or eight to ten 7.5 cm (3 in) ramekin dishes and line them all with greaseproof paper.

Soaking the livers in milk removes any bitter taste. Drain the milk from the livers and discard the milk. For the best results with this recipe you will need a food processor or liquidizer. Blitz the livers in the processor with the garlic, nutmeg, salt and pepper until smooth. Add the eggs and blitz for a further 1 minute. Add the cream, brandy and *jus,* if using. (The *jus* is optional for this recipe, but I find it gives a little depth and flavour to the parfait.) Continue to blitz for a few seconds and then check for seasoning. The parfait should now be pushed through a fine sieve to give a smoother consistency. You will now find the mix to be quite liquid.

Pour the mix into the prepared terrine or moulds and cover with a lid. Stand in a tray filled with warm water to come half-way up the sides of the terrine to ensure a slow, steady cooking, and cook in the pre-heated oven for about 1½ hours. Make sure the parfait is checked after 30 minutes and 1 hour. After 1 hour, check every 10 minutes until the parfait is just firming to the touch. It will, of course, continue to cook once removed from the oven until it has completely cooled. Remove from the water bath and leave to cool then chill for 2–3 hours.

To serve the parfait, dip the mould into hot water and turn it over on to a chopping board. Remove the greaseproof paper and slice as needed. The parfait can be wrapped in cling film and kept in the fridge for 2–3 days.

Grilled Ham, Cheese and Tomato Toasts

This recipe is a designer sandwich which I often make from left-overs or as a complete supper meal. The cooked ham I'm using here is from my Boiled Bacon recipe (see p. 113) – there always seems to be some left over. Of course, you don't have to cook bacon or ham just for this recipe; I'm sure you can buy some good cooked ham at the shops. Welsh rarebit, however, is a must for this dish. Plain melted cheese just isn't the same.

SERVES 4

4 slices crusty bread
50 g (2 oz) unsalted butter
4 slices cooked bacon or ham (see above)
4 plum or salad tomatoes, sliced
Freshly ground black pepper
175 g (6 oz) Welsh Rarebit mix (see p. 48)
4 eggs, poached (see p. 56)
1 teaspoon chopped fresh parsley
50 ml (2 fl oz) Basic Vinaigrette
    (see p. 245)

Pre-heat the grill to hot. Butter the slices of bread and toast them on both sides. Lay the ham on to the buttered side. Cover with the sliced tomatoes and season with pepper. Split the rarebit into four pieces, pat out on your hands to the size and shape of the toast and lay on top of the tomatoes. Sit the toasts under the hot grill and colour the rarebit mix golden brown.

Warm the poached eggs for a few minutes in a bowl of boiling water. Put the toasts on individual plates and top each one with a poached egg. Mix the chopped parsley with the vinaigrette and spoon over the top.

The Rhodes
'Open' Club Sandwich

A club sandwich was one of the first dishes that I ever had to make – this was at the Amsterdam Hilton. The coffee shop was always packed, and the club sandwich was one of its most popular choices. This is my version and I hope you enjoy it (see p. 27). It's having just one slice of toast that makes this 'Open'. Make it as a starter for dinner parties – nobody will expect to be served a sandwich!

MAKES 2 sandwiches

2 slices bread of your choice
soft butter
1 chicken breast, skinned
Salt and freshly ground white pepper
1 tablespoon olive oil (if necessary)
2 rashers smoked or green back bacon,
   rinded
½ iceberg lettuce, shredded

1 tablespoon finely chopped onion
2 tablespoons Mayonnaise
   (see p. 248)
2–3 tomatoes, thinly sliced
2 tablespoons Basic Vinaigrette
   (see p. 245)
1 teaspoon chopped fresh parsley
2 poached eggs, warmed (see p. 56)

Pre-heat the grill to hot. Butter the bread on both sides and then toast it under the grill until golden brown.

Split the chicken breast lengthways through the middle and season with salt and pepper. Grill, or pan-fry in the olive oil, for a few minutes on each side until cooked. Grill the bacon until crisp. Mix the shredded lettuce and onion with the mayonnaise and season with salt and pepper.

Lay the tomato slices on top of the two pieces of toast and sprinkle with some of the vinaigrette. Divide the lettuce mixture between the two and top with the bacon and chicken breast halves. Sit the warmed poached eggs on the chicken breasts and mix the chopped parsley with the remaining vinaigrette and sprinkle over them.

Beef Carpaccio

This dish originated in the 1950s and was named after the Italian painter, Vittore Carpaccio, known for the reds and whites in his work. It has now become a favourite starter across the world. Here is my version (see p. 67).

SERVES at least 8

900 g (2 lb) topside of beef
50 g (2 oz) Parmesan
Freshly ground black pepper

For the Marinade

150 ml (5 fl oz) balsamic vinegar
5 tablespoons soy sauce
5 tablespoons Worcestershire sauce
4 garlic cloves, chopped
1 bunch of fresh basil

½ bunch of fresh thyme
15 black peppercorns, crushed
300 ml (10 fl oz) dry white wine
600 ml (1 pint) olive oil
15 g (½ oz) coarse sea salt

Trim the beef of any fat and sinew, which will leave you with 750–800 g (1½–1¾ lb) of meat.

Mix together all the marinade ingredients, reserving a few basil leaves to finish the dish. Roll the beef in the marinade, cover and leave to steep in the fridge for 4–5 days to achieve the maximum taste. The beef should be turned in the marinade every day. If the beef is kept in the oil in the fridge, you could leave it for up to 10–12 days.

After the marinating process, remove the meat from the marinade and wrap in cling film. Freeze it, if you like, to use later, or it can even be sliced from frozen on a slicing machine. It can also be kept in the fridge and sliced very thinly with a sharp knife as you want it. Push the marinade through a sieve to use as the dressing.

To serve the carpaccio, slice it very thinly and place the slices on to the serving plate, covering the whole surface (about three to four slices if cut by hand, four to five if cut on a machine). Chop the remaining basil leaves and add to the dressing. Brush this over the meat and twist on some freshly ground black pepper. The Parmesan can be sliced from a piece into shavings and laid on top, or it can be grated and served separately.

*66 I don't stop at
British dishes.
A lot of my favourites
are Italian and
French, and most
of them are just too
good to ignore. 99*

*Beef Carpaccio with
shavings of
Parmesan cheese
(see p. 65).*

Breast of Pigeon
Wrapped in Cabbage on
a Warm Potato Salad

Try to find squab pigeons to make this dish. These are specially reared young pigeons, and are very tender and plump. By doubling the quantities this could also be served as a main course. As a variation, a pigeon red wine sauce can be made by adding the pigeon carcasses to the reduction of the Red Wine Sauce (see p. 236) and then continuing with the recipe. The legs and carcass will infuse the sauce, giving it a rich, gamey flavour.

Serves 4

2 squab pigeons

225 g (8 oz) mushrooms, minced or finely chopped

2 chicken livers, chopped

4 chicken hearts (optional), chopped

50 g (2 oz) wild mushrooms (optional), chopped

Salt and freshly ground black pepper

1 egg yolk

4 large green cabbage leaves

100 g (4 oz) pig's caul, soaked in cold water for 24 hours (optional)

50 g (2 oz) unsalted butter

For the Warm Potato Salad

450 g (1 lb) new potatoes, cooked

2 tablespoons olive oil

300 ml (10 fl oz) Red Wine Vinaigrette (see p. 248)

½ teaspoon chopped fresh parsley

½ teaspoon chopped fresh tarragon

½ teaspoon snipped fresh chives

Remove the legs and breasts from the carcasses. Skin the breasts but keep them whole. Cut up all the meat on the legs.

Place the minced or chopped mushrooms in a pan and cook over a low heat until almost dry. Allow to cool. Mix in the chopped leg meat, and the chopped chicken livers, hearts and wild mushrooms, if using. Season with salt and pepper and bind with the egg yolk.

Blanch the cabbage leaves quickly in boiling salted water then refresh in cold water and dry on a cloth. Lay them flat and sit the pigeon breasts on top of each one. Spread about 5 mm (¼ in) of the minced filling on top of each breast and fold over the cabbage until you have a small cabbage parcel. Cut the pig's caul into four and wrap a piece around each cabbage parcel. The parcels are now ready.

Heat the butter in a frying-pan and cook the pigeon parcels for about 5–6 minutes on each side until golden brown.

While the cooked potatoes for the salad are still warm, peel and slice them and mix with the olive oil, then season with salt and pepper. Keep them warm. Mix the red wine vinaigrette with the chopped herbs. Divide the potatoes between four plates and spoon the dressing over each portion. Make two or three cuts through the breasts, arrange them on top of the potatoes and serve.

Main Courses

It is in these main course recipes that you will find some of my favourite Great British Classics (although there are, admittedly, quite a few in the pudding section, too). They're arranged in various categories – fish, meat and poultry, and vegetarian and vegetable dishes – which will, I hope, help you find more easily what you're looking for.

ABOVE *Cod with a Parsley Crust (see p. 74) served on Mashed Potatoes (see p. 142) with Lemon Butter Sauce (see p. 243).*
LEFT *Jambonette de Volaille (see p. 96) served with Ratatouille Sauce (see p. 76) or Braised Butter Beans (see p. 99).*

Fish

Most chefs seem to prefer cooking fish to meat, but whether that's because it cooks so quickly or because it is so adaptable and versatile, I'm not quite sure. Most of the fish used here are easily available from good fishmongers or fish counters in supermarkets, but if you can't find, say, skate or tuna, you can always substitute with something similar.

When buying fish, there are some obvious signs that will alert you as to its freshness. Most fresh flat fish have what is almost a wet slime over their skins. All fish should have bright, rounded (*not* sunken) eyes, and the flesh should be firm to the touch. Some older fish, or fish that have been frozen, have flesh that is full of water, so soft that it almost falls apart.

I love using fresh cod, mostly from British waters, which has a firm, white and very meaty flesh. Some of the best sea bass, turbot and red mullet comes from Brixham in the West Country. And Scotland, of course, is the origin of some of the best smoked fish, particularly haddock and salmon. Herrings are another Scottish speciality and there's plenty more where all these came from.

Cod with a Parsley Crust was one of my first fish dishes. The nicest thing about it is all the different textures – the crisp breadcrumb topping, the flesh of the fish, and then the creamy mashed potatoes. The whole thing is finished with a light lemon sauce. Salmon Fish Cakes are another old favourite. I took them off the menu at the Greenhouse for a little while, but had to restore them after a lot of harassment from customers – they had to make a return visit. If you can't get salmon – or think it's too expensive for a fish cake – then use cod instead; the recipe works just as well.

One of the dishes that has travelled with me is the Steamed Fillet of Turbot on Green Vegetables. The flavours of ginger and lime work so well together, and act almost as a seasoning for the vegetables. If you want to go even more oriental, then just add a few drops of soy sauce to spice it up. The dish is successful because all the flavours you need are in the vegetables, accompanying the natural flavour of the fish.

Whole sautéed herrings and mustard sauce is a real British Classic, but it was always rather hard to eat the fish itself, with all those bones. I've adapted the recipe to make the fish easier to handle, and hopefully better to eat. The fish have been filleted and as many bones as possible removed, which immediately makes life a lot easier. The braised lentils aren't particularly traditional, but they eat very well with mustard, and add a whole new texture to the dish.

The fresh tuna dish is very summery in feel, with a warm onion and potato salad. The fish would taste wonderful if cooked over barbecue coals in the garden, but of course can be grilled or pan-fried in the kitchen.

There are many books with detailed instructions on how to scale, fillet and skin fish. But do remember that you can ask your fishmonger to prepare fish for you. He is an expert, will do it more quickly, and if he wants a return visit, he'll do it willingly. This will make it all much easier for you. Ask for a few extra bones to take home and make into a stock.

Cod with a Parsley Crust

The cod for this recipe is best cut from the middle of large fillets, giving good, thick, rectangular pieces of fish. The best way to serve the fish is sitting on a bed of mashed potatoes with a lemon butter sauce around (see p. 71). Finishing the dish this way creates three complementary textures with the crust, the fish and the potatoes.

SERVES 4

75 g (3 oz) unsalted butter
2 shallots, finely chopped
4 tablespoons chopped fresh parsley
½ large white sliced loaf, crusts removed
   and crumbed
Salt and freshly ground white pepper
4 cod fillet pieces, each about 175–225 g
   (6–8 oz)

To serve

1 quantity Mashed Potatoes (see p. 142)
1 quantity Lemon Butter Sauce (see
   p. 243)

Pre-heat the grill to medium, pre-heat the oven to 180–200°C/350–400°F/gas 4–6, and butter and season a flameproof dish.

Melt the butter with the chopped shallots, which should just soften them, then remove from the heat. Add the chopped parsley to the breadcrumbs and season with salt and pepper. Gradually mix this with the shallot butter to form a light paste. Place the fish on the prepared dish and cover each cod fillet with the parsley crust. Cook the cod under the grill, not too near the heat. It will take about 8–10 minutes. As the crust slowly colours, the fish will be cooking. When the fish under the crust turns opaque and milky and the crust is golden brown, it is ready. Finish in the pre-heated oven for a few minutes to make sure the fish is completely cooked.

Divide the mashed potatoes between four hot plates, sit the fish on top and spoon the warm sauce around.

Cod with Cabbage, Bacon and Peas

This dish holds all the simplest ingredients, yet is packed with textures and tastes. We all keep cabbage, bacon and peas, so all you have to do now is buy the cod.

SERVES 4

4 smoked back bacon rashers, rinded and cut into strips
2 onions, finely shredded
100 g (4 oz) unsalted butter
1 tablespoon olive oil
600 ml (1 pint) Chicken Stock (see p. 228)
½ green cabbage, finely shredded

100 g (4 oz) cooked fresh or frozen peas
Salt and freshly ground white pepper
1 tablespoon plain flour
4 cod fillet pieces, each about 175–225 g (6–8 oz), skinned
A little vegetable oil

To serve

1 quantity Mashed Potatoes (see p. 142)

Cook the bacon and onions in 25 g (1 oz) of the butter and the olive oil until soft. Add the chicken stock and bring to the boil. Allow to simmer for a few minutes then re-boil and add the cabbage. This will only need to cook for a few minutes until it is tender but with a little bite to it; it must be kept boiling to prevent the cabbage from stewing. Now add the peas and 50 g (2 oz) of the remaining butter in pieces. Check for seasoning.

Lightly flour the skinned side of the cod and brush with the remaining soft butter. Brush a frying-pan with a little oil. Pan-fry the cod, skinned side down, for about 5–6 minutes. The underside, or skinned side, is the presentation side.

Divide the hot mashed potato between four hot plates. Sit the fish on top of the potato and spoon the broth and vegetables around.

Grilled Sea Bass with Fettucine and Ratatouille Sauce

This is a very colourful dish which features many styles – English, Italian and French – many textures and, of course, many flavours. If you do not have the time to make your own pasta, there are many good-quality fresh and dried pastas available in the shops.

SERVES 4

450 g (1 lb) Pasta Dough (see p. 249)
50 g (2 oz) unsalted butter
Salt and freshly ground black pepper

4 sea bass fillets, each about
175–225 g (6–8 oz)
25 ml (1 fl oz) olive oil

For the Ratatouille Sauce

1 red pepper, seeded
1 green pepper, seeded
2 shallots
½ aubergine
1 courgette

25 g (1 oz) unsalted butter
25 ml (1 fl oz) olive oil
300 ml (10 fl oz) Red Pepper Coulis
(see p. 240)

To make the fettucine, roll the dough through a pasta machine several times until it becomes about 1 mm (1/16 in) thick, then pass through the noodle cutter and leave to rest. If you do not have a pasta machine, it can be divided, rolled several times until very thin then cut by hand into ribbons; a pizza wheel is the easiest way to cut the pasta.

Pre-heat the grill to medium and butter and season a flameproof baking tray.

To make the ratatouille, cut the vegetables into 5 mm (¼ in) dice. Melt the butter with the olive oil in a large pan. Add the diced vegetables and cook for about 3–4 minutes until just softened. In another pan, warm the red pepper coulis then add the vegetables. Season with salt and pepper.

Lay the sea bass fillets on the prepared tray skin side up and cook under the medium grill for about 8 minutes.

While the fish is cooking, boil a large pan of water with the olive oil and a pinch of salt. When boiling, drop in the pasta and move it around with a fork. If it is fresh, it will only take a few minutes to cook. For dried pasta, just follow the instructions on the packet. Drain through a colander, season with salt and pepper and toss with the remaining butter to loosen.

Warm the ratatouille sauce and spoon it on to hot plates. Sit the fettucine in the middle and lay the grilled sea bass on the top.

Steamed Fillet of Turbot on Green Vegetables with Ginger and Lime

Once you have all the ingredients together for this, it's so quick and easy to cook. This is my own version of a Chinese stir-fry for fish. If you find turbot too expensive or difficult to buy, you can substitute cod, or any of your favourite fish.

SERVES 4

4 turbot fillets, each about 175 g (6 oz)
Salt and freshly ground white pepper
150 ml (5 fl oz) dry white wine
50 g (2 oz) unsalted butter or goose fat
450 g (1 lb) oyster or button mushrooms, sliced
450 g (1 lb) leeks, sliced

450 g (1 lb) fresh spinach, stalks removed
½ teaspoon grated fresh root ginger
½ bunch of fresh flatleaf parsley, picked
8 asparagus spears, blanched and cut into 5 cm (2 in) lengths
Juice of 1 lime

Pre-heat the oven to 220°C/425°F/gas 7 and grease and season a shallow baking tray. Place the turbot fillets in the tray, add the white wine and cover with buttered greaseproof paper. Place the tray into the pre-heated oven and the fish will begin to steam. They will take only 5–6 minutes to cook and will be just firm to the touch.

Meanwhile, heat a wok or frying-pan and add the butter or goose fat. Add the sliced mushrooms, leeks, spinach and ginger and stir-fry for about 2–3 minutes until almost cooked. Add the parsley and asparagus, season with salt and pepper and add the lime juice.

To serve, divide the vegetables between four hot plates. Sit the turbot on top of the vegetables and spoon a little of the fish cooking liquor over the top.

*Grilled Tuna
on Potato and
Onion Salad*

Grilled Tuna on Potato and Onion Salad

Fresh tuna is a beautiful, meaty fish, but if you would prefer not to use it or just can't find anywhere to buy it, this dish can work very well with turbot, brill, bass and many other fish. The tuna medallions have a very similar texture to fillet of beef, and are cooked in a similar fashion. Tuna fillet eats best when cooked medium rare to medium.

SERVES 4

8 large onions, sliced
2 tablespoons water
350 g (12 oz) new potatoes, boiled
175–200 ml (6–7 fl oz) Basic Vinaigrette (see p. 245)

A few fresh basil and tarragon leaves, chopped
4 medallions of tuna fillet, each about 175 g (6 oz)
1 curly endive, separated, or a handful of lettuce leaves per person

Place the onions and water in a pan and allow to cook very slowly until the natural sugar from the onions starts to caramelize and then brown, stirring occasionally. This will take at least 1 hour of slow cooking.

Pre-heat the barbecue or grill to hot. Slice the warm new potatoes and sprinkle liberally with some of the vinaigrette. Mix with the onions and chopped herbs. This mixture should be kept just slightly warm.

The tuna would now best be cooked on an open barbecue to give a good grilled taste, but it can also be cooked under a pre-heated grill (or pan-fried in some butter and olive oil). It will take about 3–4 minutes per side, depending on the thickness of the fillet.

Spoon the potato and onion salad on to the centre of the plates. Dress the salad leaves with some of the vinaigrette. Sit some leaves on top of the potatoes and finish with the tuna. Spoon some of the dressing over and serve.

Grilled Herrings with Braised Lentils and Mustard Seed Sauce

Grilled herrings whole on the bone with a separate hot English mustard sauce was one of the very first dishes I was taught as a young chef. They were very nice to eat, but hard work. So, to simplify everything for the diner, I decided to take them off the bone and try them just with the sauce. I then needed something to eat with them, and mashed potatoes worked very well, but I find lentils even tastier.

SERVES 4

8 large herring fillets

For the Braised Lentils

50 g (2 oz) unsalted butter
25 g (1 oz) carrot, finely diced
25 g (1 oz) celery, finely diced
25 g (1 oz) onion, finely diced
25 g (1 oz) leek, finely diced
1 small garlic clove, crushed

100 g (4 oz) green lentils (*lentilles de Puys*)
450 ml (15 fl oz) Chicken Stock (see p. 228) or Vegetable Stock (see p. 229)
Salt and freshly ground black pepper

For the Mustard Seed Sauce

2 shallots, finely chopped
1 celery stick, chopped
½ leek, chopped
1 bay leaf
50 g (2 oz) unsalted butter

300 ml (10 fl oz) dry white wine
600 ml (1 pint) Fish Stock (see p. 227)
300 ml (10 fl oz) double cream
About 2 teaspoons Meaux grain mustard

Pre-heat the oven to 200°C/400°F/gas 6 and butter and season a small flameproof baking tray.

To cook the lentils, melt the butter in a small ovenproof braising pan. Add the diced vegetables and garlic and cook for a few minutes. Add the lentils, stirring well. Cover with the stock and bring to the simmer. Cover with a lid and braise in the pre-heated oven for about 30–35 minutes until the lentils are tender and all the stock has been absorbed. Make sure they are tender before taking them from the oven. Season with salt and pepper.

To make the sauce, sweat the vegetables and bay leaf in the butter for a few minutes. Add the white wine and boil to reduce until almost dry. Add the fish stock and continue to boil until reduced by three-quarters. Pour on the cream and cook slowly until the sauce is thick enough to coat the back of a spoon. Strain through a fine sieve. Stir in the mustard a teaspoon at a time until the right taste is achieved, mustardy but not overpowering.

To cook the herring fillets, place them on to a greased baking tray and brush with butter. Cook under the hot grill for about 5–6 minutes. As soon as the fillets have coloured they will be ready to serve.

To serve, spoon the lentils on to the centre of four hot plates, pour the mustard sauce around and sit the fillets on top of the lentils. The dish is now complete!

Fillet of Red Mullet on Tapenade Toasts

Red mullet is perfect for this dish, which looks and certainly tastes very good and very Mediterranean. I particularly like to use an onion bread for the toasts.

SERVES 4

4 red mullet fillets, each about 175 g
    (6 oz), scaled and all bones removed
25 g (1 oz) unsalted butter, melted
Salt and freshly ground black pepper
4 slices onion or crusty bread
4 tablespoons Tapenade (see opposite)
½ curly endive, separated into leaves
150 ml (5 fl oz) Vierge Dressing (see
    p. 249)
2 tomatoes, skinned, seeded and diced
6 fresh basil leaves, chopped

Pre-heat the grill to hot and butter a flameproof tray. Lay the mullet fillets on the buttered tray, skin side up, brush with the butter and season with salt and pepper. Place the fish under the hot grill and allow the red skin to crisp. This will only take 3–4 minutes.

Toast the slices of bread and spread the tapenade on to each slice. Place the toasts on hot plates. Toss the curly endive in a little of the vierge dressing and sit on top of the toasts. Place the fillets on top of the lettuce. Mix the diced tomatoes and basil with the remaining vierge dressing and spoon over and around the fish.

Tapenade

Tapenade comes from the word tapeno with means 'caper' in Provençal. This paste is absolutely delicious and can be used for so many things. I like to spread it on toast to serve with the red mullet dish, left, but it is also great just to have on toast as a snack with drinks.

MAKES about 350 g (12 oz)

225 g (8 oz) black olives, stoned
1 small garlic clove, crushed
50 g (2 oz) tinned anchovy fillets, drained
25 g (1 oz) capers, drained
2 tablespoons olive oil
1 teaspoon lemon juice
Freshly ground black pepper

Place the olives, garlic, anchovies and capers into a food processor and blitz to a purée. While the motor is still running, slowly add the olive oil until the mix is pliable. You may need a little more olive oil. Add the lemon juice and season to taste with pepper. The tapenade is now ready to use or will keep for about a week in the fridge.

Fingers of Skate
with Potatoes, Fennel and
Braised Artichokes

This dish really doesn't have to be difficult. The potatoes and fennel are quick and easy to prepare, and if the artichokes sound like too much hard work (but it's worth a try), there are good-quality tinned artichoke bottoms available. Mixed bags of salad leaves are also available in supermarkets.

SERVES 4

225 g (8 oz) new potatoes, boiled	1 quantity Braised Artichoke Bottoms
1 onion, finely chopped	(see opposite)
100 ml (3½ fl oz) Basic Vinaigrette	50 g (2 oz) unsalted butter
(see p. 245)	700 g (1½ lb) skate wing fillets
2 fennel bulbs, trimmed	Plain flour for coating
Salt and freshly ground white	1 tablespoon olive oil
pepper	A handful of green salad leaves (rocket,
Juice of ½ lemon	curly endive, lamb's lettuce etc.)

For the Dressing

1 egg	Juice of 1 lemon
25 g (1 oz) capers, drained	½ teaspoon chopped fresh thyme
6 tinned anchovy fillets, drained	A pinch of sugar
1 garlic clove	50 ml (2 fl oz) warm water
1 × 2.5 cm (1 in) piece fresh ginger root,	225 ml (7½ fl oz) olive oil
peeled	225 ml (7½ fl oz) ground-nut oil
1 bunch of fresh basil leaves	Salt and freshly ground black pepper

To make the dressing, place all the ingredients except the oils into a food processor and blitz to a paste. With the motor running, slowly add the oil, as you would for mayonnaise. Push the dressing through a fine sieve then season to taste with salt and pepper.

Slice the new potatoes while still warm and mix with the chopped onion. Add about 2 tablespoons of the vinaigrette to moisten.

To cook the fennel, plunge it into boiling, salted water with the lemon juice and simmer for about 20 minutes until tender. Allow to cool in the liquor. When cool, halve the fennel and slice into long strips.

Warm the potatoes, fennel and artichokes together in half the butter.

Cut the skate into fingers, allowing five pieces per portion. Lightly flour the skate and fry in the remaining butter and the olive oil for a few minutes on each side.

Mix the dressing with the potatoes, fennel and artichokes and spoon on to the centre of the plates. Sit the skate fingers on top and finish with some salad leaves tossed in the remaining vinaigrette. Any left-over dressing can be kept in the fridge and used for simple mixed salads.

Braised Artichoke Bottoms

There are so many things you can do with artichoke bottoms, from adding them to a mixed salad to stuffing and braising. This recipe will help you cook them, the rest is up to you.

SERVES 4

2 large globe artichokes	1 tablespoon olive oil
Juice of ½ lemon	1 bay leaf
1 shallot, chopped	1 sprig of fresh thyme
1 carrot, chopped	6 black peppercorns
1 celery stick, chopped	6 coriander seeds
25 g (1 oz) unsalted butter	4 tomatoes, chopped

Firstly remove the stalks from the artichokes and then cut around the base, removing the leaves. Now cut across about 4 cm (1½ in) from the base and cut off any excess stalk or green left on. The centre of the bottom will still be intact. Rub with lemon juice.

Sweat the chopped shallot, carrot and celery in the butter and olive oil for a few minutes, then add the bay leaf, thyme, peppercorns, coriander seeds and chopped tomatoes. Pour in just enough water to cover. Bring to a simmer and cook for 10 minutes. Add the artichoke bottoms and about 1 teaspoon of lemon juice and simmer for 20–30 minutes until tender. When cooked and cooled, remove and discard the bristly centres. Cut each bottom in half, and each half into four or five slices. They are now ready to use.

Salmon Fish Cakes (see p. 88) served with Lemon Butter Sauce (see p. 243)

66 *These are fish cakes with a difference.* **99**

Salmon Fish Cakes

These are fish cakes with a difference. They are simple to make, but good to look at and great to eat (see previous page). They go very well with a green salad.

SERVES 4–6

2 shallots, finely chopped
Salt and freshly ground white pepper
450 g (1 lb) salmon, filleted and skinned
1 tablespoon unsalted butter
150 ml (5 fl oz) dry white wine
1 tablespoon chopped fresh parsley
350 g (12 oz) Mashed Potatoes without
    cream or butter (see p. 142)

2 tablespoons plain flour
2 eggs, beaten
100 g (4 oz) fresh breadcrumbs for
    coating
Vegetable oil for deep-frying
1 quantity Lemon Butter Sauce
    (see p. 243)

Pre-heat the oven to 200°C/400°F/gas 6 and butter and season a baking tray.

Sprinkle the finely chopped shallots on to the prepared baking tray, sit the salmon on top and season again with salt and pepper. Add the white wine, cover with foil and cook in the pre-heated oven for about 8–10 minutes until the fish is just cooked. The salmon should be just firm on the outside and still pink in the middle.

Sit the salmon in a colander over a pan to collect all the cooking juices. When all the juices have been collected, boil to reduce them to a syrupy consistency.

Break up the salmon with a wooden spoon, then add the syrupy reduction and the chopped parsley. Fold in 225 g (8 oz) of the potato, and then add it a spoonful at a time until you have a binding texture. Check for seasoning then roll into 12 to 18 balls about 4 cm (1½ in) in diameter. Three cakes per portion will be enough. Lightly pass through the flour, beaten eggs and then the breadcrumbs; repeat the process of egg and breadcrumbs once more.

The fish cakes are now ready for deep-frying which cooks them well and gives a good all-round colour. Heat the vegetable oil to 180°C/350°F then fry the fish cakes for about 4–5 minutes. Drain well on kitchen paper.

To serve, just pour the warm lemon butter sauce into individual serving dishes or bowls and sit three fish cakes in the middle of each one.

Poultry and Meat

It is in this section of the main course recipes that we can start to imagine that murmuring and bubbling *daube* mentioned at the beginning of the book. And it is here that you will find most of the basic techniques of Great Old British cookery that have become so much a personal and professional passion.

Some of the recipes are what you might expect – Braised Oxtail, Beef Stew and Dumplings, Boiled Bacon, Irish Stew and Lancashire Hot-pot. But a couple are a little different, using cuts of meat that are not eaten so much now – although in the good old days they were very popular. Faggots are a regional dish using kidney, liver and ox heart wrapped in caul fat (just like the classic French *crépinettes*); they're delicious with my Onion Gravy. Pigs' cheeks should not be too difficult to find. They are pure meat, and when braised are so succulent and tasty – I think they are a lot more flavoursome than pork chops, loins or even fillets. If you can't get them, just substitute chunks of pork; it's not quite the same, but the recipe still works. When they have been slowly braised, they're so soft and tender. You might find some difficulty in obtaining lambs' tongues but this is where having a good, friendly and understanding butcher comes in handy.

Most dishes here are on the British theme, apart from one or two. The Confit of Duck and all its variations are French, as is the Jambonette de Volaille. The Chicken with Paprika, Lemon and Soy Sauce is eastern in flavour, the Chicken Breast with Noodles and the Fillets of Lamb on Aubergine more Italian.

There's still plenty of room for all those dishes from the various culinary roads that criss-cross Britain: faggots from the west and Wales; steak and kidney pudding from the north, along with sausages and our boiled bacon. Although the boiled bacon is my own recipe, I've found a very similar Cumbrian version which uses orange lentils and split peas instead of green lentils and pearl barley.

One of my own favourite British specialities is the good old Cornish pasty, but when I published my own version under that name in a newspaper article, I was inundated with letters saying mine was nothing like the real thing. So I now call my version a Home-made Lamb Pasty! Apparently, or so I'm told, the way to test a real Cornish pasty is to drop it 100 feet down a mine; if the pastry doesn't break, then it's genuine!

Chicken with Wild Mushrooms, Grapes and Tarragon

This dish can be a fricassee, as here, or the chicken can simply be roasted and the sauce served separately. Oyster or pleurote mushrooms have become fairly common, but if you have any problem finding them, just substitute with button mushrooms.

SERVES 4

1 chicken, 1.5–1.75 kg (3–4 lb)
350 g (12 oz) oyster or button
   mushrooms
1 bunch of fresh tarragon

25 g (1 oz) unsalted butter
1 tablespoon olive oil
175 g (6 oz) seedless grapes, peeled
Salt and freshly ground white pepper

For the Sauce

4 shallots, chopped
1 carrot, chopped
2 celery sticks, chopped
1 bay leaf
1 sprig of fresh thyme

50 g (2 oz) unsalted butter
300 ml (10 fl oz) dry white wine
1.2 litres (2 pints) Chicken Stock (see
   p. 228)
450 ml (15 fl oz) double cream

For a fricassee, the chicken must be cut into four portions, removing the breasts and legs from the carcass. Split the drumsticks from the thighs, but leave the breasts whole. The carcass should be chopped and used in making the sauce.

Pre-heat the oven to 200°C/400°F/gas 6.

Pick over the oyster mushrooms, removing and reserving the stalks, and slice the mushroom caps. Remove the stalks from the tarragon and reserve them for the sauce.

To make the sauce, sweat the tarragon stalks, chopped shallots, carrot, celery, bay leaf and thyme in half the butter. Add the chopped chicken carcass and the mushroom trimmings and cook for a few minutes. Pour on the white wine and boil to reduce until almost dry. Add the chicken stock and boil to reduce by three-quarters. Add the cream and simmer for 20 minutes. Strain the sauce through a sieve.

Fry the chicken pieces in the butter and olive oil until coloured then transfer to the pre-heated oven and cook for 20 minutes, checking the breasts after 10 minutes; they may be ready and can be removed. When the chicken is cooked, leave it to rest for 15 minutes. Add the sliced mushroom caps, tarragon leaves and grapes to the sauce and warm them through until the mushrooms are tender. Season with salt and pepper.

Cut the chicken breasts in half and divide the chicken, giving a piece of breast and leg for each portion. Spoon over the sauce and serve.

Chicken with Paprika, Lemon and Soy Sauce

This dish eats very well with my Mashed Potatoes (see p. 142), which can be spiced up with a little olive oil, chopped onion, garlic, even chopped parsley for that extra taste and colour.

SERVES 4

1 chicken, about 1.5–1.75 kg (3½–4 lb)	2 heaped tablespoons paprika
1 garlic clove, halved	2 tablespoons plain flour
150 ml (5 fl oz) olive oil	Juice of 3 lemons
Salt and freshly ground white pepper	50 ml (2 fl oz) soy sauce
1 sprig of fresh thyme, chopped	50 g (2 oz) unsalted butter

Pre-heat the oven to 220°C/425°F/gas 7.

Cut the chicken into eight pieces: split the legs in half; remove the breasts from the carcass and cut each into two pieces. Rub the chicken pieces with the garlic and some of the olive oil. Season with salt and pepper and sprinkle with chopped thyme. Mix the paprika and flour together and cover the chicken pieces liberally with the mixture. Mix together the lemon juice and soy sauce and cover the chicken with half of this mixture.

Pre-heat a large flameproof baking pan and add some of the olive oil and half the butter. Add the chicken and fry over a high heat to crisp the skin until it is almost burnt black. Turn the chicken pieces in the pan and add the remaining lemon juice and soy sauce and a little more of the paprika mix. Place in the pre-heated oven for about 20 minutes, by which time the chicken will have a very crispy skin.

Remove the chicken from the pan and drain the liquor through a sieve into another pan. Warm this liquor and add the remaining butter. The sauce will now almost have a sweet and sour taste from the lemon, soy sauce and paprika. Simply pour it over the chicken and serve. Or, if you are serving the dish with mashed potatoes, divide the potato between individual plates, sit the chicken on top and pour the juices over.

Grilled Chicken Breast with Noodles in Creamy Mushroom Sauce

This is a variation on a great old Italian classic: noodles, mushrooms and a cream sauce (see p. 119 and pp. 230–1). It's a great way of turning a simple chicken breast into a wonderful dish, and is best served with a mixed or green salad. The marinated chicken breasts can be cooked on an open barbecue and served with a salad, and the cream sauce can be used with other dishes, even just with noodles on their own. If you don't have time to make your own fettucine, you can use shop-bought fresh or dried.

SERVES 4

4 chicken breasts
Salt and freshly ground white pepper
450 g (1 lb) Fettucine (see p. 76)
A little olive oil
1 teaspoon chopped fresh parsley

For the Marinade

300 ml (10 fl oz) olive oil
Juice of 2 lemons
1 garlic clove, crushed

½ teaspoon chopped fresh thyme
½ teaspoon chopped fresh basil
½ teaspoon chopped fresh tarragon

For the Cream Sauce

4 chicken wings (optional)
1 carrot, coarsely chopped
1 onion, coarsely chopped
2 celery sticks, coarsely chopped
1 small leek, coarsely chopped
50 g (2 oz) unsalted butter
1 small garlic clove

1 sprig of fresh thyme
1 bay leaf
A few fresh basil leaves
300 ml (10 fl oz) dry white wine
900 ml (1½ pints) Chicken Stock
   (see p. 228)
600 ml (1 pint) double cream

For the Garnish

2 large onions, sliced
6 smoked back bacon rashers, rinded
   and chopped
225 g (8 oz) button mushrooms, sliced
50 g (2 oz) unsalted butter

Mix together all the marinade ingredients, season with salt and pepper and pour over the chicken breasts. The breasts are best left in the marinade for 48 hours to allow them to take on the tastes.

Pre-heat the grill to medium.

To make the cream sauce, cook the chicken wings and chopped vegetables in the butter with the garlic and herbs until softened. Add the white wine and boil to reduce until almost dry. Add the chicken stock and boil to reduce by two-thirds. Add the cream, slowly bring to the simmer then simmer the sauce gently for about 30 minutes. Push the sauce through a sieve, check for seasoning and keep to one side in a large pan.

Remove the chicken breasts from the marinade and grill them until cooked through and tender, or pan-fry them in a little butter and olive oil.

The pasta can be made as for the sea bass recipe (see p. 76), or finer spaghetti noodles can be made or bought for this. It just needs to be boiled in salted water with a little oil until tender.

For the garnish, cook the sliced onions, bacon and mushrooms in the butter until they are soft.

To serve, place the pasta and garnish into the sauce, bring to the simmer and allow it to warm through for 2 minutes. Divide the pasta and garnish between four large bowls and spoon some of the sauce over each one. The grilled or pan-fried chicken can now be carved into two pieces, cutting at an angle through the middle. Slightly divide the chicken and sit it on top of the noodles. Pour 8–10 tablespoons of the marinade through a sieve into a bowl and add the chopped parsley. Spoon a little over each chicken breast just before serving.

66*The preparation is as important as the cooking.***99**

Dicing the bacon for Jambonette de Volaille (see p. 96).

Jambonette de Volaille

This is a classic French dish and really is just a stuffed chicken leg. When totally finished, the shape resembles a small ham, which is where the name jambonette comes from (see pp. 70–1). This recipe may look time-consuming, but it is very straightforward and worth every effort. The jambonette eats well with Braised Butter Beans (see p. 99) Ratatouille (see p. 76), or Tomato and Onion Flavoured Gravy (see p. 239).

SERVES 4

4 chicken legs
225 g (8 oz) pig's caul, soaked in cold
    water for 24 hours (optional)
2 tablespoons olive oil

For the Stuffing

225 g (8 oz) button mushrooms, minced
    or finely chopped
2 small chicken breasts, skinned
50 g (2 oz) fresh spinach, stalks removed,
    blanched and drained
1 large onion, finely chopped
2 smoked bacon rashers, rinded and
    finely diced

1 garlic clove, crushed
A few fresh basil leaves, chopped
100 g (4 oz) oyster mushrooms
    (optional), sliced
25 g (1 oz) unsalted butter
Salt and freshly ground white
    pepper
1 egg

To serve

Braised Butter Beans (see p. 99) or
    Ratatouille (see p. 76)
Tomato and Onion Flavoured Gravy
    (see p. 239)

Firstly, the chicken legs must be boned. Lay the leg, skin side down, and cut along the thigh bone only. Scrape down the bone towards the joint and the thigh meat will start to fall from the bone. Continue to scrape until the bone is free of any meat. Keep the point of the knife close to the knuckle joint and cut round carefully. The joint will now be clean. Continue the same process and scrape down to the next joint. At this point, the bone can be broken or cut and the leg will be boned. Repeat the same process for all the legs, just leaving the knuckle on the end of each one.

    To make the stuffing, heat the minced mushrooms on their own in a pan until they become totally dry. Allow to cool. Mince or finely chop the chicken breasts with the blanched spinach then mix into the mushrooms and chill in the fridge. Heat the onion, bacon, garlic, basil and oyster mushrooms, if using, in the butter for a few minutes until softened, then allow to cool. Add to the chicken and mushroom mixture, season with salt and pepper and mix in the egg.

Fill the boned legs with the stuffing, filling them enough to re-shape into a chicken leg, and folding the skin and meat under to seal the leg. They can now be wrapped in pig's caul, if using, or simply use wooden cocktail sticks to hold the legs together. Leave the legs to rest for at least 1 hour in the fridge to set, then they will be ready to roast.

Pre-heat the oven to 200°C/400°F/gas 6.

Fry the legs on the curved side in the olive oil in a flameproof baking pan until golden brown then turn in the pan and cook in the pre-heated oven for 20–25 minutes.

Serve the hot butter beans or ratatouille on to hot plates. Cut the jambonette into 4–5 slices and arrange on the beans or vegetables and serve with the tomato and onion sauce poured around.

Confit of Duck

Confit comes from the French word meaning 'to preserve'. It is a classic regional dish from Gascony in south-west France. The technique can be applied to various different meats, but duck, goose and pork are the most common. So many tastes and textures can be achieved in the dish, but it will, of course, depend on how long you marinate the meat, how slowly you cook it, how you store it and what actually goes into the marinade. I'm going to give you my version, with various ways of serving it. I cook it in goose fat, which is quite expensive to buy, but the dish will work very well with rendered pork fat or lard. It really is worth making the effort for a good confit. The recipes that follow are just a few ideas of what to eat with confit. If you don't fancy any of these, confit is wonderful with a good salad.

SERVES 4

4 duck legs
2 teaspoons rock salt
1–1.5 kg (2–3 lb) goose or pork fat to
    cover
4 tablespoons clear honey

For the Marinade

A few sprigs of fresh thyme
1 bay leaf
6 fresh basil leaves
12 black peppercorns
1 garlic clove, sliced
2 shallots or 1 onion,
    chopped

2.5 cm (1 in) fresh root ginger, peeled
    and grated
2 teaspoons Worcestershire sauce
2 teaspoons soy sauce
2 teaspoons balsamic vinegar
1 tablespoon white wine vinegar
1 tablespoon extra virgin olive oil

Mix together all the ingredients for the marinade. Rub each duck leg with the rock salt. Place the legs in the marinade, cover and leave for at least 3–4 days in the fridge. The longer the legs marinate, the stronger the flavour will become.

Pre-heat the oven to 160–180°C/325–350°F/gas 3–4.

To cook the duck legs, melt the fat in a deep flameproof baking dish or tray. Add the duck legs to the fat and cook in the pre-heated oven for about 2 hours. When cooked slowly the legs take on more flavour. Check them during cooking: if you try to separate the leg from the thigh and it starts to give easily, then they are ready. Leave to cool in the fat.

The legs can be eaten immediately after cooking. Or at this stage, they can be transferred to a suitable container, covered with the cooking fat and chilled. They will keep for weeks, even months, and the flavour will be developing all the time. When you are ready to serve them, simply remove them from the fat and cook in the low oven for about 20 minutes. I always like to finish my confit with a tablespoon of honey on each leg and then crisp it under the grill.

Braised Butter Beans

Braised butter beans go well with many other dishes as well as confit (see pp. 70–1).

SERVES 4

1 onion, chopped
2 smoked bacon rashers, rinded and cut into strips
1 tablespoon olive oil
1 tablespoon unsalted butter
1 garlic clove, crushed
8 fresh basil leaves, chopped

1 bay leaf
100 g (4 oz) dried butter beans
600–900 ml (1–1½ pints) Chicken Stock (see p. 228)
2 tomatoes, skinned, seeded and diced
Salt and freshly ground black pepper

To serve

A few curly endive leaves
1 quantity Confit of Duck (see left)
2–3 tablespoons Basic Vinaigrette (see p. 245)
1 quantity Red Wine Sauce (see p. 236)

Pre-heat the oven to 180°C/350°F/gas 4.

Sweat the chopped onion and bacon in a flameproof dish in the olive oil and butter for a few minutes, then add the garlic, basil, bay leaf and butter beans. Cover with 600 ml (1 pint) of chicken stock and bring to the simmer. Cover and cook in the pre-heated oven for 1–1½ hours until the beans are tender; they may need a little more stock added during the cooking process.

When the beans are tender they will have created a thick sauce. Add the tomatoes, salt and pepper and spoon on to hot plates. Mix the curly endive with the vinaigrette and sit some on top of the beans. Finish with the hot, glazed duck confit and pour some red wine sauce around.

Confit of Duck
with Cabbage, Onions and
Beansprouts

The flavours in the dish give an oriental taste similar to the classic Peking duck.

SERVES 4

½ green cabbage, shredded
225 g (8 oz) beansprouts
2 onions, sliced
25 g (1 oz) goose fat or unsalted butter
2 tablespoons olive oil
Salt and freshly ground black pepper
A pinch of five-spice powder
300 ml (10 fl oz) Veal *Jus* (see p. 232) or
     bought alternative (see p. 225)
1 quantity Confit of Duck (see p. 98)
1–3 tablespoons Plum Purée Sauce
     (see p. 242)

Blanch the cabbage and beansprouts separately in boiling salted water then refresh under cold water and drain well. Fry the onions in the goose fat or butter and olive oil until softened and brown. Add the cabbage and beansprouts and season with salt, pepper and five-spice powder. Continue to cook for 3–4 minutes until slightly softened.

Bring the veal *jus* to the simmer and gradually add the plum purée sauce until a rich, spicy plum flavour is achieved. One tablespoon may well be enough, the quantity all depends on your taste buds.

Spoon the cabbage mixture on to the hot plates, sit the hot, glazed confit on top and pour the sauce around.

Confit of Duck with Red Cabbage and Apples

SERVES 4

4 apples, peeled and cored
½ red cabbage, shredded
2 onions, sliced
65 g (2½ oz) unsalted butter
150 ml (5 fl oz) red wine vinegar
25 g (1 oz) demerara sugar
150 ml (5 fl oz) red wine
Salt and freshly ground black pepper

To serve

1 quantity Confit of Duck (see p. 98)
1 quantity Red Wine Sauce (see p. 236)

Chop two of the apples. Sweat the red cabbage and onions in 50 g (2 oz) of the butter for a few minutes until softened. Add the chopped apples and cook for a further few minutes. Add the wine vinegar and cook until it evaporates. Add the sugar and red wine and season with salt and pepper. Cover with a lid and continue to cook for about 30 minutes until the cabbage is tender.

Slice the remaining apples in to 12 rings. Melt the remaining butter and fry the apple rings in a hot pan, browning on both sides.

Spoon the cabbage on to hot plates and sit three apple rings on top. Arrange the hot, glazed duck confit on the apples and pour the red wine sauce around.

Calves' Liver with
Onion Gravy and Mashed Potatoes

This has to be the most popular main course on my menu. It's simple, it's tasty, but of course calves' liver isn't the easiest offal to find. I also enjoy lambs' liver, so this recipe can be used with the liver of your choice. The liver also eats very well with the bacon just plain, without the sauce or potatoes. You can then serve your own choice of vegetables to go with it.

SERVES 4

700 g (1½ lb) calves' liver
700 g (1½ lb) Mashed Potatoes (see p. 142)
600 ml (1 pint) Onion Gravy (see p. 233)
4 smoked middle bacon rashers, rinded
50 g (2 oz) unsalted butter

The liver can be bought already sliced, but if you wish to cut your own, make sure the film of soft sinew covering the meat is removed first. Cut the liver into about eight thin slices.

Pre-heat the grill to hot.

Prepare the mashed potatoes and onion gravy and keep them hot on the stove. Grill the bacon until crispy.

The ideal way to cook the liver is on an open grill for the maximum taste. If you don't have a grill, pan-fried liver will be equally good. Pre-heat a frying-pan very hot. Add the butter and the liver. If the liver has been sliced 6 mm (¼ in) thick, it will only take 1½ minutes on both sides. It will now be a good colour and still slightly pink inside, making it moist to eat.

To serve the dish, spoon the potatoes towards the top of hot plates and cover the rest of the plate with onion gravy. Lay the liver on the potatoes and gravy, allowing two slices per portion. To finish, just sit the bacon rashers on top.

OPPOSITE
*Calves' Liver with Onion Gravy
and Mashed Potatoes.*

Faggots in Onion Gravy

I usually use the trimmings from cuts of beef for this when I make them (see pp. 106–7). Pig's caul (the lining of a pig's stomach) is the classic wrapping for faggots, and your butcher should be able to get some for you. (It needs to be soaked in cold water for 24 hours before use.) Alternatively, you can fry the faggots without the caul, as for meatballs, but the finish and flavour won't be quite the same. The best dishes to serve with faggots are Colcannon (see p. 142) or Mashed Potatoes (see p. 142).

SERVES 4

2 onions, finely chopped
1 garlic clove, crushed
½ teaspoon fresh thyme leaves
½ teaspoon chopped fresh sage
½ teaspoon chopped fresh parsley
50 g (2 oz) unsalted butter
300 ml (10 fl oz) Veal *Jus* (see p. 232) or bought alternative (see p. 225)

175 g (6 oz) lean beef rump or topside, well trimmed
175 g (6 oz) ox heart, trimmed
175 g (6 oz) ox kidney, trimmed
175 g (6 oz) lambs' liver, trimmed
Salt and freshly ground black pepper
1 egg
450 g (1 lb) pig's caul, soaked in cold water for 24 hours

To finish

1.2 litres (2 pints) thin Veal *Jus* or Stock (see p. 232)
25 g (1 oz) beef dripping
1 quantity Onion Gravy (see p. 233)

Cook the chopped onions, garlic and herbs in the butter until soft. Add the veal *jus* and boil to reduce by two-thirds. Leave to cool, then allow to set in the fridge.

Mince the meats through a medium cutter. Place all the minced meat in a mixer and beat slowly, adding salt and pepper to taste. The salt will also thicken the meat, giving a gelatinous texture. Add the egg and the reduced, cool onion mix. The faggot mixture is now ready, and is best left chilled for 2–3 hours to set more firmly.

To form the faggots, squeeze any excess water from the caul and cut it into 8 × 20 cm (8 in) squares. Spoon about 75 g (3 oz) of the faggot mixture into the centre of each square and wrap and turn the caul around the meat to form firm ball shapes.

When you are ready to cook the faggots, warm the veal *jus* or stock. Fry the faggots in the dripping until brown on all sides, then place them in the *jus* or stock and simmer very gently for 12–15 minutes until just starting to firm up. Remove the pan from the heat and leave to rest. The faggots can now be allowed to cool, left in the cooking liquor, and chilled. The liquor will set like a jelly and keep the faggots for up to a week in the fridge.

When you want to serve the faggots, remove them from the jelly and heat through for 15–20 minutes in the onion gravy on top of the stove. To serve, lift the faggots from the gravy and arrange on hot plates. Sit the onions on top and spoon over the gravy.

LEFT Stage 1:
Preparing the pig's caul.
RIGHT Stage 2:
Spooning in the filling.

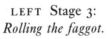

LEFT Stage 3:
Rolling the faggot.

ABOVE
*Faggots simmering in
Onion Gravy
(see p. 104).*

Pigs' Cheeks Stew

Pigs' cheeks are certainly an unusual cut of meat, not very often used. You'll have to know your butcher and ask him to save some for you. What you want is just the meaty part of the cheek. This is a classic recipe for stewing them, but if cheeks are unavailable, replace with large chunks of lean pork. The cheeks are best served with Mashed Potatoes (see p. 142) and Glazed Carrots (see p. 161) or Spinach with Cream and Garlic (see p. 153).

SERVES 4

1.5 kg (3 lb) pigs' cheeks, trimmed of all sinews

Salt and freshly ground black pepper

50 g (2 oz) plain flour

25 g (1 oz) beef dripping or lard

450 g (1 lb) shallots or onions, sliced

225 g (8 oz) bacon rind, cut into strips

6 garlic cloves, halved

A few black peppercorns

1 bottle red wine

600 ml (1 pint) Veal *Jus* (see p. 232) or bought alternative (see p. 225)

1 bouquet garni (1 bay leaf, 1 sprig of fresh thyme, 2 sprigs of fresh sage wrapped and tied in a strip of leek) or bouquet garni sachet

For the Garnish

225 g (8 oz) button onions

100 g (4 oz) unsalted butter

225 g (8 oz) button mushrooms

175 g (6 oz) smoked bacon, rinded and cut into strips

Season the cheeks with salt and pepper and lightly dip in flour. Pre-heat the lard in a frying-pan and fry the cheeks until coloured on both sides. Remove from the pan and place in a large flameproof casserole. Add the sliced shallots or onions to the frying-pan and fry until tender. Transfer the shallots or onions to the casserole using a slotted spoon. Add the bacon rind to the frying-pan and fry for a few minutes then transfer to the casserole. Add the garlic and peppercorns to the frying-pan and pour on the red wine and *jus*. Bring to the simmer, then pour over the cheeks and add the bouquet garni. Cover and allow to cook gently for about 1½–2 hours until the cheeks are tender.

Meanwhile, prepare the garnish. Fry the button onions in the butter until softened and golden brown. Add the mushrooms and bacon strips and continue to fry for a few more minutes. Leave to drain of any excess fat in a sieve or colander.

When the cheeks are tender, remove them from the sauce and strain the sauce through a sieve into a pan. Boil the sauce until reduced to a thicker consistency, skimming once or twice, if necessary, to remove any impurities. Once re-boiled, mix with the cheeks again, add the drained garnishes and re-heat gently before serving.

Duck Variation

This recipe can also be used for duck legs. Allowing one leg per portion, simply remove the skin, separate the thigh from the drumstick and quickly fry in fat. Soak the legs in red wine and chill for a few days to enhance the taste, or cook straightaway as for the cheeks. The legs will take about 2 hours to cook in the liquor, and they eat particularly well with the Spinach with Cream and Garlic (see p. 153)

Braised Oxtail

This dish is more than just traditional British, in fact it has become my signature dish. I find it exciting to cook and even more exciting to eat. You can pick up the tails and eat them with your hands and just dip your bread in the sauce to collect all the tastes. The tails are also very good served with creamy Mashed Potatoes (see p. 142).

*Braised Oxtail
with Mashed Potatoes
(see p. 142).*

SERVES 4–6

4 oxtails, trimmed of fat
Salt and freshly ground black pepper
100 g (4 oz) beef dripping
225 g (8 oz) carrots, chopped
225 g (8 oz) onions, chopped
225 g (8 oz) celery sticks, chopped
225 g (8 oz) leeks, chopped

450 g (1 lb) tomatoes, chopped
1 sprig of fresh thyme
1 bay leaf
1 garlic clove, crushed
600 ml (1 pint) red wine
2.25 litres (4 pints) Veal Stock (see
    p. 232) or bought alternative (see
    p. 225)

For the Garnish

1 large carrot, finely diced
1 onion, finely diced
2 celery sticks, finely diced

1 leek, finely diced
6 tomatoes, skinned, seeded and diced
2 tablespoons chopped fresh parsley

For this recipe, the veal stock should not have been reduced to a sauce consistency, as this tends to become too strong when braising the tails. Oxtails can be used in place of veal bones when making the stock for extra beef flavour.

Pre-heat the oven to 200°C/400°F/gas 6.

Firstly, separate the trimmed tails between the joints and season with salt and pepper. In a large pan, fry the tails in the dripping until brown on all sides, then drain in a colander. Fry the chopped carrot, onion, celery and leek in the same pan, collecting all the residue from the tails. Add the chopped tomatoes, thyme, bay leaf and garlic and continue to cook for a few minutes. Place the tails in a large braising pan with the vegetables. Pour the red wine into the pan and boil to reduce until almost dry. Add some of the stock then pour on to the meat in the braising pan and cover with the remaining stock. Bring the tails to a simmer and braise in the pre-heated oven for 1½–2 hours until the meat is tender.

Lift the pieces of meat from the sauce and keep to one side. Push the sauce through a sieve into a pan, then boil to reduce it, skimming off all impurities, to a good sauce consistency.

While the sauce is reducing, quickly cook the diced garnish carrot, onion, celery and leek in a tablespoon of water until soft. When the sauce is ready, add the tails and vegetable garnish and simmer until the tails are warmed through. Add the diced tomato and spoon into hot bowls, allowing three or four oxtail pieces per portion. Sprinkle with chopped parsley and serve.

Braised Lambs' Tongues

Lambs' tongues are a cheap cut of meat which don't get used very often. They take a while to cook, but are simple and worth every minute. This recipe is similar to the Irish Stew (see p.129) in its basic ingredients, but there are many additions that can change the whole dish: Meaux mustard can be added at the end; mushrooms and bacon can be cooked with the vegetables; celeriac, swede and parsnip can all be used to lift the dish. This eats very well with the Mashed Potatoes (see p. 142) or just some crusty bread.

SERVES 4–6

12 lambs' tongues
1.75 litres (3 pints) Chicken Stock (see p. 228)
3 large onions
450 g (1 lb) carrots
8 celery sticks
675 g (1½ lb) potatoes, peeled
50 g (2 oz) unsalted butter

2 tablespoons olive oil
2 garlic cloves, crushed
1 bouquet garni (1 bay leaf, 1 sprig each of fresh thyme, rosemary and sage, wrapped and tied in a strip of leek) or bouquet garni sachet
Salt and freshly ground black pepper
1 tablespoon chopped fresh parsley

Cover the tongues with cold water in a large pan and bring to the boil. Drain, then refresh under cold water. Return the tongues to the same pan and cover with chicken stock. Bring to the simmer, cover and cook slowly for 2–2½ hours in the stock. Make sure they are covered with liquid all the time, adding more stock or water if necessary. Check after 2 hours. Remove one tongue from the stock and pinch or pierce with a knife; it will either give slightly or the knife will pierce easily if it is cooked. If not, continue to cook for a further 30 minutes then re-check. When cooked and still warm, remove them from the stock and take off the skins. These will peel off very easily. Strain and reserve the cooking liquor.

Cut the vegetables into 2.5 cm (1 in) pieces. Melt the butter and olive oil in a separate pan and cook the vegetables, garlic and bouquet garni for 5–10 minutes. Add the reserved cooking liquor, season with salt and pepper, bring to the simmer and cook for 15 minutes.

Cut the tongues into two or three pieces and add to the vegetables. Bring back to the simmer and continue to cook for a further 5–10 minutes. Remove the bouquet garni and taste for seasoning. Sprinkle with parsley and the stew is ready. The tongues will be tender and the vegetables will have taken on the flavours of the cooking liquor.

Boiled Bacon with Pearl Barley and Lentils

There are so many alternative ways of serving boiled bacon. It eats well with split peas, broad beans and even just parsley sauce, but this is one of my favourite ways of serving it. It could even be used as a winter soup. The bacon can also be served with Braised Split Peas (see p. 154), with just a little stock spooned over. Any left-over stock can be frozen for soup-making, some sauces, or even your next boiled bacon.

SERVES 4

1.8 kg (4 lb) unsmoked rolled bacon collar, rind removed	50 g (2 oz) pearl barley
5 carrots	1 large swede
4 onions	2 parsnips
2 celery sticks	100 g (4 oz) unsalted butter
1 leek	1 garlic clove, crushed
1 sprig of fresh thyme	50 g (2 oz) Braised Lentils (see p. 80)
1 bay leaf	1 tablespoon chopped fresh parsley
About 1.75–2.25 litres (3–4 pints) Chicken Stock (see p. 228)	Salt and freshly ground black pepper
	1 quantity Mashed Potatoes (see p. 142)

Soak the bacon in water for 24 hours before cooking. This will reduce the salt content.

Put the bacon in a large pot. Coarsely chop two of the carrots, one of the onions, the celery and leek and add to the pot with the herbs. Cover with chicken stock, bring to the simmer, skim off any impurities, cover and cook gently for about 1½ hours until cooked. Allow to rest for 30 minutes in the stock.

Cook the pearl barley in some of the cooking liquor for about 15–20 minutes until soft. Cut the remaining vegetables into 1 cm (½ in) dice and sweat in half the butter with the garlic. Add the pearl barley and a little more stock, if necessary, to give a soup consistency. Allow this to simmer for about 15 minutes until all the vegetables are tender. Add the cooked lentils, the remaining knobs of butter and the chopped parsley to create a barley, lentil and vegetable stew. Check for seasoning.

To serve, sit the warm mashed potatoes in the centre of the serving plates and spoon some of the stew around. Slice the bacon, allow two slices per portion, and place on the potatoes. Finish with a spoonful of stock on top of the meat and serve.

Jellied Bacon with Parsley

This is a very tasty, traditional English dish. It can simply be spooned on to a plate and served with lettuce leaves and a potato salad, the recipe for which is to be found on p. 141.

SERVES 4

1.8 kg (4 lb) unsmoked bacon collar
2 carrots
1 onion
2 celery sticks
1 leek
1 bay leaf
1.2–1.75 litres (2–3 pints) Chicken Stock (see p. 228)

6 shallots or 3 onions, finely chopped
150 ml (5 fl oz) dry white wine
150 ml (5 fl oz) white wine vinegar
2 teaspoons chopped fresh parsley
Salt and freshly ground black pepper

Cooking the bacon is best done either in the morning or the day before. Put the bacon, carrots, onion, celery, leek, bay leaf and chicken stock in a pan, making sure the stock covers the meat. Bring to the simmer, cover and simmer gently for 1 hour until the bacon is cooked. Allow the bacon to cool in the stock then transfer it to a clean container. Pass the cooking liquor through a fine sieve; it will set to a jelly.

While the stock is setting, cover the chopped shallots with the white wine and wine vinegar in a small pan. Boil to reduce until dry then leave to cool.

Taste the jelly, and if it is a little bland, it may now need to be re-boiled and reduced for a stronger taste. When it is ready, sit it on a bowl of ice and allow it to cool almost to setting point. It will have almost jellied.

Trim the bacon of any excess fat; the meat will be nice and moist. Slice and shred the bacon into thin strips and mix with the parsley and shallots. Check for seasoning and add the stock. Pour the mix into a bowl or tray and chill in the fridge until set.

OPPOSITE
*Jellied Bacon with Parsley
served with New Potato Salad
(see p. 141).*

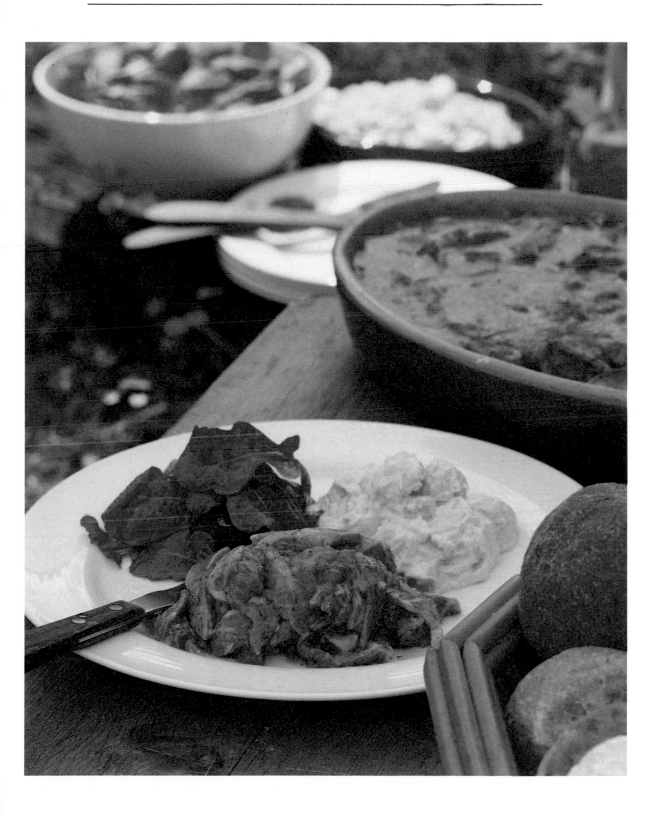

Home-made Pork Sausages

There are so many varieties of sausage available in the shops, good ones, too, that you're probably wondering why I'm making my own. Well, they've become a Great British Classic, and I like making classic dishes. They give me a great sense of achievement and taste really good too (see p. 119)!

If you do decide to make the sausages, speak to your butcher a day or two before and order the pigs' cheeks and sausage skins. The cheeks are totally fat free and have great flavour; you need just the centre, meaty part. Also make sure the shoulder is boned and rindless. You can make life even easier, however, by replacing the shoulder, cheeks and back fat with trimmed pork belly. I like to serve the sausages with Split Pea Fritters (see opposite), arranging two sausages on top of each fritter. I also like to serve them with an Onion Gravy (see p. 233) which you may well want to pass through a sieve for a smoother sauce.

MAKES about 16 sausages

900 g (2 lb) boned and rinded shoulder
    of pork
4 pigs' cheeks, trimmed
225 g (8 oz) rinded pork back fat
2 onions, very finely chopped
25 g (1 oz) unsalted butter
¼ teaspoon chopped fresh thyme
¼ teaspoon chopped fresh sage
1 garlic clove, crushed

Salt and freshly ground black
    pepper
A pinch of ground mace
2 slices white bread, crusts removed
    and crumbed
1 egg, beaten
Worcestershire sauce
About 4 metres (4½ yards) sausage skins,
    soaked in cold water
50 g (2 oz) lard

Mince the shoulder, cheeks and back fat through a medium mincer. I like to keep the mix fairly coarse and only mince the meat once. If you prefer a smoother texture then mince once more.

Sweat the chopped onions in the butter with the herbs and garlic for 2–3 minutes until soft. If there is any excess liquid once the onions are cooked, turn up the heat and boil to reduce until dry. Leave to cool. When the onions are cold, mix them with the pork meat and season with salt, pepper and ground mace. Add the breadcrumbs and egg. A few drops of Worcestershire sauce will now finish the taste.

The skins will have been preserved in salt and will need to be well soaked and rinsed in cold water. Cut the skin into sixteen 25 cm (10 in) lengths and tie a knot in one end. Fill a piping bag with the sausage meat and pipe into the skin. Fill to the size of a standard pork sausage, then tie a knot in the other end. This will leave 5–8 cm (2–3 in) of spare sausage skin which will shrink during cooking. Repeat the process with the remaining sausage mix. Rest the sausages in the fridge for 30 minutes.

The sausages are now ready to cook. They must be treated carefully during cooking and not fried on a high heat. Melt the lard and cook the sausages over a medium heat for about 10 minutes until browned on all sides. The sausages are now ready to eat. They can be simply placed on top of the pea fritters and the onion sauce poured around, or even just eaten in a roll!

Split Pea Fritters

Serves 4

100 g (4 oz) plain flour	1 teaspoon chopped fresh parsley
A pinch of salt	8 tablespoons Braised Split Peas
1 egg	(see p. 154)
300 ml (10 fl oz) milk	Salt and freshly ground white pepper
1 tablespoon unsalted butter, melted	2 tablespoons vegetable oil

Sieve the flour and salt into a bowl. Beat the egg with half the milk then fold the mixture into the flour. Gradually add more of the milk until the mixture is thick enough to coat the back of a spoon. Add the melted butter and chopped parsley.

The split peas must be cold. Slowly fold some of the batter into the peas until you have a thick pancake mix; not all the batter may be needed. Season with salt and pepper.

Heat a little oil in a 15 cm (6 in) pancake pan and pour in the batter to about 6 mm (¼ in) thick. Fry until golden brown, then turn over in the pan and fry the other side. Keep warm while you make three more fritters.

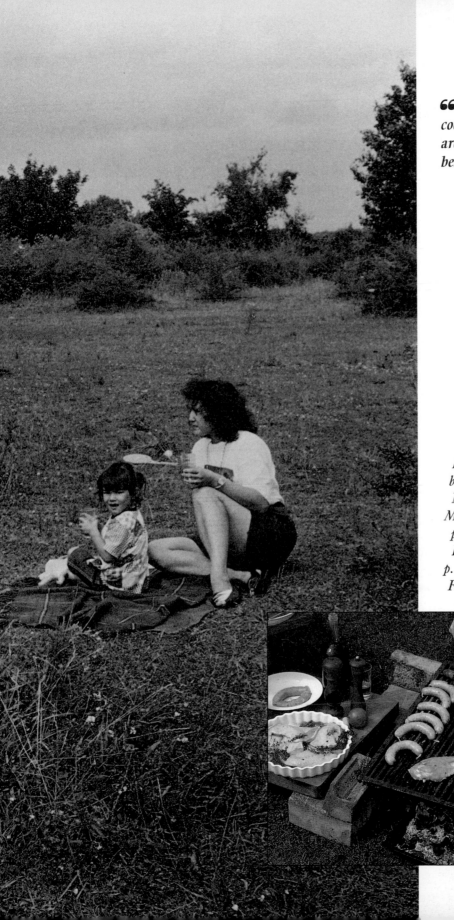

66 *The simplest cooking techniques are still the best.* **99**

Barbecuing chicken breasts to serve with Noodles in Creamy Mushroom Sauce (see p. 92), Home-made Pork Sausages (see p. 116) and Split Pea Fritters (see p. 117).

Fillet of Venison Wellington

This dish is usually associated with fillet of beef, but I've tried it with venison, added some chestnuts to the stuffing, and served it with a slightly sweetened sauce and found it really delicious. You can, of course, follow this recipe for fillet of beef but omit the chestnuts and cook for an extra 20 minutes. Two dishes from one recipe! Ask your butcher to bone the venison for you and trim the fillet of all sinew. Take the bones home to add flavour to the sauce.

Another way to serve this is to make the Bubble and Squeak on p. 147, either cooked as per the recipe or in individual cakes. The venison slices can then be placed on top of the cakes and the sauce poured around.

SERVES 4

1 × 450–750 g (1–1½ lb) boned loin of venison from a saddle of fallow deer
275 g (10 oz) Puff Pastry (see p. 216)
50 g (2 oz) unsalted butter

Salt and freshly ground white pepper
4–6 thin Savoury Pancakes (see p. 208)
1 egg, beaten

For the Stuffing

225 g (8 oz) mushrooms, minced or finely chopped
1 onion, finely chopped
2 smoked back bacon rashers, rinded and finely diced
1 garlic clove, crushed
A pinch of chopped fresh sage
A pinch of chopped fresh thyme

25 g (1 oz) unsalted butter
50 g (2 oz) shelled chestnuts, chopped
25 g (1 oz) fresh white breadcrumbs
1 teaspoon chopped fresh parsley
1 large chicken breast, skinned and minced or very finely chopped
Salt and freshly ground white pepper
1 egg, beaten

For the Sauce

Venison bones (optional)
600 ml (1 pint) Red Wine Sauce (see p. 236)
1–2 teaspoons cranberry jelly

To make the stuffing, cook the mushrooms on their own in a pan until almost dry. Cook the chopped onion, bacon, garlic, sage and thyme in the butter for a few minutes without colouring. Leave to cool. Add the chestnuts, breadcrumbs and parsley. Season the chicken with salt and pepper, gradually mix in the egg and mix until firm to the touch. Stir in the mushrooms and the onion mixture and check for seasoning.

The sauce can be made in advance. If you have the venison bones, pre-heat the oven to 220°C/425°F/gas 7. Chop the bones and roast in the pre-heated oven for about 30 minutes until browned. Add them to the reduction for the red wine sauce (see p. 236) before adding the veal *jus*, then cook in the normal way. Once the sauce has been pushed through a sieve a good venison flavour will have developed. Stir in the cranberry jelly to give a slightly sweeter taste.

Roll out the pastry until large enough to wrap the venison; the thinnest should be 3 mm (⅛ in) and the absolute thickest is 5 mm (¼ in). Leave to rest in the fridge.

Season the venison and fry in the butter in a hot pan until coloured on all sides but not cooked. Leave to cool.

To make the Wellington, lay two of the pancakes on the centre of the pastry and spread some of the stuffing over to cover them. Lay the meat on top and spread some more of the stuffing on top. Fold the pancakes around the meat and lay the other two on top. Brush the edges of the pastry with beaten egg and fold over to enclose the meat and stuffing. Trim off any excess pastry and turn the parcel over on to a dampened roasting tray. Leave to rest in the fridge for 30 minutes.

Pre-heat the oven to 220°C/425°F/gas 7.

Brush the pastry with a little more beaten egg. The pastry can be decorated with pastry trimmings or left plain. Roast in the pre-heated oven for 20–25 minutes. This will leave the meat still pink inside. Leave to rest for 10–15 minutes.

Slice the Wellington, allowing three slices per portion, and serve with the hot, rich sauce.

Steak and Kidney Pudding

There are many recipes for steak and kidney puddings. This one is a little more involved, but I think gets the best results (see pp. 126–7). It's best to have some fresh and some dried suet, but if not you can use just the dried.

SERVES 6–8

900 g (2 lb) braising steak, trimmed and cut into 2.5 cm (1 in) dice

450 g (1 lb) ox or lambs' kidneys, trimmed and cut into 2.5 cm (1 in) dice

50–75 g (2–3 oz) beef dripping

6 celery sticks, diced

6 carrots, diced

8 onions, diced

225 g (8 oz) mushrooms, quartered (optional)

1 garlic clove, crushed

½ teaspoon chopped fresh thyme

50 g (2 oz) unsalted butter

300 ml (10 fl oz) Guinness

1.75 litres (3 pints) Veal *Jus* (see p. 232) or bought alternative (see p. 225)

Salt and freshly ground white pepper

For the Suet Paste

450 g (1 lb) plain flour

25 g (1 oz) baking powder

100 g (4 oz) fresh suet, chopped

100 g (4 oz) dried suet

300 ml (10 fl oz) water

Grease two 1.2 litre (2 pint) pudding basins or six 400 ml (14 fl oz) moulds.

For the steak and kidney filling, fry the beef and kidney in the dripping, allowing it to colour well on all sides.

In a separate large pan, sweat the diced vegetables and mushrooms, if using, garlic and herbs in the butter for a few minutes until soft. Add the Guinness and boil to reduce until almost dry. Add the meat and cover with the *jus*. Bring to the simmer, cover, and simmer for 1–1½ hours until the meat is tender. Check the seasoning and allow to cool.

While the meat is cooking, make the suet paste. Sieve the flour, baking powder and a pinch of salt into a bowl. Mix in the suets then fold in the water to form a fairly firm paste. Allow the paste to rest for about 20 minutes. Roll out the paste and use the majority to line the pudding moulds; you will need some left for the lids. Keep in the fridge until needed.

When the filling is cold, fill the moulds with the meat mixture, using a slotted spoon. You need only a little liquid in the filling. Roll out the remaining suet paste and cover the moulds, trim and press together. Top with pieces of buttered foil.

Stand the puddings in a steamer or a pan half-filled with hot water, cover and steam for about 1 hour for the smaller puddings and 1½–2 hours for the larger ones, topping up with boiling water as necessary.

The liquid left from the stew can be re-boiled, pushed through a sieve and used as the gravy.

To serve, trim round the tops. Turn the individual puddings out on to hot plates and cover with the gravy. From the larger basins, cut and spoon on to hot plates and cover with gravy.

Beef Olives with Black Pudding

The stuffing for the beef olives is made from the same base as for the Jambonette de Volaille (see p. 96), using onions, mushrooms, garlic and herbs. The black pudding works very well in the recipe, and can be broken down with a wooden spoon if mincing is impossible. The beef olives can be served plain or some garnish can be added. I've chosen the button onions, mushrooms and bacon to give extra flavours and texture to the dish.

SERVES 4

700 g (1½ lb) lean beef topside or rump
Salt and freshly ground white pepper
225 g (8 oz) pig's caul, soaked in cold
    water for 24 hours (optional,
    see method)

1.2 litres (2 pints) Red Wine Sauce
    (see p. 236) or Veal *Jus* (see p. 232)
50 g (2 oz) beef dripping

For the Stuffing

225 g (8 oz) black pudding, skinned and
    minced
1 chicken breast, minced or finely
    chopped
1 egg
3 onions, finely chopped
2 garlic cloves, crushed

A few fresh sage leaves, chopped
½ teaspoon chopped fresh thyme
50 g (2 oz) unsalted butter
175 g (6 oz) button mushrooms, minced
    and cooked until dry

For the Garnish

100 g (4 oz) button onions
100 g (4 oz) unsalted butter
100 g (4 oz) bacon, rinded and diced
100 g (4 oz) button mushrooms
2 teaspoons chopped fresh parsley

To make the stuffing, mix together the black pudding and chicken breast, season with salt and pepper and add the egg. Fry the chopped onions, garlic and herbs in the butter until softened, then allow to cool. Cook the mushrooms in a separate pan until dry then leave to cool. When cold, mix all the ingredients and beat together well. Check for seasoning and adjust to taste with salt and pepper.

Cut the meat into eight thin slices and sit each slice between two sheets of cling film. These can now be batted with a rolling pin to stretch the meat. Divide the filling between the slices then roll them up, folding in the sides to form a cylindrical beef olive shape. Wrap them individually in the pig's caul, if using, to keep the shape of the meat, or pierce and hold them in shape with cocktail sticks.

Start to warm the red wine sauce or *jus* in a large, lidded braising pan, making sure the sauce is not too thick; when the olives are slowly cooking in the sauce, it will thicken.

Fry the beef olives in the dripping for a few minutes until well coloured on all sides. Drain off any excess fat and sit the beef olives in the red wine sauce or gravy. Bring to the simmer and cook gently for about 1½ hours. Check the meat: it should start to feel soft and give when pinched. Simmer for a further 30 minutes, then the olives will be tender and ready.

Drain the sauce into a pan and re-boil, skimming off any excess fat or impurities if necessary. Return the beef olives to the sauce to warm through.

To make the garnish, fry the onions in butter until soft and golden brown. Remove from the pan and add the bacon and mushrooms. These can be fried together on top of the stove until the bacon is brown and crispy. Add the garnishes to the sauce.

To serve, remove the cocktail sticks, if using, from the beef olives, and serve the olives into hot bowls, allowing two per portion. Spoon the garnish and sauce over and sprinkle with the chopped parsley.

OVERLEAF
*Four classic dishes: top left, Steak and
Kidney Pudding (see p. 122),
top right, Irish Stew (see p. 129),
below left, Beef Stew and Dumplings
(see p. 128) and
below right, Home-made Lamb Pasties
(see p. 134).*

Beef Stew and Dumplings

This is a classic British dish which is a total meal in itself (see previous page). You've got the meat, the vegetables and the dumplings all in one dish. The chestnuts are optional but I really enjoy the nutty taste they give the dish.

SERVES 4–6

900 g (2 lb) braising steak, trimmed and
    cut into 2.5 cm (1 in) dice
Salt and freshly ground black pepper
100 g (4 oz) beef dripping
4 large onions, diced
1 garlic clove, crushed
1 sprig of fresh thyme
25 g (1 oz) unsalted butter

½ bottle red wine
1.75 litres (3 pints) Veal *Jus* (see p. 232)
    or bought alternative (see p. 225)
6 carrots
6 celery sticks
4 large potatoes, peeled
350 g (12 oz) button mushrooms
1 tablespoon tomato purée (optional)

For the Dumplings

1 onion, finely chopped
4 smoked back bacon rashers, rinded
    and diced
1 teaspoon chopped fresh thyme
25 g (1 oz) unsalted butter
100 g (4 oz) chestnuts, cooked, shelled
    and chopped (optional)

225 g (8 oz) plain flour
2 teaspoons baking powder
100 g (4 oz) fresh or dried beef suet,
    shredded
150 ml (5 fl oz) water
Chicken Stock (see p. 228)
    or water

Season the meat with salt and pepper and fry in the beef dripping until brown. Leave to drain in a colander. Meanwhile, in a large flameproof casserole, sweat the diced onions, garlic and thyme in the butter for a few minutes until soft. Add the red wine and boil until reduced by two-thirds. Add the *jus*, bring to the boil, and add the steak. Cover and leave to simmer gently for 1½ hours.

Cut the carrots, celery and potatoes into large dice and add them to the stew with the whole button mushrooms and tomato purée. Continue to cook for another 15–20 minutes until the vegetables are soft. Check for seasoning.

Meanwhile, make the dumplings. Sweat the chopped onion, bacon and thyme in the butter until soft. Add the chopped chestnuts, if using, then allow the mixture to cool.

Mix together the flour, baking powder and suet. Add a pinch of salt and the onion mixture and mix to a dough with the water. The dumplings can now be rolled into balls 2.5–4 cm (1–1½ in) in diameter. Bring the chicken stock or water to the boil, add the dumplings and simmer for 20 minutes. Serve the stew in hot bowls, and to finish top with the dumplings.

Irish Stew

This dish can be prepared and cooked in many different ways. You can look in a dozen cookery books and you'll find a dozen varying recipes. Well, this is my version (see pp. 126–7).

SERVES 4

750 g (1½ lb) middle neck of lamb, cut into cutlets
100 g (4 oz) unsalted butter
4 onions, sliced
450 g (1 lb) potatoes, peeled and cut into 2.5 cm (1 in) dice
1 garlic clove
1 bouquet garni (1 bay leaf, 1 sprig each of fresh rosemary and thyme tied in a square of muslin or strip of leek) or bouquet garni sachet

1.5 litres (2½ pints) Chicken Stock (see p. 228) or water
175 g (6 oz) carrots, diced
6 celery sticks, cut into 2.5 cm (1 in) dice
225 g (8 oz) Savoy cabbage, shredded
Salt and freshly ground white pepper
2 teaspoons chopped fresh parsley

Cover the meat with cold water in a large pan and bring to the boil. Drain off the water and refresh the meat in cold water. Drain well.

Melt the butter in a large braising pan and add the sliced onions, half the diced potatoes and the garlic. Add the bouquet garni to the pan and sweat for 2 minutes. Add the lamb cutlets and cover with the chicken stock. Bring the stock to the simmer, cover and cook for 30 minutes. The meat will be half-cooked and the potatoes will have started to purée and thicken the stock. Add the diced carrots and continue to cook for a further 10 minutes. Add the remaining potatoes and the diced celery and cook for 15–20 minutes. At this stage we do not want to purée the potatoes but just cook them until soft. Add the cabbage and cook for another 2–3 minutes until the meat and vegetables are tender. Season with salt and pepper, remove the bouquet garni and serve in individual bowls or one large bowl. Finish with the chopped parsley. You now have a complete meal.

My own version of
a traditional
Lancashire Hot-pot
(see p. 132).

Lancashire Hot-pot

This is a Great British Classic. It's usually just neck of lamb, kidneys, onions, potatoes and gravy, but I've tried to refine it, by adding more textures and tastes. It also looks a lot nicer when presented, and just shows how good ordinary lamb chump chops can be (see previous page). The chops should be lean with the little bone and fat left on. The vegetables have to be chopped into very small dice, which may sound tiresome but it's worth doing. You will need a shallow flameproof braising dish to hold the chops in one layer.

SERVES 4

2 carrots, finely diced
2 celery sticks, finely diced
2 onions, finely diced
1 leek, finely diced
50–75 g (2–3 oz) unsalted butter
½ garlic clove, crushed
2 large sprigs of fresh rosemary
4 thick, lean lamb chump chops

150 ml (5 fl oz) dry white wine
900 ml (1½ pints) Veal *Jus* (see p. 232)
    or bought alternative (see p. 225)
4 large potatoes, peeled
1 tablespoon lamb fat or beef dripping
Salt and freshly ground white pepper
A sprinkling of chopped fresh
    parsley

Pre-heat the oven to 200°C/400°F/gas 6.

Lightly cook the diced vegetables in the butter with the garlic and rosemary for a few minutes until softened. Drain and keep to one side. Fry the chops in the butter remaining in the pan for about 3–4 minutes on each side until golden. Remove and drain. Add the white wine to the pan and boil to reduce until almost dry. This will help release all the flavours into the sauce. Add the *jus*, bring just to the boil, then strain through a sieve.

Shape the potatoes into cylinders and slice them 3 mm (⅛ in) thick. You will need about ten slices per chop. Fry the potatoes in the fat or dripping until golden, then drain well.

Place the chops in the braising dish and spoon the vegetables on top, covering all the lamb. Season with salt and pepper. Layer the potatoes on top of the vegetables, overlapping them almost to resemble fish scales. Pour the gravy around and bring to the simmer. Place in the pre-heated oven and allow to braise for about 40–45 minutes. The potatoes should be crisp and golden.

Remove the chops with the vegetables and potatoes still on top. Bring the sauce to the boil, skimming off any impurities. It should be rich and dark, just thick enough to coat the back of a spoon. Place the chops in hot bowls, pour the sauce around and sprinkle with chopped parsley.

Chump of Lamb
Marinated with Red Wine and Orange

There are many ways of cooking and serving this dish. The lamb cooks beautifully on a barbecue grill, leaving it nicely burnt outside and still pink in the centre. This gives a lovely bitter-sweet taste that will eat well with a mixed or green salad. But for this recipe, I'm going to roast the lamb and make a sauce with the marinade.

Lamb chumps are taken from the saddle of lamb towards the tail end. They can be cut into chump chops or left as one piece, rolled and tied. For this recipe they are going to be just that, like individual roasts. One of my favourite dishes to go with this is Buttered Spetzli with Leeks (see p. 155).

SERVES 4

4 chumps of lamb, each about 225–275 g (8–10 oz), rolled and tied	600 ml (1 pint) Veal *Jus* (see p. 232) or bought alternative (see p. 225)
25 g (1 oz) lard	(optional)

For the Marinade

½ bottle red wine	1 sprig of fresh thyme
2 shallots or 1 onion, chopped	1 sprig of fresh rosemary
2 garlic cloves, sliced	1 sprig of fresh tarragon
Zest of 1 orange	A few black peppercorns, crushed

Mix all the marinade ingredients together in a dish large enough to hold the chumps in one layer. Add the chump roasts, cover and leave to marinate. The flavour gets better if left longer. I prefer to marinate in the fridge for up to 5 days for the best results. You will find that the lamb is now deep red in colour.

Pre-heat the oven to 220°C/425°F/gas 7. Pre-heat a roasting tray and fry the chumps in the lard on top of the stove until almost burnt and crisp. Then place the tray in the pre-heated oven and roast for 15–20 minutes. Remove from the oven and leave to rest for 6–8 minutes.

While the lamb is roasting, boil the marinade until reduced by three-quarters. Add the *jus*, if using, then leave to simmer for 15 minutes. Pass the sauce through a sieve.

The lamb chumps can now be sliced and served with the sauce.

Roast Celeriac

Probably one of my favourite vegetable dishes is roast parsnips, but celeriac makes a great alternative and change.

SERVES 4–6

900 g (2 lb) celeriac
2 tablespoons beef dripping, lard or
        vegetable oil
50 g (2 oz) unsalted butter
Salt and freshly ground white pepper

Pre-heat the oven to 200°C/400°F/gas 6.

Celeriac has very thick skin which has to be cut off with a knife rather than peeled. Cut the flesh into large 4 cm (1½ in) pieces. This should be cut just before cooking to prevent them from discolouring.

Pre-heat a roasting tray on top of the stove and add the dripping or lard. Start to fry the celeriac, turning the pieces in the pan until golden brown on all sides. When coloured, add the butter and roast in the pre-heated oven for 25–30 minutes until the celeriac is tender and crispy. Season and serve.

That is the basic recipe. To add a bit more, during the last 5–10 minutes of roasting, some pieces of smoked bacon and/or some garlic, sage and thyme will lift the dish, giving lots of extra taste.

Roast Parsnips with Honey

Parsnips are a vegetable that are far too often ignored. When roasted, they're always crisp, sweet and tender, and I find these parsnips eat particularly well with roast lamb.

SERVES 6

900 g (2 lb) parsnips, peeled and
  quartered
2 tablespoons olive oil
50 g (2 oz) unsalted butter
2 tablespoons clear honey
Salt and freshly ground black pepper

Pre-heat the oven to 220°C/425°F/gas 7.

If the parsnips have slightly woody centres, cut these out before cooking.

Pre-heat a roasting tray on top of the stove and add the olive oil and butter. Fry the parsnips in the oil until golden brown on all sides then roast them in the pre-heated oven for 20 minutes, turning occasionally. Pour the honey over the parsnips and carefully turn them, making sure they have all been covered. Season and put back in the oven for 5 minutes. The parsnips will now be tender and sweet. Stir them in a serving dish and spoon some of the honey glaze from the pan over the top to finish.

Puddings

This will be a lot of people's favourite chapter. We all love puddings, and we probably all eat far too many of them! The British are well known for their national sweet tooth, and there is a wealth of great traditional recipes for puddings, creams, fruit tarts and pies, and ices etc. It is said we liked sweet things so much that we had to invent an extra meal at which to enjoy them – afternoon tea – and so there are a few recipes here for teacakes and pastries (Gingerbread Cake, Banana and Pecan Nut Bread, Chocolate Flan and Semolina Tart among them).

ABOVE *Glazed Lemon Tart*
(see p. 202).
LEFT *Summer Pudding with cream*
(see p. 178).

Most of the recipes here are British in origin, with one or two exceptions. The easiest of them all is the Lemon Posset: just cream, lemon and sugar. The finished texture eats just like a mousse, so if you're looking for a quick pudding for some unexpected visitors or for a dinner party, then this is the one for you. Crumbles are very British, and are a great excuse for experimenting with any seasonal fruit. Rice puddings can be eaten hot or cold, a sherry trifle is wonderful when made well, and I love steamed sponge puddings, especially when served with a home-made custard.

A lot of the most famous British puddings are made with bread – Summer Pudding, Queen of Puddings, and one of my own favourites, Bread and Butter Pudding. Now this pudding really has seen some changes. It's usually associated with stale bread, butter, a couple of eggs, sugar and milk, and then it's baked on its own in the oven until firm – ugh! That's not what I call bread and butter pudding. I think of it as almost sponge-like in texture with thick fresh custard just oozing out between the layers. The best thing to do is just turn to page 184, follow the recipe, and then I promise you'll never look back. Here's wishing you happy puddings!

Crème Brûlée

I've never been quite sure if this originates from France or England, but I've always called it crème brûlée *(see overleaf). It sounds a lot tastier than 'burnt cream'. This recipe is very similar to the Anglaise Sauce (see p. 220) but is cooked in a slightly different way and certainly has a different finish.*

SERVES 6

8 egg yolks
50 g (2 oz) caster sugar
600 ml (1 pint) double cream

1 vanilla pod, split, or a few drops of
   good vanilla essence
Icing sugar

Pre-heat the oven to 180°C/350°F/gas 4.

Mix the egg yolks and sugar together well in a bowl. Bring the cream to the boil with the vanilla pod, if using. Remove the vanilla pod and scrape the insides into the cream. Now whisk the cream into the egg yolks and sugar. Sit the bowl over a pan of hot water and heat until the custard begins to thicken, stirring all the time. It should have the consistency of single cream. It is now ready for the next stage.

Divide the custard between six 7.5 cm (3 in) ramekins or moulds. Sit these in a roasting tin and add warm water until it comes three-quarters up the sides of the moulds. Finish in the pre-heated oven until just setting, about 20–30 minutes. To test, remove one of the moulds from the water after 20 minutes and shake gently. There should still be slight movement in the centre of the custard. If it is still runny, put it back in the oven and check after another 5 minutes. Remove from the oven and allow to cool. I prefer to eat these at room temperature, so I do not put them in the fridge.

To finish the brûlées, when set sprinkle them liberally with icing sugar. If you have a blow torch, this is great for achieving a quick and even glaze! If not, then colour them under a pre-heated hot grill, having the moulds as close as possible to the heat. As the sugar is heating, it will bubble and start to colour. More sugar may need to be added and then continue to colour until deep golden brown. The brûlée is now ready to serve.

Variation

You can make chocolate brûlées by simply adding grated chocolate to the mix before putting it into the ramekins. About 100 g (4 oz) of good-quality plain chocolate should be enough for this recipe – but of course if you prefer it stronger, just add some more! The brûlées can be finished with icing sugar, but I think they are better when topped with chocolate shavings.

Cappuccino Mousse

I always enjoy a cappuccino coffee – it's lovely with the frothy milk on top – so I thought, why not have a pudding to match? Chocolate and coffee go so well with each other, and the lightly whipped cream on top is a really good finish to the dish.

If you make your own biscuits it would be very nice to offer cappuccino mousse and biscuits for pudding. Why not try the home-made Palmier Biscuits (see p. 218)?

SERVES 4

175 g (6 oz) plain chocolate	50 g (2 oz) caster sugar
3 tablespoons strong black coffee	2 egg yolks
5 egg whites	150 ml (5 fl oz) double cream, whipped

Break 150 g (5 oz) of the chocolate into small pieces and melt with the coffee in a bowl over a pan of hot water. Beat the egg whites with the sugar to a meringue consistency, creating soft peaks. Fold the egg yolks into the melted chocolate, making sure it is not too hot, add one-third of the egg white meringue and whisk into the chocolate. Carefully fold in the remaining egg whites and half of the whipped cream.

The mousse can now be spooned into glasses, ramekin dishes or one large bowl and placed in the fridge for 2–3 hours to set. The remaining cream can be piped or forked on top of the mousse. To finish the dish, just finely grate the remaining chocolate over the top. So now we have a cappuccino coffee pudding with extra chocolate taste.

Chocolate Sponge Cake with Cappuccino Mousse

If you would like to be more adventurous, here is a way to make the mousse even more exciting. The sponge adds a good texture to the mousse, but of course can be used with any mousse or other puddings.

PREVIOUS PAGE
*Finishing the Crème Brûlée: if you don't
own a blow torch then a pre-heated
hot grill will achieve the same deep golden
brown colour (see p. 169).*

Serves 4

1 quantity Cappuccino Mousse
   (see left)
Rum or liqueur to taste
1 quantity Coffee Sauce
   (see p. 220) or Clementine or
   Orange Sauce (see p. 221)
1 sprig of fresh mint

For the Sponge

175 g (6 oz) plain chocolate
3 tablespoons strong black coffee
5 eggs, separated
100 g (4 oz) caster sugar
Pinch of salt

Pre-heat the oven to 180°C/350°F/gas 4 and line a 30 × 25 cm (12 × 10 in) baking tray and four 6 cm (2½ in) flan rings with greaseproof paper to come up 5–7 cm (2–3 in) round the sides.

To make the sponge, melt the chocolate with the coffee in a bowl over a pan of hot water. Leave to cool slightly. Beat the egg yolks until smooth then add the caster sugar. Continue to beat until pale and the mixture trails off the whisk in ribbons. In a separate bowl, beat the egg whites and salt until they form soft peaks. Add the melted chocolate to the egg yolk mix then fold in the egg whites. Spread on to the lined baking tray to between 5 mm (¼ in) and 1 cm (½ in) thick. Bake in the pre-heated oven for 15 minutes. Remove from the oven and allow to cool.

Make the mousse but do not allow it to set. Cut out four rings from the sponge the same diameter as the flan rings, and place them in the bottom of the rings. The sponge can now be flavoured with a little rum or liqueur, if required. Spoon the mousse into the moulds on top of the sponge, chill and leave to set.

When the mousses are set, lift off the flan rings and carefully take off the paper. Finish with the whipped cream and grated chocolate of the mousse recipe. Place the mousses on plates and serve with your chosen sauce and a sprig of mint.

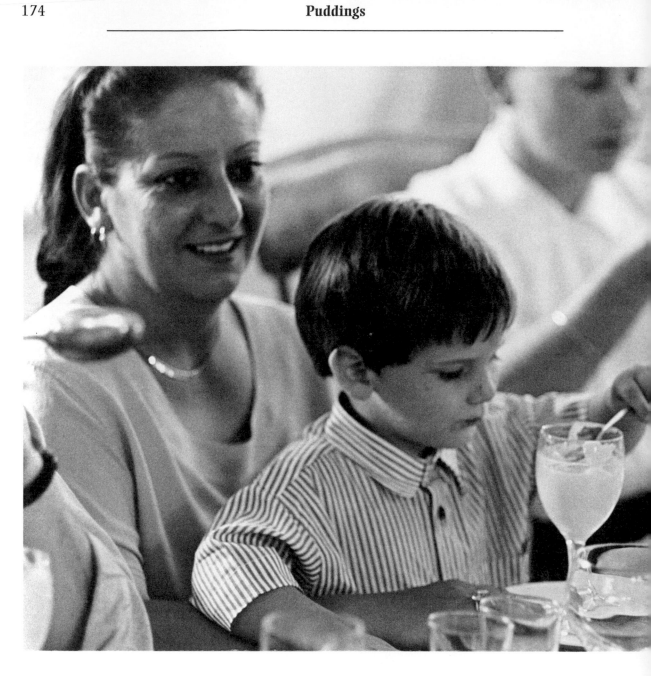

ABOVE AND OPPOSITE
*Lemon Posset – a simple pudding
for everyone to enjoy
(see p. 176).*

*If you're stuck for a pudding
And pushed for time,
Then turn to this recipe
And you'll be fine.*

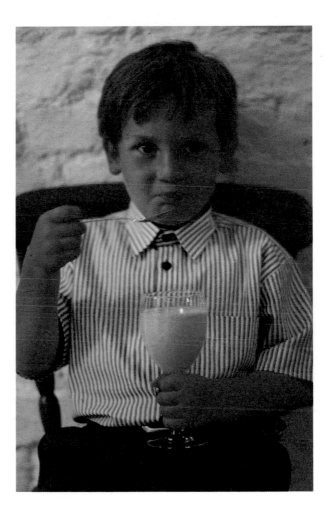

Lemon Posset

This must be the easiest pudding to prepare and cook, which is why I've included it in the book (see previous page).

SERVES 6

900 ml (1½ pints) double cream
250 g (9 oz) caster sugar
Juice of 3 lemons

Boil the cream and sugar together in a pan and cook for 2–3 minutes. Add the lemon juice and mix in well. Leave to cool slightly then pour into six glasses and leave to set in the fridge. The pudding is now ready. It is nice to pour a little more liquid cream on top before serving.

Sherry Trifle

Trifle over the years has taken on many variations. The word itself comes from an old term, 'trifling', which meant layering different sponges, fruits and jellies, and finished with a sabayon rather than a custard. Of course, most home-made trifles still have all those ingredients, even sometimes blancmange too, but as with most other things, I like good old-fashioned simplicity, and this recipe has plenty of taste and texture, without all the extras.

The custard below can be used solely for this pudding, but I like to go halves with Anglaise Sauce (see p. 220) to give a richer and fresher taste. (I don't use all Anglaise because it wouldn't set.)

SERVES 4

For the Sponge

3 eggs
75 g (3 oz) caster sugar
75 g (3 oz) plain flour
40 g (1½ oz) unsalted butter, melted

For the Syrup

225 g (8 oz) caster sugar
300 ml (10 fl oz) water
4–5 tablespoons sweet sherry

For the Custard Sauce

600 ml (1 pint) milk
50 g (2 oz) custard powder
50 g (2 oz) caster sugar

For the Filling and Topping

Raspberry jam to cover the sponge
300 ml (10 fl oz) double cream, whipped
100 g (4 oz) plain chocolate, grated

Pre-heat the oven to 200°C/400°F/gas 6 and grease and line a 20 cm (8 in) flan tin or flan ring and baking sheet.

To make the sponge, whisk the eggs and sugar in a bowl over a pan of hot water until the mixture has doubled in bulk and is light and creamy. Very gently fold in the flour and melted butter. Pour the mix into the lined flan tin or ring and bake in the pre-heated oven for 30 minutes. Turn out and allow to cool.

To make the syrup, boil the sugar and water together for about 2 minutes to a syrup, then add sherry to taste – more than above if you like the taste.

To make the custard sauce, mix some of the milk with the custard powder in a pan. Bring the remaining milk to the boil in another pan. Pour this on to the custard powder, whisking all the time. Return to the heat and bring back to the boil. While stirring, the sauce will thicken. Add the sugar, cover with buttered greaseproof paper and allow to cool.

Split the sponge in half horizontally and spread jam on both pieces. Place one half into a bowl and soak with half the sherry syrup. Sit the other sponge on top and again soak with sherry syrup. Pour the custard on top and allow to set in the fridge. When set, spoon the whipped cream on top and sprinkle with grated chocolate.

You can also make individual trifles in 10 cm (4 in) soufflé dishes. Bake little sponges to fit, or cut to fit, and assemble in exactly the same way.

Summer Pudding

I've listed quantities and varieties of fruits below but, of course, the beauty of this dish is that the choice of red berries is entirely your own, so use what is easily available (see pp. 166–7). I have found that these fruits work well together. You need about 1.4 kg (3 lb) of soft fruit altogether. If there is a lot of the fruit mix left over it can be kept for a few days and served as it is with ice-cream or cream – or make some more puddings!

SERVES 8–10

2 punnets raspberries	1 punnet blackcurrants
2 punnets strawberries	1 punnet blueberries
1 punnet tayberries or loganberries	2 tablespoons crème de
1 punnet blackberries	framboises
1 punnet redcurrants	1 loaf thinly sliced white bread

For the Raspberry Purée

450 g (1 lb) fresh or frozen raspberries
50 g (2 oz) icing sugar

For the Sugar Syrup

600 ml (1 pint) water
350 g (12 oz) caster sugar

To serve

Clotted or whipped cream

Lightly butter a 1.5 litre (2½ pint) basin or eight 150 ml (5 fl oz) moulds.

Trim and wash all the fruits and leave to drain.

To make the raspberry purée, simply blitz the berries and sugar together in a blender, then push through a sieve.

To make the sugar syrup, simply boil the water and sugar together for a few minutes to a clear syrup. Leave to cool.

Mix half of the raspberry purée with the sugar syrup and bring to the simmer. Add the fruits and the crème de framboises to the sauce, then remove from the heat and leave to rest. The fruits should have all softened but will still have kept their shape. When cool, pour some of the syrup into a separate bowl.

Remove the crusts from the bread and cut each slice into three. Dip these in the reserved raspberry syrup and line the basin or moulds with the soaked bread, overlapping slightly with each slice. When the basin or all the moulds are lined, fill with the fruits and a little of the sauce and cover with more bread. Cover with a plate, press down with a weight and leave in the fridge for a few hours.

Mix the remaining raspberry purée with a little of the remaining pudding juices until you have a sauce consistency. Turn out the summer puddings on to plates or divide the large one into wedges, and spoon the finished raspberry sauce over them. Garnish with some of the remaining fruit mix, purée and clotted or whipped cream.

OVERLEAF
Summer fruits for
Summer Pudding.

Vanilla Ice-cream

Many alternatives can be made from this basic vanilla ice-cream recipe, a few of which I have outlined below.

In the basic recipe, vanilla pods are used. These can be quite expensive, but if you buy two or three pods and keep them in an airtight container with caster sugar, you will have all the taste you want in the sugar for the recipe. You can, of course, use the pods again and again by just topping up the container with more sugar. Failing this, a good, thick vanilla essence will also work.

SERVES 4–6

1 vanilla pod
300 ml (10 fl oz) double cream
300 ml (10 fl oz) milk
6 egg yolks
175 g (6 oz) caster sugar

Split the vanilla pod and scrape the insides into the cream and milk in a pan. Bring to the boil.

While the milk and cream are heating, mix the egg yolks and sugar together in a bowl and beat until pale. When the cream has boiled, pour slowly on to the egg yolks and sugar, beating all the time. Continue to stir until the ice-cream mixture has cooled. Once cooled, chill until totally cold. The mix is now ready to make into ice-cream.

Pour into an ice-cream maker and turn until the cream has thickened, increased in volume and, of course, frozen. If you do not have an ice-cream maker, pour the mix into a suitable container and place in the freezer, stirring well every 30 minutes until frozen. The beating is important to get the correct, smooth texture. You should now have a thick dairy ice-cream which will be best served as soon as made or frozen for a minimum time.

Variations

This recipe can now be used for many alternatives. To make fruit ice-creams add a fruit purée. Or, the vanilla can be replaced with cinnamon sticks left in the mixture until cold, or 1–2 teaspoons of ground cinnamon. This can be served with apple fritters, apple tart, or even a good old-fashioned apple crumble (see p. 198 and 200).

Fruit Ice-cream

This is a simple recipe which uses a stock syrup (also used in sorbet-making). Crème fraîche is French 'fresh' cream, and is now available in most supermarkets. It is cream that has been treated with a special culture which gives it a longer life and an almost sour taste. It works very well in ice-creams, giving a full body to the taste.

SERVES 4–6

300 ml (10 fl oz) fruit purée (strawberry,
    raspberry, mango etc.)
1–2 heaped tablespoons crème fraîche

For the Stock Syrup

300 ml (10 fl oz) water
225 g (8 oz) caster sugar, flavoured with
    vanilla (see left)
1 tablespoon liquid glucose (optional)

To make the stock syrup, simply bring all the ingredients to the boil and cook for 2–3 minutes. This will leave you with a thick, sweet syrup. Leave until cold.

To make the fruit ice, mix the fruit purée with the cold stock syrup and add the crème fraîche. The mix is now ready to freeze, either in a machine or freezer, churning by hand every now and again.

Praline

Another lovely ice-cream is made with praline, a toffee-type mixture of sugar and hazelnuts boiled together. Simply crush the praline pieces in a bowl and add to the vanilla ice-cream mix when it's ready to be churned or frozen. This will be very sweet so it's best to omit 50 g (2 oz) of caster sugar from the basic ice-cream recipe.

100 g (4 oz) shelled hazelnuts, chopped
100 g (4 oz) caster sugar

Place the nuts and sugar together in a pan and slowly cook until the sugar is golden brown. Pour the mixture on to a lightly oiled tray and leave until set and cold. The praline is now ready to break.

Sorbets

Sorbets are also known as water ices. They are good as a light pudding or to serve between courses as a palate cleanser. All you need is to mix equal quantities of stock syrup and fruit purée, exactly as the fruit ice-creams, but without the crème fraîche.

For example, 300 ml (10 fl oz) each of stock syrup and an apple purée mixed together and turned through an ice-cream maker will produce a simple sorbet. This, of course, can be improved by adding a squeeze of lemon juice to enrich the taste and some cider or calvados to make it even stronger.

All sorbets can be made and varied in this way. A raspberry sorbet can be really tasty with a little raspberry liqueur added in place of some of the stock syrup.

These sorbets can be used as a main item for puddings. How does a pear sorbet with chocolate sauce and fresh thick cream sound?

Bread and Butter Pudding

Bread and butter pudding has become one of our great classics. It was always a good way of using up stale bread with milk, sugar and eggs, but this would often result in a firm and tasteless pud, which left it with a bad name. This recipe will give you quite a different dish (see pp. 186–7). I'm using just egg yolks and half milk and double cream, which is obviously a little more expensive to make, but once you've tried it you'll never want to make it any other way!

SERVES 6–8

12 medium slices white bread
50 g (2 oz) unsalted butter, softened
8 egg yolks
175 g (6 oz) caster sugar
1 vanilla pod or a few drops of vanilla
   essence

300 ml (10 fl oz) milk
300 ml (10 fl oz) double cream
25 g (1 oz) sultanas
25 g (1 oz) raisins

To finish

Caster sugar

Grease a 1.75 litre (3 pint) pudding basin with butter.

Firstly, remove the crusts and butter the bread. Whisk the egg yolks and caster sugar together in a bowl. Split the vanilla pod and place in a pan with the milk and cream. Bring the milk and cream to the simmer, then sieve on to the egg yolks, stirring all the time. You now have the custard.

Arrange the bread in layers in the prepared basin, sprinkling the sultanas and raisins in between layers. Finish with a final layer of bread without any fruit on top as this tends to burn. The warm egg mixture may now be poured over the bread and cooked straightaway, but I prefer to pour the custard over the pudding then leave it to soak into the bread for 20 minutes before cooking. This allows the bread to take on a new texture and have the flavours all the way through.

Pre-heat the oven to 180°C/350°F/gas 4.

Once the bread has been soaked, place the dish in a roasting tray three-quarters filled with warm water and place in the pre-heated oven. Cook for about 20–30 minutes in the pre-heated oven until the pudding begins to set. Because we are using only egg yolks, the mixture cooks like a fresh custard and only thickens; it should not become too firm.

When ready, remove from the water bath, sprinkle liberally with caster sugar to cover, and glaze under the grill on medium heat. The sugar should dissolve and caramelize and you may find that the corners of the bread start to burn a little. This helps the flavours, though, giving a bittersweet taste, and certainly looks good. The bread and butter pudding is now ready to serve and when you take that first spoonful and place it into a bowl you will see the custard just seeping from the dish – it's delicious!

Bread and Butter Pudding
(see p. 184).

Glazed Pear and Almond Zabaglione

This dish looks very simple and almost like a crème brûlée, but just think of all those textures and tastes. When you break through the sugar topping it's into the warm zabaglione then on to the cooked pears and finally the moist almond sponge. I've chosen Comice pears because they have a good, sweet taste and texture. Other varieties will work but may need more cooking and more sugar to taste. This dish comes in a very close second to the bread and butter pudding!

The frangipane or almond sponge recipe is wonderful for home-made bakewell tart, bakewell and apple tart, or prune, Armagnac and almond tart. Because of the high ratio of ground almonds, it's very moist and keeps a lot longer than a traditional sponge.

SERVES 4–6

6 Comice pears
50 g (2 oz) icing sugar
1 tablespoon unsalted butter

For the Almond Sponge (Frangipane)

225 g (8 oz) unsalted butter
225 g (8 oz) caster sugar
50 g (2 oz) plain flour
175 g (6 oz) ground almonds
4 eggs

For the Zabaglione

5 egg yolks
40 g (1½ oz) caster sugar
25 ml (1 fl oz) Poire Williams (Marsala
    or Calvados will both work)
25 ml (1 fl oz) dry white wine

Pre-heat the oven to 200°C/400°F/gas 6 and grease and line a 20 cm (8 in) square baking tray.

To make the sponge, beat the butter and sugar until creamed. Add the flour and ground almonds and stir until well blended. Add one egg at a time, making sure it is completely beaten in before adding the next. This process can be done in a food processor or mixer, or with a plain wooden spoon. When everything is thoroughly folded in, spread the mix 1 cm (½ in) thick in the prepared baking tray. Bake in the pre-heated oven for 20–30 minutes until firm and set. Allow to cool.

Meanwhile, prepare the pears. Peel and chop two of the pears and cook quickly in a pan with a tablespoon of icing sugar and the butter. These pears need to cook to a purée. When very soft, push them through a sieve. Peel and cut the remaining pears into 1 cm (½ in) dice. Bring the purée to the boil and add the diced pears. Cook for just 2–3 minutes on a high heat then allow to cool slightly.

Cut the sponge into rounds to fit four 9 cm (3½ in) soufflé moulds or one 23 cm (9 in) bowl. Spoon the warm pears on top of the sponge.

To make the zabaglione, beat together the egg yolks and sugar until light in colour. Add the Poire Williams and white wine and whisk in a bowl over a pan of hot water until light, thick and frothy. This will take 5–10 minutes. The zabaglione should be thick enough to make soft peaks when the whisk is drawn from the mix. Spoon over the pears in the moulds or bowl.

Sieve the remaining icing sugar on top of each mould or on to the bowl. Place under a hot grill for a few minutes until golden brown. If you are very generous with the icing sugar, it will also give a crunchy topping.

Caramel Rice Pudding

This recipe shows how a simple pudding can become a great dessert!

Serves 6

For the Caramel

225 g (8 oz) caster sugar
300 ml (10 fl oz) water

For the Pudding

225 g (8 oz) short-grain rice
1.2 litres (2 pints) milk
100 g (4 oz) caster sugar
50 g (2 oz) unsalted butter
8 egg yolks
300 ml (10 fl oz) double cream

Pre-heat the oven to 180°C/350°F/gas 4.

Prepare the caramel for the moulds first. Dissolve the sugar in three-quarters of the water, bring to the boil then boil for a few minutes without shaking the pan until the caramel is golden brown. Add the remaining water and re-boil. The caramel is now ready and can be divided between six 9 cm (3½ in) soufflé dishes. Leave to set.

To make the pudding, place the rice in cold water to cover, bring to the boil, then drain, refresh under cold water and drain again. Boil 1 litre (1¾ pints) of the milk, half the sugar and the butter in a large pan and add the rice. Bring to the simmer and cook for about 8–10 minutes until tender. Beat the egg yolks and remaining sugar together in a bowl. Boil the cream with the remaining milk. Pour the milk on to the yolks, stirring all the time. Mix this with the rice, then pour carefully into the caramel-lined moulds. Stand the moulds in a baking tray three-quarters filled with hot water and bake in the pre-heated oven for about 20–30 minutes until set. When set, remove from the water bath and leave to cool.

The puddings must now be chilled until firm and totally set. Release from the dishes with a warm knife and turn out. The rice puddings will hold together with the custard, and the caramel will pour over the top.

Rhubarb Rice Pudding

This is a delicious pudding which combines a traditional rice pudding with the slightly sharp taste of the rhubarb.

SERVES 6

450 g (1 lb) rhubarb
25 g (1 oz) unsalted butter
100 g (4 oz) caster sugar
1 quantity Rice Pudding mixture
    (see left)
75 g (3 oz) icing sugar

Pre-heat the oven to 180°C/350°F/gas 4.

Lightly peel the rhubarb and cut into 2.5 cm (1 in) pieces. Melt the butter in a pan and cook the rhubarb and caster sugar over a high heat for about 4–5 minutes until soft, stirring frequently. This should now be tasted to see if it is sweet enough. Allow the rhubarb to drain through a sieve, keeping any syrup. Spoon the rhubarb into six 9 cm (3½ in) soufflé dishes, only filling them about one-third deep.

Make the rice pudding mix as described in the previous recipe, then add the reserved syrup to the rice pudding mixture and use this to cover the rhubarb. Stand the moulds in a baking tray three-quarters filled with hot water and bake in the pre-heated oven for about 20–30 minutes until set.

Remove the moulds from the water bath, sprinkle liberally with the icing sugar and glaze under a hot grill. Unlike the caramel rice pudding, this can be served hot and left in the moulds.

Manchester Pudding
(Queen of Puddings)

This is a really sweet pudding, the one you want to eat plenty of but always regret afterwards! Here are two recipes which both work very well. The one using breadcrumbs is the more traditional, but the sponge and jam one is also delicious. The beauty of using sponge is that you can use up your Madeira cake when it's past its best.

SERVES 4–6

RECIPE 1

600 ml (1 pint) milk
Zest of 1 lemon
50 g (2 oz) unsalted butter
50 g (2 oz) caster sugar

100 g (4 oz) fresh white breadcrumbs
6 egg yolks
4 tablespoons raspberry jam

For the Meringue

4 egg whites
225 g (8 oz) caster sugar

Pre-heat the oven to 180°C/350°F/gas 4 and prepare six 7.5 cm (3 in) soufflé dishes or one 1.75 litre (3 pint) soufflé dish.

Bring the milk and lemon rind to the boil in a pan, then remove from the heat and leave to stand for 15 minutes. Remove the zest and add the butter and sugar. Bring back to the simmer and remove from the heat. Stir in the breadcrumbs and allow to cool slightly. Beat the egg yolks and add to the mix. Pour it into the soufflé dish or dishes and stand them in a roasting tray filled three-quarters full of hot water. Bake in the pre-heated oven for 30–40 minutes until set. When the puddings have just set, remove from the oven and the water bath and leave to rest for 10 minutes.

Increase the oven temperature to 230°C/450°F/gas 8. Divide the jam between the tops of the puddings. To make the meringue, whisk the egg whites with the sugar until they form firm peaks. Pipe or spoon the meringue over the top of the puddings and return them to the hot oven, or place under a pre-heated grill, for about 6–8 minutes until golden brown. The queen of puddings is now ready to serve.

RECIPE 2

½ baked Vanilla Sponge (see p. 214)
Raspberry jam
4 eggs
75 g (3 oz) caster sugar

300 ml (10 fl oz) milk
300 ml (10 fl oz) double cream
1 vanilla pod, split (optional)

For the Meringue

4 egg whites
225 g (8 oz) caster sugar

Pre-heat the oven to 160°C/325°F/gas 3 and prepare six 7.5 cm (3 in) soufflé dishes or one 1.75 litre (3 pint) soufflé dish.

Split the sponge into three layers and sandwich together again with the raspberry jam. Cut into 1 cm (½ in) squares and divide between the soufflé dishes or arrange in the base of the large dish.

Whisk the eggs and sugar together and add the milk, cream and the scraped out insides of the vanilla pod, if using. Strain through a sieve and pour on top of the sponge sandwich. Sit the moulds in a roasting tray three-quarters filled with hot water and cook in the pre-heated oven for 30–40 minutes until the custard has just set. Remove from the oven and the water bath and leave to rest.

Increase the oven temperature to 230°C/450°F/gas 8.

To make the meringues, whisk the egg whites with the sugar until they form firm peaks. Pipe or spoon the meringue over the top of the puddings and return them to the hot oven for about 6–8 minutes until golden brown.

So here are two ways, now you can decide which one to try!

Toffee and Banana Crumble

We've all had apple, rhubarb or apricot crumbles, but this one is almost a banana and toffee pie, which makes it a crumble with a difference!

SERVES 4

1 × 200 g (7 oz) tin condensed milk
225 g (8 oz) Puff Pastry (see p. 216)
225 g (8 oz) plain flour
100 g (4 oz) unsalted butter
100 g (4 oz) caster sugar
3 bananas

To make the toffee, place the unopened tin of condensed milk in a pan of water and boil for 3 hours, topping up with boiling water as necessary. Leave the tin to cool, and the toffee is ready!

Pre-heat the oven to 180°C/350°F/gas 4 and dampen a 25 cm (10 in) flan tin or individual flan rings on a baking sheet.

While the tin is boiling, roll out the pastry and use to line the flan tin or rings. Line the pastry with greaseproof paper, fill with baking beans and bake blind in the pre-heated oven for 15 minutes. Remove the beans and paper and leave to cool. Increase the oven temperature to 220°C/425°F/gas 7.

To make the crumble, rub the flour and butter together until the mix is like fine crumbs, then add the sugar. Chop the bananas and spoon into the flan cases. Top with the toffee from the tin and sprinkle with the crumble. Bake in the pre-heated oven for about 15–20 minutes until the crumble is golden brown. The pudding is ready to serve, and will eat very well with fresh cream or custard, or even both!

OPPOSITE
*Toffee and Banana Crumble
with Anglaise Sauce (see p. 220) and cream.*

Steamed Victoria Plum Pudding

A lemon sponge was the first of my steamed puddings, and I still think it can never be repeated. But here's one that comes very close! It is best served with a warm Anglaise Sauce (see p. 220).

SERVES 6

225 g (8 oz) caster sugar
300 ml (10 fl oz) water
750 g (1½ lb) Victoria plums, stoned
    and chopped

For the Sponge

100 g (4 oz) unsalted butter
150 g (5 oz) caster sugar
1 vanilla pod, split
2 eggs
1 egg yolk
200 g (7 oz) self-raising flour
Finely grated zest and juice of ½ lemon

Grease six 150 ml (5 fl oz) moulds or one 900 ml (1½ pint) basin with butter.

Dissolve the sugar in the water then bring to the boil and boil for a few minutes to make a syrup. Add the plums and cook gently for about 8–10 minutes to a lumpy, marmalade consistency.

To make the sponge, mix the butter and sugar together until almost white, then add the insides of the vanilla pod and beat in the eggs and egg yolk. Fold in the flour, lemon juice and zest. Spoon some of the plums and their syrup into the bottom of the moulds or basin. Cover with the sponge mix to come three-quarters up the sides. Cover with buttered foil and place in a steamer or a pan half-full of hot water. The small puddings will only need 40 minutes in the hot steamer, the large pudding will need 1–1½ hours.

When cooked, turn the puddings out on to a plate or plates and spoon some more of the hot Victoria plum syrup over each portion. The dish is now ready to serve and will eat well with either fresh cream or Anglaise Sauce (see p. 220).

Walnut and Maple Syrup Sponge

Sweet suet sponges have a thicker and denser texture, so I always think they need stronger tastes. The syrup helps the taste, the walnuts help the texture.

SERVES 6

175 g (6 oz) self-raising flour
75 g (3 oz) dried suet
75 g (3 oz) caster sugar
1 egg
1 egg yolk
About 2 tablespoons milk
175 g (6 oz) shelled walnuts, chopped
8 tablespoons maple syrup

Grease a 900 ml (1½ pint) or six 150 ml (5 fl oz) pudding basin(s) with butter.

Mix the flour, suet and sugar together. Beat the egg with the egg yolk then mix it into the dry ingredients. Add a little milk to give the mixture a pudding consistency when the mix just drops from the spoon. Add half the walnuts and half the maple syrup. Pour into the prepared pudding basin, cover and cook in a hot steamer or a pan half-filled with hot water for 1¼–1½ hours.

Warm the remaining walnuts in the maple syrup. Turn out the puddings on to one large or several individual plates, spoon the syrup and nuts over and serve with cream or custard.

Apple Fritters with Apricot Sauce and Vanilla Ice-cream

If it's a hot pudding you're after, this must be one of the easiest. So many other fruits can be used – bananas, apricots, pears – but I find apples go so well with the ice-cream and apricot sauce.

SERVES 4

1 quantity Vanilla Ice-cream (see p. 182)

For the Apricot Sauce

225 g (8 oz) caster sugar
300 ml (10 fl oz) water
350 g (12 oz) fresh apricots, stoned and
    quartered
2 tablespoons apricot jam (optional)

For the Fritters

300 ml (10 fl oz) sweet cider
100 g (4 oz) plain flour plus a little extra
    for coating
25 g (1 oz) caster sugar
4 Granny Smith apples, peeled
    and cored
Vegetable oil for deep-frying
1 sprig of fresh mint (optional)

To make the apricot sauce, dissolve the sugar in the water over a low heat then bring to the boil and boil for a few minutes to make a syrup. Cook the apricots in the syrup and jam for about 10 minutes until they have puréed. Push through a sieve and keep warm.

To make the fritter batter, mix the cider, flour and sugar together. Cut each of the apples into five wedges and lightly flour each piece. Dip them in the batter and deep-fry in hot oil for about 5 minutes until golden and crispy. Drain well.

To serve, lay the fritters on a plate and pour the apricot sauce next to them. Serve a large spoonful of vanilla ice-cream with each portion. For extra colour, decorate with a sprig of mint.

*Apple Fritters
with Apricot Sauce and
Vanilla Ice-cream.*

Apple Tart with its own Sorbet

This recipe gives you a tart that is hot, thin and crisp, and if you can't imagine the sorbet melting all over it you're just going to have to try it! For a variation, try flavouring the sorbet with calvados or replacing the water with cider.

SERVES 4

For the Tart

225 g (8 oz) Puff Pastry (see p. 216) or bought
50 g (2 oz) unsalted butter
8 Granny Smith apples

4 teaspoons caster sugar
4 tablespoons apricot jam
2 tablespoons water

For the Sorbet

225 g (8 oz) caster sugar
300 ml (10 fl oz) water

10 Granny Smith apples, peeled, cored and chopped

Grease one large or two smaller oven trays.

To make the tart bases, roll out the puff pastry as thinly as possible and leave to rest in the fridge. Cut the pastry into four 20 cm (8 in) circles, each forming one portion. Lay the tart bases on to the oven trays and return to the fridge.

The next step is to make the sorbet. Dissolve the sugar in the water over a low heat then bring to the boil and boil for a few minutes to make a syrup. Add the apples and simmer gently for about 10–15 minutes until they start to purée. When ready, push them through a sieve and wait for the mix to cool. This can now be made into a sorbet by freezing in an ice-cream maker or in the freezer, when you'll have to whisk it every 15–20 minutes until frozen.

Pre-heat the oven to 230°C/450°F/gas 8.

To make the tarts, peel, core and quarter the apples. Slice the apple quarters into three or four pieces, and start to overlap them on the pastry discs all the way round until each circle of pastry is totally covered. Chop the butter and divide between the tarts. Sprinkle each one with caster sugar and bake in the pre-heated oven for about 15 minutes until the pastry is crisp and the apples have started to colour.

Boil the apricot jam with the water and brush on to the tarts to give a glazed finish. The apple tarts are now ready to serve. The sorbet may be shaped between two spoons to make a quenelle shape or simply served separately in a bowl.

Sticky Toffee Pudding

This is a good old English pudding which is made all over the country. I think this recipe originated with Francis Coulson of Sharrow Bay in Ullswater, and it works better than any of the other recipes I have tried. The best dates to use are Medjool, which come from India; they are plump and meaty, with almost a treacle taste.

SERVES 4

175 g (6 oz) dates, stoned and chopped
300 ml (10 fl oz) water
1 teaspoon bicarbonate of soda
50 g (2 oz) unsalted butter
175 g (6 oz) caster sugar
2 eggs, beaten
175 g (6 oz) self-raising flour
1 teaspoon vanilla essence

For the Sauce

300 ml (10 fl oz) double cream
50 g (2 oz) demerara sugar
2 teaspoons black treacle

Pre-heat the oven to 180°C/350°F/gas 4 and grease a 28 × 18 cm (11 × 7 in) baking tin.

Boil the dates in the water for about 5 minutes until soft, then add the bicarbonate of soda. Cream the butter and sugar together until light and fluffy, then add the eggs and beat well. Mix in the dates, flour and vanilla essence then pour into the greased baking tin and cook in the pre-heated oven for about 30–40 minutes until just firm to the touch.

To make the sauce, simply place all the ingredients in a pan over a low heat and stir together until blended, then bring to the boil. Some of this can be poured over the sponge and finished under the grill, or it can be kept totally separate and ladled over the sponge when portioned. Good, fresh, thick cream is just right for this pudding.

66 *Probably the most popular of classic American dishes – lovely tastes with a lovely texture.* **99**

Pecan Pie (see p. 205).

Sweet and Savoury Pancakes

It certainly doesn't have to be Pancake Day to make these pancakes, which can be made both savoury and sweet. Perhaps their most classic sweet use is the flambéed Crêpes Suzettes, great for a bit of show at your dinner party. Or, of course, you can use savoury ones in your main course Fillet of Venison Wellington (see p. 120).

SERVES 4

225 g (8 oz) plain flour
A pinch of salt
2 eggs
600 ml (1 pint) milk
50 g (2 oz) unsalted butter, melted
Vegetable oil
2 teaspoons chopped fresh parsley or
　　　herbs (optional)

Sift the flour and salt into a bowl. Beat the eggs into the milk, then whisk into the flour. Add the melted butter and whisk into the mix, which can now be used for sweet pancakes. For savoury pancakes, add the chopped herbs.

To cook the pancakes, pre-heat a 20 cm (8 in) or 15 cm (6 in) frying-pan; I prefer to make smaller pancakes. Lightly oil the pan and pour in some of the mixture, making sure the pan has only a thin layer of mix. Cook for 10–15 seconds until brown, turn in the pan and cook for a further 10–15 seconds. The pancake is now cooked. Keep warm while you make the remainder. Three small pancakes or two large will be enough for one portion.

Pancakes can be filled with anything you like – fruit or ice-cream for the sweet, seafood or vegetables for the savoury. Pancakes to be filled can, of course, be prepared in advance and then simply microwaved for 1–2 minutes to heat them through.

Apple Pancakes

I'm using apples for these filled pancakes, but pears or any other fruit can be used.
There are also a few other additions you can make, some of which I list below.

SERVES 4

1 quantity Sweet Pancakes (see left)
6 ripe apples
50 g (2 oz) unsalted butter
50 g (2 oz) icing sugar

Peel, core and chop two of the apples and cook in half the butter and sugar until puréed. Peel and quarter the remaining apples then cut each quarter into four or five slices. Melt the remaining butter and toss the apple slices in this for a few minutes until just softening. Add the apple purée and bring to the simmer. The filling is now ready.

Allowing three pancakes per portion, divide the purée between the pancakes and either fold them in half or in quarters. Sit them in bowls and sprinkle with the remaining icing sugar. They can now be glazed under a hot grill to give a crispy topping. You can serve them with clotted or double cream, but here are a few ideas of how to enhance all the flavours.

1 When making the purée, some calvados or reduced sweet cider can be added.
2 Serve the pancakes with home-made Apple Sorbet (see p. 200) or Vanilla Ice-cream (see p. 182).
3 Add calvados or reduced cider to some Anglaise Sauce (see p. 220) to serve as a sauce.
4 For the ultimate dessert, serve a calvados anglaise and Apple Sorbet with the pancakes.

*Banana and Pecan Nut Bread
(see p. 213) and
Gingerbread Cake (see
p. 212).*

Gingerbread Cake

This gingerbread can be served as a warm pudding or simply as a cold cake (see pp. 210–11). I like to use it as both, and find that it eats really well with Clementine or Orange Sauce (see p. 221) and clotted cream.

SERVES 4

225 g (8 oz) self-raising flour
¾ tablespoon ground ginger
A pinch of salt
100 g (4 oz) demerara sugar
100 g (4 oz) unsalted butter
100 g (4 oz) treacle
175 g (6 oz) golden syrup
1 egg
150 ml (5 fl oz) milk

Pre-heat the oven to 180°C/350°F/gas 4 and grease and line a 900 g (2 lb) loaf tin.

Mix together the flour, ginger and salt in a bowl. Warm the sugar, butter, treacle and golden syrup together in a pan. Beat the egg into the milk, then mix all the ingredients in the bowl. The gingerbread is made. Pour the mixture into the lined tin and spread evenly. Simply bake in the pre-heated oven for 45 minutes–1 hour. Remove from the tin and leave to stand for a few minutes before serving warm, or just leave to cool.

Banana and Pecan Nut Bread

This can be served as an afternoon teacake (see pp. 210–11), or eats very well with clotted cream and warm Chocolate Sauce (see p. 221) as a pudding.

MAKES 1 × 450 g (2 lb) loaf

3 large ripe bananas
225 g (8 oz) self-raising flour
A pinch of salt
175 g (6 oz) caster sugar
100 g (4 oz) unsalted butter, softened
2 eggs
2 tablespoons golden syrup
50 g (2 oz) pecan nuts

Pre-heat the oven to 160°C/325°F/gas 3 and grease a 450 g (2 lb) loaf tin.

Peel and mash the bananas in a bowl then add the remaining ingredients and beat vigorously for a minute to make sure they are well combined. Spoon the mixture into the loaf tin and spread it to the sides. Sprinkle the top with the pecan nuts and bake in the pre-heated oven for 1¼ hours until well risen and firm to the touch. Leave the loaf to rest for 10–15 minutes in the tin and then turn on to a cooling rack and leave to rest and become cold or just serve warm as a pudding.

Vanilla Sponge
(Genoise)

This sponge can be used for many things: cakes, gâteaux, trifles or Manchester Pudding are just a few.

MAKES 1 × 20 cm (8 in) sponge

6 eggs
175 g (6 oz) caster sugar, flavoured with
    vanilla (see p. 182)
175 g (6 oz) plain flour, sifted
75 g (3 oz) unsalted butter, melted

Pre-heat the oven to 200°C/400°F/gas 6, grease a 20 cm (8 in) round cake tin and dust with flour.

Whisk the eggs and sugar together in a bowl over a pan of hot water. Continue to whisk until the mixture has doubled in volume and is light and creamy. Remove from the heat and continue to whisk until cold and thick. This is called the ribbon stage as the mixture will trail off the whisk in ribbons when you lift it out of the mixture. Lightly fold in the flour and melted butter. Gently pour the mix into the prepared tin and bake in the pre-heated oven for about 30 minutes. The easiest way to test is with a skewer, which will come out clean when the sponge is ready.

Allow to cool for 10 minutes in the tin and then turn out on to a wire rack.

Breakfast Muesli

This is a recipe I couldn't resist. It really is good just with cold milk for breakfast, or it can be mixed with chocolate to make a biscuit to be eaten with ice-cream and Anglaise Sauce (see p. 220) as a pudding.

350 g (12 oz) jumbo oats
100 g (4 oz) sunflower seeds
100 g (4 oz) wheatgerm
75 g (3 oz) demerara sugar
75 ml (3 fl oz) olive oil
100 g (4 oz) clear honey

40 g (1½ oz) dried apple, coarsely
    chopped
40 g (1½ oz) dried apricots, coarsely
    chopped
75 g (3 oz) flaked almonds, toasted
75 g (3 oz) All-Bran (optional)
100 g (4 oz) raisins

Pre-heat the oven to 180°C/350°F/gas 4.

Place the first six ingredients in a small roasting tray, mix together, then cook in the pre-heated oven, stirring regularly, for 15–20 minutes until golden brown. Remove from the oven and leave to cool, stirring all the time.

When cold, stir in the remaining ingredients. Mix them together well, then store in an airtight container. This will keep for up to two weeks. The muesli is now ready to use.

Crunchy Chocolate Muesli Biscuits

MAKES about 30 biscuits

225 g (8 oz) plain or milk chocolate
½ quantity Breakfast Muesli (see above)

Melt the chocolate in a bowl over a pan of hot water. Remove from the heat and leave to cool for a few minutes. Stir in enough muesli so that the mixture will be just held together by the chocolate.

To make sweets, spoon the mixture into small paper cases, or just on to a tray. Cool, then chill until set.

To make biscuits, the mix can be spread on to a tray lined with waxed paper. When set, it can be cut into fingers. Alternatively, spread the warm melted chocolate on to waxed paper, then sprinkle the muesli liberally over the top. Set this in the fridge, and the resulting biscuits could almost be called 'country florentines'. When set, the mix can be cut into rounds or fingers and served with home-made ice-creams.

Puff Pastry

This recipe is used for the Apple Tarts (see p. 200), Home-made Pasties (see p. 134), and could also be used for a steak and kidney pie. It's very simple to do, just place the steak and kidney filling from the pudding recipe (see p. 122) in a pie-dish, cover with the puff pastry and bake in a pre-heated oven at 200°C/400°F/gas 6 for about 30 minutes until the pastry is golden and crisp.

MAKES about 450 g (1 lb)

225 g (8 oz) unsalted butter
225 g (8 oz) strong plain flour
A pinch of salt
150 ml (5 fl oz) cold water
A few drops of lemon juice

Cut off 50 g (2 oz) of the butter, melt it then leave it to cool. The remaining 175 g (6 oz) block should be left out to soften. Sift the flour and salt together into a large bowl and make a well in the centre. Pour the water, lemon juice and cooled, melted butter into the well in the flour and gently fold in the flour to make a pliable dough. Allow to rest for 20 minutes.

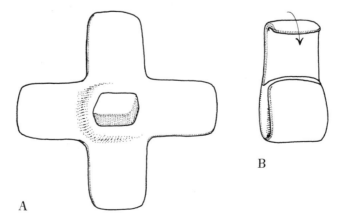

A　　　B

On a lightly floured board, roll the pastry from four sides, leaving a lump in the centre. The dough should look like a crossroads. The remaining block of butter should have softened to a similar texture to the dough; it should be easy to roll without melting and not so hard that it will break the pastry.

Sit the butter on the centre lump of the dough (A) and fold over each pastry flap (B). Pat the pastry into a 30 × 15 cm (12 × 6 in) rectangle and leave to rest in the fridge for 10–15 minutes.

Roll the pastry lengthways to make it double in length to about 60 cm (24 in) but the same width (C). Fold in both ends to the centre (D) and then fold once more (E). This is called a double turn and should be completed a further 3 times, each time rolling out the same length and then finishing with a double turn. Always roll with the folded edge on the left, and always leave to rest for 20–30 minutes in the fridge before each turn. The pastry should now be rested for a minimum of 30 minutes in the fridge before using.

Palmier Biscuits

When using puff pastry for different recipes there are always some trimmings left over which quite often just get thrown away. Well, here is a way of using them all up and making great biscuits to serve with Cappuccino Mousse (see p. 172), Vanilla Ice-cream (see p. 182), sorbets (see p. 184) or petits fours.

Puff pastry trimmings, rolled together
Icing sugar

Pre-heat the oven to 220°c/425°f/gas 7 and dampen a baking sheet.

Sprinkle icing sugar liberally on to the work surface and give the pastry one more double turn with the sugar. Rest in the fridge for 15 minutes.

Once chilled, sprinkle more icing sugar on to the surface and roll out the pastry to 3 mm (⅛ in) thick. Trim the edges. If this makes a large square, then cut the pastry in half (A) and double turn each strip (B). Rest in the fridge or freezer for 20 minutes until set.

When set, cut each folded strip into pieces about 5 mm (¼ in) thick (C), lay them flat on the work surface, dust with more icing sugar and flatten lightly with a rolling pin (D). Lay them on the baking sheet and cook in the pre-heated oven for about 5 minutes. Turn them over on the tray and cook for a further 5 minutes until golden and crisp. Leave to cool on a wire rack. The biscuits will keep in an airtight container for 24 hours, but are best eaten on the same day.

Sweet (and Savoury) Pastry

This sweet pastry cooks to a light and crumbly texture and, of course, if you omit the icing sugar and vanilla you have an instant savoury pastry for all your flans and pies. In the Glazed Lemon Tart recipe (see p. 202), I use this basic recipe with the addition of lemon zest for extra taste. For a shorter pastry texture replace half of the buttter with lard.

MAKES about 800 g (1¾ lb)

450 g (1 lb) plain flour
150 g (5 oz) icing sugar
A pinch of salt
1 vanilla pod (optional)
225 g (8 oz) unsalted butter
1 egg
1 tablespoon milk

Sift the flour, icing sugar and salt together. Split the vanilla pod, if using, scrape out the seeds and mix into the flour. This is an optional extra but it gives a wonderful taste to the pastry for any pudding flans.

Rub in the butter to give a breadcrumb texture. Beat the egg with the milk and work into the mix to form a dough. Wrap in cling film and leave to rest in the fridge for 20–30 minutes before using.

Anglaise (Fresh Custard) Sauce

This so-called Anglaise Sauce is really just a fresh custard sauce. It's great with steamed puddings, tarts and trifles.

MAKES 750 ml (1¼ pints)

8 egg yolks
75 g (3 oz) caster sugar flavoured with
    vanilla (see p. 182)
1 vanilla pod, split (optional)
300 ml (10 fl oz) milk
300 ml (10 fl oz) double cream

Beat the egg yolks and sugar together in a bowl until well blended. Scrape the insides of the vanilla pod into the milk and cream and bring to the boil. Sit the bowl over a pan of hot water and whisk the cream into the egg yolks and sugar. As the egg yolks cook, the custard will thicken. Keep stirring until it starts to coat the back of a spoon, then remove the bowl from the heat and stir the sauce occasionally until cool. The custard is now ready to serve.

It can also be brought back up to heat over a pan of hot water, but must never boil. If that happens, the sauce will separate.

Coffee Sauce

The custard recipe above can also be used to create rich coffee sauce which tastes good with the Cappuccino Mousse (see p. 172) or a home-made Vanilla Ice-cream (see p. 182).

Just replace the vanilla pod with 2 teaspoons of fresh, ground coffee, and bring to the boil with the milk and cream. Cook as above, and when ready, pour through a sieve to remove any coarse granules. The sauce will have taken on a light coffee colour with very fine granules left in.

Chocolate Sauce

This sauce goes very well with pear sorbet, banana ice-cream, Vanilla Ice-cream (see p. 182), or a steamed chocolate pudding.

MAKES about 350 ml (12 fl oz)

225 g (8 oz) plain chocolate
150 ml (5 fl oz) milk
75 ml (3 fl oz) double cream
40 g (1½ oz) caster sugar

Melt the chocolate in a bowl over a pan of hot water. Do not allow it to get too hot or this will make it grainy. Boil the milk, double cream and sugar together and stir into the chocolate. Allow the mixture to cool, stirring occasionally. The sauce is now finished and ready to use.

To enrich the taste and consistency, 25 g (1 oz) of unsalted butter can be added while the sauce is still warm.

Clementine or Orange Sauce

This is a good sauce for ice-creams, sorbets (see p. 184), Gingerbread Cake (see p. 212), or even Cappuccino Mousse (see p. 172).

MAKES about 600 ml (1 pint)

2.25 kg (5 lb) clementines or oranges
15 g (½ oz) arrowroot
Icing sugar to taste

Squeeze the juice from the clementines or oranges then push the juice through a sieve. This should leave you with at least 600 ml (1 pint) of juice. Bring to the boil and boil until reduced by half; in fact, whatever quantity of juice you have, always reduce it by half. Mix the arrowroot with a little water to soften it, then add it to the reduced juice a little at a time, stirring continuously until you have a sauce that will lightly coat the back of a spoon. Allow the sauce barely to simmer for 3–4 minutes. Remove from the heat and leave to cool.

When the sauce is cold, it should be a rich orange colour and have a full taste. If you feel it needs to be a little sweeter, just stir in some icing sugar.

Sauces, Stocks and Pickles

I't's in this section that you will find all the bits and pieces – the stocks, sauces, gravies, dressings, chutneys etc. – that are so important to good cooking. It's a shame to lump them together almost as an afterthought, because they are so basic to so many of the recipes, but it is the most convenient way to place them. You will find some other similar recipes in other chapters of the book, as I see some of the recipes as an integral part of a particular main course or starter.

ABOVE *Grilled Mackerel with Stewed Tomatoes, Pesto and Onions (see p. 44).*
LEFT *Foreground, Chicken Liver Parfait (see p. 62), back right, Grape Chutney (see p. 251), back left, Piccalilli (see p. 252).*

Vinegar

Malt vinegar is probably the best-known, especially for sprinkling on your fish and chips! Malt vinegar is made from malted barley (as, of course, is whisky), and gets its colour from caramel. The strongest of vinegars, it is used mostly for pickling, and I've used it here in a chutney recipe where it helps achieve the right acidity for the ingredients. Don't use it in basic dressings, as its strength is just too much for salads.

Red and white wine vinegars are the ones to use for most general dressings and purposes. Red wine vinegar is the best. Wine vinegars are allowed to mature slowly in barrels until the vinegars have turned the alcohol into acetic acid. They can be made more swiftly by heating, but this tends to destroy some of the flavours.

Balsamic vinegar must be the most-used vinegar in modern cookery, which doesn't surprise me as it really is astounding. There are many cheap copies on the market, which aren't worth buying. Real balsamic vinegar is made from Trebbiano grapes, and should be a mimimum of five years old to have any true flavour. The older it gets, the better and stronger it tastes but, of course, the more expensive it is to buy. Twelve-year-old balsamic is a great medium and although it's pricey, you need very little because of its immense flavour. Some balsamics can be as old as forty years, but this is very rare, and you'll probably have to wait another forty years to try one!

Oils

The oils that I generally use are olive oil (extra virgin) and ground-nut (peanut) oil.

Ground-nut oil is a very basic oil which is used in France (*huile à la arachide*) as a base in most dressings and in frying. It's very similar to sunflower oil, and has quite a bland flavour. In the basic dressing here, I mix it with olive oil, which prevents the dressing from being too overpowering. It is also cheaper to make, and works well on all simple salads.

Virgin olive oil is an oil from the first pressing, which is totally pure, without any heating or chemical processing. The 'extra' in front applies to its low acidity grade. Extra virgin oil has 1 per cent acidity, which is the lowest and the best.

Alternative Stocks and Sauces

These may look really hard work, but they're not at all. They may not always be practical to make in the home, though, so I've been out doing some homework on stocks and sauces, in search of some good commercial alternatives to make the cooking of some of my dishes a little easier.

Fish and Chicken Stocks

Alternatives to these can be found in the chill cabinet of most Sainsbury's and other quality supermarkets. They are sold in plastic tubs, each containing about 284 ml (about 9–10 fl oz). The beauty of these is a) they taste great, b) they have good colour and jelly texture, and c) they are sold as stocks ready to use. They really are the best I've found, but if you can't get hold of them, there are also some good-quality stock cubes.

Beef and Veal *Jus*

In the basic recipe, these start out as stocks, and then for use in other recipes, they are reduced to a sauce consistency. I've found a sauce which will cut out all of this, and is an instant *jus* to use as a base sauce in many of the recipes asking for veal or beef *jus*. Madeira Wine Gravy or White Wine Gravy are both made by Crosse & Blackwell in their Bonne Cuisine range, and should be available in just about every supermarket or good grocery shop. The Madeira flavour gives it good body and, when made, it has a lovely glossy finish. I've tried it with the Braised Oxtails and in Onion Gravy, and my only advice is to mix it with 600 ml (1 pint) of water instead of 300 ml (10 fl oz). This way, when slow braising or stewing, there's room for reduction and it won't become too thick. If you are cooking oxtail for four to six people, then I would use two packets and 1.2 litres (2 pints) of water. This would make a stock consistency, but once the meat is cooked, you'll finish with a good, rich sauce.

Chicken Stock

Chicken stock is one of our most important bases. It's used for most soups and many cream sauces. It's also very simple to make. I'm sure your local butcher will help you out with some chicken bones. If not, then cook a boiling fowl with vegetables in water and you will have an instant tasty stock and the bird to eat as well. If you do not have a large stock pot, you can easily reduce the quantities. (For information on ready-made alternatives see p. 225.)

MAKES 2.25 litres (4 pints)

2 onions, chopped
2 celery sticks, chopped
2 leeks, chopped
25 g (1 oz) unsalted butter
1 garlic clove, crushed
1 bay leaf
1 sprig of fresh thyme
A few black peppercorns
1.8 kg (4 lb) chicken carcasses, chopped
3.4 litres (6 pints) water

In a large stock pot (about 8.5 litres (15 pint) capacity), lightly soften the vegetables in the butter without colouring. Add the garlic, bay leaf, thyme, peppercorns and chopped carcasses. Cover with the cold water and bring to the simmer, skimming all the time. Allow the stock to simmer for 2–3 hours, then drain through a sieve. The stock is now ready to use and will keep well chilled or frozen.

Vegetable Stock

This stock is a great substitute for chicken and fish stock in lots of the recipes in this book. It's easy to make and works very well in vegetarian risottos or soups. This is a very basic recipe, but many other flavours can be added, such as mushrooms or tomatoes – both would add different tastes for different dishes.

MAKES about 1 litre (1¾ pints)

225 g (8 oz) carrots
225 g (8 oz) celery sticks
1 large onion
1 leek
50 g (2 oz) unsalted butter
1 bay leaf
1 sprig of fresh thyme
1 small garlic clove, crushed
1.2 litres (2 pints) water
Salt and freshly ground black pepper

Cut the vegetables roughly into 1 cm (½ in) dice. Melt the butter in a large pan and add the diced vegetables, herbs and garlic. Cover with a lid and cook over a low heat for 6–8 minutes, stirring from time to time. Add the water, bring to the simmer and cook for 20–30 minutes. Remove from the heat and allow the vegetables to stand in the stock until cool.

Pour the stock through a sieve, squeezing out all the juices from the vegetables but not puréeing them. Taste, and season with salt and pepper. The stock is now ready to use. If you find it's not strong enough, then just boil to reduce it until you are happy with the taste. Check again for seasoning after reduction.

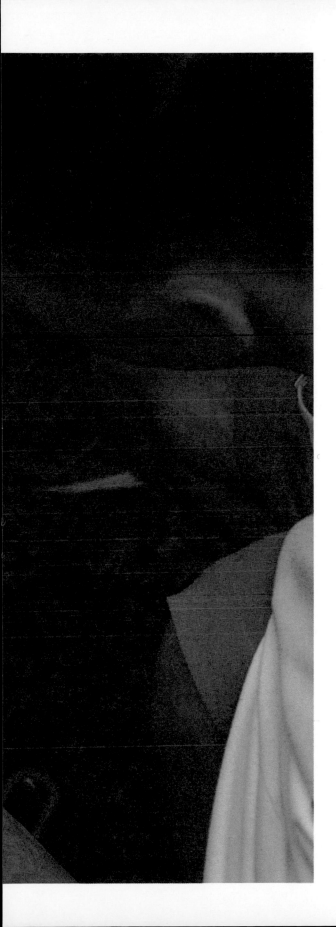

*Noodles in Creamy Mushroom
Sauce to be served with
chicken breasts (see p. 92).
The mushroom sauce is made
with chicken stock
(see p. 228).*

Veal or Beef Stock
and *Jus*

This stock is a base to a lot of cooking, and really holds the essence of a good dish. Reading this recipe may well make you want to think twice about it, but it is worth making and so satisfying once made. It will give you great sauces and, of course, will store well in your freezer, so go on, have a go! It is best started in the morning, which will allow the stock to cook throughout the day.

If this really is too much, then a lot of good gravy bases can be found but do use them carefully, not making them too thick and strong. (For information on ready-made alternatives see p. 225.)

MAKES 4.5–5.5 litres (8–10 pints) stock
or 600 ml–1.2 litres (1–2 pints) *jus*

3 onions, halved	3 celery sticks, coarsely chopped
2–3 tablespoons water	1 leek, chopped
2.25 kg (5 lb) veal or beef bones	3–4 tomatoes, chopped
225 g (8 oz) veal or beef trimmings from the butcher	1 garlic clove, halved
	1 bay leaf
225 g (8 oz) carrots, coarsely chopped	1 sprig of fresh thyme

Pre-heat the oven to 110°C/225°F/gas ¼–½. Lay the onion halves flat in a roasting tray with the water. Place the onion into the very cool oven and allow to slowly caramelize until they have totally softened and coloured. This process will take 1–2 hours. The sugars in the onions will slowly cook and give a wonderful taste. Pop the onions into a large stock pot and leave on one side. Increase the oven temperature to 200°C/400°F/gas 6.

Place all the bones and trimmings in a roasting tray and roast for about 30 minutes until well coloured. Roast the chopped carrots and celery in another roasting tray for about 20 minutes until lightly coloured.

When ready, add the bones, trimmings and vegetables to the onions in the pot, along with the leeks, tomatoes, garlic, bay leaf and thyme. Fill the pot with cold water – you'll need about 5.5–6.5 litres (10–12 pints). Bring the stock to the simmer and skim off any impurities. Allow to cook for 6–8 hours, and with this you will achieve the maximum taste. If it seems to be reducing too quickly during cooking, top up with cold water.

When ready, drain and discard the bones and vegetables. This is now your veal stock, and you can cool it and freeze it in convenient quantities.

Or you can make a veal *jus* with the stock. Allow the liquid to boil and reduce down to 600 ml–1.2 litres (1–2 pints), skimming all the time. The stock should be thick and of a sauce consistency. Make sure that you taste all the time during reduction. If the sauce tastes right but is not thick enough, thicken it lightly with cornflour. (Of course, I do hope that won't be necessary!) You now have a veal *jus*, a classic sauce.

Onion Gravy

I use this simple gravy to accompany the Home-made Pork Sausages on p. 116 and also serve it with Calves' Liver with Onion Gravy and Mashed Potatoes (see p. 102), a dish that has become a bit of a classic. The gravy is also a vital component of my faggot recipe on p. 104.

SERVES 4

8 onions, thinly sliced
2 tablespoons water
600 ml (1 pint) Veal *Jus* (see left) or
    bought alternative (see p. 225)

Place the sliced onions in a pan with the water and cook very slowly, stirring all the time. The sugar from the onions will slowly caramelize and become brown and sweet-tasting. The process will take 1½–2 hours.

Add the veal *jus* and simmer for a further 30 minutes. The gravy will now be even richer in taste and colour with a lovely shiny finish.

OVERLEAF
*'Saucing the plates' for, left, Grilled
Sardine Fillets on Tomato Toasts
(see p. 45) and, right,
Calves' Liver with Onion Gravy
and Mashed Potatoes
(see p. 102).*

Red Wine Sauce

This sauce tastes good with almost any meat – chicken, beef, pork, veal – and even eats well with baked fish.

MAKES about 1.2 litres (2 pints)

4 shallots, chopped
1 large carrot, chopped
2 celery sticks, chopped
25 g (1 oz) unsalted butter
1 garlic clove, crushed
1 bay leaf
1 sprig of fresh thyme
225 g (8 oz) beef skirt or trimmings from
    the butcher (optional)
1 tablespoon olive oil (optional)
1 bottle red wine
1.2 litres (2 pints) Veal *Jus* (see p. 232)
    or bought alternative (see p. 225)
Salt and freshly ground white pepper

In a large pan, cook the chopped vegetables in a little butter with the garlic and herbs, allowing them to colour. In a frying-pan, fry the meat, if used, in the oil, colouring on all sides, then add the meat to the vegetables. Pour the red wine into the frying-pan to release any flavours from the trimmings. Scrape and stir, then pour the wine on to the meat and vegetables and boil to reduce until almost dry.

Add the veal *jus* and bring to the simmer, skim off any impurities, then simmer the sauce gently for 30 minutes. Pass through a sieve, squeezing all the juices from the vegetables and meat. Check for seasoning, and you now have a rich, glistening red wine sauce.

Curry Cream Sauce

This recipe will provide a slightly yellow, creamy curry sauce with just enough strength to flavour the kedgeree (see p. 46). Any left-over sauce can be kept in the fridge for a few days. It's good added to any curry.

MAKES 600 ml (1 pint)

1 onion, chopped
1 carrot, chopped
½ leek, chopped
2 celery sticks, chopped
1 garlic clove, chopped
½ teaspoon ground ginger or a small
    piece of fresh root ginger, grated
A few coriander seeds (optional)
A few cardamom seeds (optional)
A few black peppercorns
50 g (2 oz) unsalted butter
2 teaspoons medium curry powder
600 ml (1 pint) Chicken Stock (see
    p. 228) or Vegetable Stock (see
    p. 229)
300 ml (10 fl oz) double cream
Salt and freshly ground white pepper

Cook all the chopped vegetables, garlic and spices in the butter for 10 minutes. Add the curry powder and continue to cook for 15 minutes. Add the chicken stock and bring to the simmer. Simmer the stock until reduced by half. Now add the cream and cook for 10–15 minutes. Season with salt and pepper. Push the sauce through a sieve; it is now ready to use.

Tomato and Onion Flavoured Gravy
to accompany Jambonette de Volaille
(see p. 96).

Tomato and Onion Flavoured Gravy

This sauce has a delicious variety of flavours, and goes particularly well with lamb and chicken dishes.

MAKES 1.5 litres (2½ pints)

4 onions, sliced
1–2 tablespoons water
8 tomatoes, chopped
1 garlic clove, crushed
1 small sprig of fresh rosemary
8 fresh basil leaves
300 ml (10 fl oz) Noilly Prat or white
    vermouth
300 ml (10 fl oz) dry white wine
1.2 litres (2 pints) Veal *Jus* (see p. 232)
    or bought alternative (see p. 225)

Cook the sliced onions with the water very slowly until they have naturally caramelized, stirring occasionally. This will take at least an hour. Add the tomatoes, garlic and herbs and continue to cook for 15–20 minutes until the tomatoes are soft. Pour in the Noilly Prat or vermouth and the white wine and boil to reduce until almost dry. Add the *jus*, bring to the simmer and cook for 30 minutes. Blitz using a hand blender or liquidizer. This will thicken the sauce and help it take on lots more tastes. Pass through a sieve and serve.

Tomato or
Red Pepper Coulis

You can use the same recipe to make either a tomato coulis (see p. 151), or a red pepper version. For a red pepper coulis, replace 350 g (12 oz) of the tomatoes with an equal weight of seeded red peppers, then follow the same procedure to make the coulis.

MAKES about 900 ml (1½ pints)

1 large onion, chopped
2 celery sticks, chopped
1 large carrot, chopped
1 garlic clove, crushed
A few fresh basil or tarragon leaves or a
    pinch of dried tarragon
1 sprig of fresh thyme or a pinch of
    dried thyme
2 tablespoons olive oil
50 g (2 oz) unsalted butter

150 ml (5 fl oz) dry white wine
450 g (1 lb) tomatoes, chopped
300 ml (10 fl oz) Chicken Stock
    (see p. 228) or Vegetable Stock (see
    p. 229)
1 tablespoon tomato purée
Salt and freshly ground white
    pepper
A few drops of Spicing Essence
    (see p. 242) (optional)

Cook the chopped onion, celery and carrot with the garlic and herbs in the olive oil and butter for a few minutes until softened. Add the white wine and boil to reduce until almost dry. Add the chopped tomatoes and cook for a few minutes, then add the stock and tomato purée, bring to the simmer, cover with a lid and continue to cook for 20 minutes. Liquidize the sauce then push it through a sieve to give a smooth sauce consistency. If the sauce is a little thick, add more stock to reach the right consistency. Season to taste with salt and pepper. The coulis is now ready. To make the sauce more spicy, add a few drops of the spicing essence at a time, if using, whisking and tasting until you have the flavour you want.

Spicy Tomato Sauce

This sauce goes so well with seafood of all types. It's almost like eating a loose, spicy tomato chutney. Once made, it can be kept chilled for up to two weeks.

MAKES about 450 g (1 lb)

85 ml (3 fl oz) olive oil
3 shallots or 2 onions, finely
    chopped
2 garlic cloves, crushed
A few fresh basil, thyme and
    tarragon leaves

900 g (2 lb) tomatoes, skinned and
    seeded
2 tablespoons red wine vinegar
1 teaspoon caster sugar
Salt and freshly ground white pepper
2–3 drops Tabasco sauce

Warm the olive oil in a pan and add the chopped shallots or onions, the garlic and the herbs. It's best to have the herbs in sprigs, as these can then be easily removed at the end of cooking. Allow the shallots and herbs to cook for 4–5 minutes until tender.

Cut the tomato flesh into 5 mm (¼ in) dice and add to the shallots. Have the pan on a very low heat, just on a light simmer, and cook for about 45 minutes. The sauce may cook a little quicker, or take a little longer – this will really depend on the water content of the tomatoes. After 45 minutes, add the wine vinegar and sugar and cook for a further 15 minutes. The tomatoes should have taken on an almost lumpy sauce texture; if the sauce is very thick, simply fold in a little more olive oil. Allow to cool until just warm then season with salt, pepper and Tabasco. The sauce is now ready.

Rouille

MAKES about 300 ml (10 fl oz)

1 red pepper, seeded and chopped
1 small dried or fresh chilli pepper,
    seeded and chopped
2 garlic cloves, crushed

50 g (2 oz) fresh white breadcrumbs
1 egg yolk
Salt
150 ml (5 fl oz) extra virgin olive oil

Place the pepper and chilli in a food processor or liquidizer with the garlic, breadcrumbs, egg yolk and salt and blitz until smooth. With the motor still running, slowly add the olive oil as if making mayonnaise. When all the oil has been added, push the sauce through a sieve. It can be kept in the fridge for a couple of days without spoiling.

Hollandaise Sauce

This is a French classic. It can be bought ready-made, but I'm going to give you two ways of making it. Both taste very good.

RECIPE 1: *The Classic*

225 g (8 oz) unsalted butter
2 tablespoons malt or white wine
    vinegar
6 white peppercorns, lightly crushed
1 tablespoon water
2 egg yolks
Salt and cayenne or freshly ground
    white pepper

Melt the butter in a pan then leave it to cool slightly so that it is just warm when added to the sauce; if it is too hot, the sauce will curdle. The butter will have separated, leaving all its solids in the base of your pan, which you can discard, so you will only be adding the butter oil to the sauce. This is clarified butter.

Boil the vinegar with the peppercorns until reduced by half. Add the cold water to cool and drain the reduction through a sieve into a bowl. Add the egg yolks and whisk together. Place the bowl over a pan of hot water and whisk to a sabayon. A sabayon is created by the cooking and thickening of the egg yolks. As they are whisked, they increase in volume to a cream consistency. When the yolks have reached this stage, remove the bowl from the heat and continue to whisk, slowly adding the warm, clarified butter. When all the clear butter has been added and whisked, the sauce should be a thick consistency which can now be seasoned with salt and cayenne or white pepper.

Should the hollandaise curdle, just take a tablespoon of warm water and very slowly whisk in the sauce. This should bring the sauce back to a nice consistency.

To increase the flavours of this sauce, a pinch of dried tarragon, basil and some chopped onion or shallot can be added to the reduction. This will leave you with a Sauce Béarnaise, which also goes well with meat dishes and even a plain grilled steak.

RECIPE 2: *The Easy Way*

225 g (8 oz) unsalted butter
2 egg yolks
1 tablespoon warm water
Juice of ½ lemon
Salt and cayenne or freshly ground
    white pepper

Clarify the butter as described in the classic recipe.

To make the sauce, just add the egg yolks to the water (this is a fake reduction) and make into a sabayon as in the previous recipe. Add the clarified butter, as before. When made, just add the lemon juice and seasoning.

This eats very nicely with Grilled Sardine Fillets (see p. 45).

So now you have two methods, the choice is yours!

Basic Vinaigrette

This basic recipe is very convenient. Once made, it can sit in your fridge and can be used at any time and for any dish you might fancy. The vinegar just gives a very slight sweetness to the taste.

MAKES 600 ml (1 pint)

300 ml (10 fl oz) extra virgin olive oil (French or Italian)
300 ml (10 fl oz) ground-nut oil
25 ml (1 fl oz) balsamic vinegar
1 bunch of fresh basil
½ bunch of fresh tarragon

3–4 sprigs of fresh thyme
12 black peppercorns, lightly crushed
3 shallots, finely chopped
2 garlic cloves, crushed
1 bay leaf
1 teaspoon coarse sea salt

Warm the olive and ground-nut oil together. Place all the remaining ingredients into a 750 ml (1¼ pint) bottle. Pour the oil into the bottle and close with a cork or screw top. For the best results, leave to marinate for a week which will allow all the flavours to enhance the oils. To help the dressing along, shake the bottle once a day. Taste for seasoning before using.

66 *Warming olive oil will help to release the maximum flavour.* **99**

A simple green salad dressed with Basic Vinaigrette (see p. 245).

Red Wine Vinaigrette

This is a very basic recipe. Many herbs can be added to the bottle to help infuse more flavours. The best to use, unchopped, are basil, tarragon and thyme. When the dressing is to be used, just add some chopped fresh chives, basil, thyme or tarragon to finish the dressing.

MAKES about 600 ml (1 pint)

4 shallots or 1 large onion, finely
  chopped
2 garlic cloves, crushed
300 ml (10 fl oz) red wine

300 ml (10 fl oz) red wine vinegar
2 teaspoons Dijon mustard
600 ml (1 pint) olive oil
Salt and freshly ground black pepper

Mix the chopped shallots or onion with the garlic in a pan and add the red wine. Bring to the boil then reduce until almost dry. Add the red wine vinegar and boil to reduce by three-quarters. Remove the pan from the heat.

While the shallots are still warm, add the Dijon mustard and blend in with the olive oil. Season with salt and pepper. The dressing can now be left to cool and then bottled. Chilled, it keeps for two to four weeks.

Mayonnaise

This is another basic recipe, but so much nicer than bought mayonnaise. Use it with potatoes in a salad, or in my version of a club sandwich (see p.64).

MAKES about 600 ml (1 pint)

3 egg yolks
1 tablespoon malt, white wine or
  balsamic vinegar
A pinch of English or Dijon mustard

Salt and freshly ground white pepper
300 ml (10 fl oz) basic olive oil
1 teaspoon hot water
A few drops of lemon juice (optional)

Whisk the egg yolks, vinegar, mustard and seasonings together, then slowly add the olive oil, whisking continuously. When all the oil is added, finish with the water and correct the seasoning. A few drops of lemon juice can be added to enhance the taste.

Vierge Dressing

This dressing has a very different taste to the basic dressing, and lends itself best to fish dishes. I was first inspired to make it whilst staying at La Côte St Jacques in Joigny, France, in the mid 80s. The restaurant now has three Michelin stars. The dressing was served with a red mullet dish, so now I've got one of my own which is very simple to make (see p. 82).

MAKES 600 ml (1 pint)

600 ml (1 pint) extra virgin olive oil (French or Italian)
15 g (½ oz) coriander seeds, crushed
1 bunch of fresh tarragon

12 black peppercorns, crushed
4 shallots, chopped
2 garlic cloves, crushed
A pinch of sea salt

Warm the olive oil with the coriander seeds. Place the remaining ingredients into a 600 ml (1 pint) jar and pour the oil and coriander on top. Leave to marinate for 1 week, shaking the bottle daily.

Pasta Dough

This pasta dough can be used for lasagne, fettucine, ravioli and many more pasta dishes. You can make it by hand or in a food processor. It also freezes very well.

MAKES 450 g (1 lb) to serve 4

250 g (9 oz) fine semolina or plain flour
A pinch of salt
½ teaspoon olive oil
2 eggs
3 egg yolks

Mix the semolina or flour with the salt and olive oil, and mix well for 1 minute. Add the eggs and egg yolks and stir well until it becomes a dough. Knead the dough for 1–3 minutes until it has a smooth texture. It should now be wrapped in cling film and chilled for 30 minutes to rest.

The pasta is now ready to use. It can be rolled, cut and cooked straightaway, or cut and left to dry and used later. If dried, the pasta will always take a little longer to cook.

Chutneys and Pickles

Ialways like a pickle or chutney in a ham or cheese sandwich, or with my ploughman's lunch. Here are a few of my favourites, which certainly have their own distinctive flavours. The grape is sweet without being sickly, and the tomato is more savoury and sharp. The piccalilli is a combination of both but also has a spicy finish. One thing's for sure, they're all delicious.

You will need a large pan or preserving pan for making chutneys. The best jars to use for this are Kilner jars with rubber seals. If you are using a screw-top lid, keep the chutneys chilled and they'll last a lot longer. Do not use metal lids as they react with the acid in the vinegar.

Grape Chutney

This chutney (see pp. 222–3) improves with time and is delicious to serve with the Chicken Liver Parfait (see p. 62).

MAKES about 1.5 kg (3 lb)

10 Granny Smith or Golden Delicious apples, peeled, cored and chopped
2 onions, finely chopped
300 ml (10 fl oz) good balsamic vinegar
300 ml (10 fl oz) drinkable brandy

2.25 kg (5 lb) seedless white grapes, picked and washed
350 g (12 oz) demerara sugar
A pinch of salt
2 teaspoons mixed spice
2 teaspoons ground cinnamon
1 teaspoon ground ginger

Simmer the apples, onions, balsamic vinegar and brandy together in a preserving pan for 30 minutes. Stir in the grapes, sugar, salt and spices and continue to simmer for 1½–2 hours over a low heat until the mixture is thick and pulpy, stirring occasionally. Should the chutney still seem a little too liquid, boil on a high heat to allow the excess liquid to evaporate.

Let the chutney cool slightly then spoon into warm, sterile jars. Seal then label and store in a cool, dark place until needed.

Green Tomato Chutney

MAKES about 1.5 kg (3 lb)

2.25 kg (5 lb) green tomatoes, cut into 8
600 ml (1 pint) malt vinegar
5 large onions, finely chopped
225 g (8 oz) raisins
450 g (1 lb) sultanas

350 g (12 oz) demerara sugar
25 g (1 oz) salt
4 teaspoons mixed spice
4 teaspoons ground cinnamon
2 teaspoons ground ginger

Place the tomatoes in a preserving pan, add the vinegar and simmer over a low heat for 30 minutes. Add the onions, raisins and sultanas and continue to cook for a further 30 minutes. Add the sugar, salt and spices and simmer gently for 1½–2 hours until thick, stirring occasionally. Leave to cool slightly, then spoon into warm, sterile jars.

Piccalilli

This has to be one of the easiest pickle recipes that I make (see pp. 222–3). There are so many variations that you can try – different vegetables, mustards and vinegars. This pickle eats particularly well with oily fish such as mackerel and herrings; its acidity works against the oils and leaves a good, clean taste.

Makes about 1.25 kg (3 lb)

1 cauliflower	300 ml (10 fl oz) malt vinegar
3 large onions	¼ teaspoon chopped dried chilli
8 large shallots, or 16 onions if	350 g (12 oz) caster sugar
unavailable	50 g (2 oz) English mustard
Salt and freshly ground white pepper	powder
1 cucumber	25 g (1 oz) ground turmeric
600 ml (1 pint) white wine vinegar	3 tablespoons cornflour

Cut the cauliflower into small florets. Peel and cut the onions and shallots into 1 cm (½ in) dice. Place in a bowl, sprinkle with 25 g (1 oz) of salt and leave to stand for 24 hours. Afterwards rinse in cold water and dry.

Peel and de-seed the cucumber and cut it into 1 cm (½ in) dice. Sprinkle with a little salt and leave to stand for 10–15 minutes. Rinse in cold water, then dry and add to the onions and cauliflower.

Boil the two vinegars together with the chilli and then leave to cool for 30 minutes. Strain through a sieve and discard the chilli.

Mix together the sugar and remaining dry ingredients in a bowl. When the vinegar is cool, mix a little of it with the dry ingredients. Bring the bulk of the vinegar back to the boil, pour into the sugar mixture, and whisk until it is all blended together. Bring this mixture back to the boil and cook for 3 minutes, then simply pour over the vegetables and mix well. Leave to cool. The piccalilli is now ready and can be put into jars and refrigerated, or served at once. It will keep refrigerated for at least a month.

Index

Page numbers in *italic* refer to the illustrations

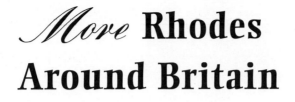

More Rhodes
Around Britain

More Rhodes
Around Britain

Gary Rhodes

Photographs by Anthony Blake

Acknowledgements

My thanks to: David, Margaret and Joseph Levin; Celia and Martin Warbrick from Kitchens of Knightsbridge; Alice Portnoy from Neff UK; Anthony Blake and Joy Skipper; Nicky Copeland and Wendy Hobson; Clare Adkins; the *More Rhodes Around Britain* production team; my *sous-chefs*, Stuart Busby and Wayne Tapsfield, and everyone at The Greenhouse; and, of course, my wife, Jenny.

This book is published to accompany the television series entitled *More Rhodes Around Britain* which was first broadcast in 1995.

This edition produced for
The Book People Ltd
Guardian House
Borough Road
Godalming
Surrey GU7 2AE
by BBC Books, an imprint of BBC Worldwide Publishing,
BBC Worldwide Ltd, Woodlands, 80 Wood Lane, London W12 0TT
First published 1995

Tested and edited by Wendy Hobson
Designed by Isobel Gillan and Tim Higgins
Illustrations by Kate Simunek
Photographs © Anthony Blake
Styling by Anthony Blake and Joy Skipper
Food prepared by Gary Rhodes
Cutlery and crockery provided by Divertimenti and Villeroy and Boch

Set in Ehrhardt and Ellington
Printed and bound in Great Britain by Butler & Tanner Ltd, Frome and London
Colour separation by Radstock Reproductions Ltd, Midsomer Norton
Jacket printed by Lawrence Allen Ltd, Weston-super-Mare

PRECEDING PAGES Gary preparing four of his favourite cod dishes (see pp.66–73).

Contents

Soups, Starters *and* Main Courses!

Looking at the title could be a little unnerving! Starters mixed with main courses? – this could be a long chapter! Well, don't worry. The reason I put them together is that almost every dish here can either be a starter or a main course, depending on how you serve it, and how much you serve.

ABOVE *Griddled Scallops with Crispy Aubergines (see p.42).*
LEFT *Grilled Tuna with Salsa Dressing (see p.34).*

All the recipes have been developed to give everybody plenty of scope and movement – some have also 'mini-features' so they include more than one dish in the basic recipe. There's everything from vegetarian to risottos and meat dishes – so I hope there's something to suit everybody and every occasion. So whether it's a light lunch you need, a summer barbecue, a family tea, or special dinner party – there's something here for you.

And don't forget that I don't want you to stop with these recipes. All the recipes should be an inspiration and spark off stacks of ideas of your own. So if you want to make the leek and Parmesan risotto but add asparagus and strips of smoked salmon and even top with a poached egg, why not?

The majority of starters are fish-based, ranging from mackerel and salmon to scallops, cockles and smoked eel. Fish is one of the bonuses of island-living; we have such wonderful fish available to us. In fact, only the tuna and king prawns are not locally fished. I didn't go out of my way to give mainly fish starters, but I do think fish starters with meat main courses does suit the British way of eating.

Gazpacho

This is a wonderful summer soup that has so many variations. My version has plenty of flavours and textures (see pp.18–19). Gazpacho can be served chunky-style or can be blitzed in a liquidizer and served smooth. It is traditionally served with everything raw, but if you want to make a winter Gazpacho, then just cook the ingredients in the olive oil first, then add the tomatoes and the rest of the ingredients to give you a spicy tomato and sweet pepper soup. To make the soups totally vegetarian, simply replace the Tomato Coulis and Chicken Stock with tomato juice.

SERVES 4

450 g (1 lb) ripe plum or salad tomatoes
1 red pepper
2 green peppers
1 yellow pepper
1 cucumber, peeled and de-seeded
1 garlic clove
1 onion
2 teaspoons tomato purée
2 tablespoons red wine vinegar

75 ml (3 fl oz) olive oil
300 ml (10 fl oz) Tomato Coulis (see p.232)
300 ml (10 fl oz) Chicken Stock (see p.222)
Salt and freshly ground black pepper
6–8 fresh basil leaves
12–16 fresh tarragon leaves

Remove the eyes from the tomatoes, then plunge them into boiling water for 8–10 seconds. Transfer to cold water and slide off the skins. This is called blanching. Once the tomatoes have been blanched, halve and de-seed them. Remove the stalks and seeds from the peppers. The tomatoes, peppers, cucumber, garlic and onion can now be minced through a medium cutter, finely diced or blitzed in a liquidizer until almost puréed.

Mix together the tomato purée and red wine vinegar. Whisk the olive oil slowly into the purée. Now add three-quarters of the tomato coulis and chicken stock. Stir in the minced ingredients and check the seasoning with salt and pepper. Lightly cut the basil and tarragon leaves and add them to the soup.

The soup can be as thick or thin as you wish. If you want to make it thinner, then add the remaining tomato coulis and stock.

Variations

A slice of white bread can be blitzed with the vegetables to give a thicker texture.

The flavour of the soup can be made hotter and more spicy by adding a few drops of Tabasco or Worcestershire sauce or even both.

Green Lentil Soup

This soup is a good winter dish. I personally like to eat it any time of the year, but on a cold winter evening a large bowl of this soup served with plenty of crusty bread in front of the fire (are you getting hungry?) is absolutely delicious. I also like to add some smoked bacon to this soup to lift the flavour and almost make it a main course dish. It can, of course, be a vegetarian soup by simply omitting the bacon and replacing the chicken stock with vegetable stock.

SERVES 4

25 g (1 oz) unsalted butter
1 tablespoon olive or vegetable oil
2 large carrots, diced
2 onions, diced
2 celery sticks, diced
4 rashers smoked streaky bacon, cut into strips

175 g (6 oz) green dried lentils
900 ml–1.2 litres (1½–2 pints) Chicken Stock (see p.222) or Vegetable Stock (see p.223)
Salt and freshly ground black pepper
150 ml (5 fl oz) milk or double cream (optional)

Melt the butter with the oil. When the butter begins to bubble, add the diced vegetables and bacon and cook for 2–3 minutes without colouring. Add the lentils and continue to cook for a few minutes. Add 900 ml (1½ pints) of the stock and bring to a simmer. The soup can now cook slowly, just ticking over for 45–60 minutes.

The lentils must be cooked all the way through, becoming tender and thickening the soup. If the soup is a little too thick, add the remaining stock. This is now a lentil broth. To help the lentils become more evenly spread through the soup, blitz gently with a hand blender or in a liquidizer to give a thick broth consistency with the bacon and vegetables not totally broken. Alternatively, the soup can be totally blended to a purée, in which case you'll need to add a lot more stock. Season to taste.

To finish either of the soups, you can add the milk or double cream to give a slightly creamy texture.

Cream of Onion Soup

This is a very simple soup to make using just a few basic ingredients. It's delicious served with thick slices of toasted French stick, finished with melting Cheddar or Parmesan. I like to serve it with Parmesan croûtons. Make these by slicing the crusts off a loaf of bread – any type you like: white, wholemeal, olive or anything else – and cutting it into 1 cm (½ in) dice. Cook the bread in a roasting pan with just enough olive oil to cover the pan in a pre-heated oven at 200°C/400°F/gas 6. As the croûtons are heating they will become golden and crispy. Every 1–2 minutes, turn the bread croûtons over to give an all-round colour. Once the croûtons are totally golden and hot they can be sprinkled with finely grated Parmesan and mixed to give an overall cheesey taste.

SERVES 4

50 g (2 oz) unsalted butter
675 g (1½ lb) onions, diced
2–3 celery sticks, diced
1 small potato, diced (optional)
1 leek (white only), diced

1 small garlic clove, chopped
900 ml (1½ pints) Chicken Stock (see p.222) or Vegetable Stock (see p.223)
2 tablespoons double cream or milk (optional)

Melt the butter in a pan. When the butter begins to bubble, add all the vegetables and cook for 8–10 minutes over a medium heat without colouring. Add the stock and bring to a simmer. Continue to cook for 20–30 minutes. The soup can now be blitzed in a liquidizer until totally puréed, then pushed through a sieve. If the soup is very thick, thin it down with a little extra stock.

As an extra added, stir in the double cream or milk to help the consistency and make a good cream of onion soup.

Lobster Bisque

Lobster bisque is regarded as the king of all soups and I don't think I can or want to argue with that. It is so rich in flavour and texture that it is really worth every effort in making it. If you make this quantity, you can freeze what you don't need.

Like all recipes, other flavours can be used. Crab, prawns or shrimp will all give you a full flavour. I use the same recipe to make a crab bisque to go with Crab Risotto (see p.60).

This recipe also holds lots of little extras – saffron, brandy, fennel – which all help to make this a better soup but can be left out for a basic bisque.

MAKES about 2.25 litres (4 pints)

1 × 450 g (1 lb) lobster
1.75–2.25 litres (3–4 pints) Fish Stock
    (see p.221)
50–75 g (2–3 oz) unsalted butter
1 tablespoon olive oil
2 large carrots, diced
4 shallots or 2 large onions, diced
2 celery sticks, diced
1 leek, diced
1 fennel bulb, diced
1 garlic clove, crushed
A few fresh basil leaves

A few fresh tarragon leaves
A pinch of saffron
6 ripe tomatoes, quartered
50 ml (2 fl oz) brandy
½ bottle white wine
50 g (2 oz) long-grain rice
Salt and freshly ground black pepper
A pinch of cayenne pepper
150 ml (5 fl oz) single cream (optional)
A few drops of lemon juice or brandy
    (optional)

If you are using a live lobster, bring the fish stock to the boil and drop in the lobster. Cook for about 5–6 minutes, then remove from the heat. The best way now is to leave the lobster in the stock until completely cooled. This will help flavour the stock and keep the lobster meat moist. If you are going to remove the lobster from the stock immediately, cook for 6–8 minutes, remove the lobster from the pan, then allow it to cool slightly before breaking the shell. Make sure you keep the cooking liquor to use in the soup.

Break off the claws and crack them with the back of a heavy knife to remove the lobster meat. Split the body and tail through the middle lengthways and remove the tail meat. Reserve the meat to garnish the soup. The lobster shells are used to flavour the soup itself. I prefer to crack the lobsters down (with a rolling pin) in a large saucepan as finely as possible, making sure I get the maximum taste. It's also possible just to break the shells down without finely crushing them.

Melt the butter with the olive oil. Add the roughly chopped carrots, shallots or onions, celery, leek and fennel with the crushed garlic, basil and tarragon leaves. Add the pinch of saffron and the tomatoes and cook for a few minutes. Add the crushed lobster shells and cook for a further few minutes. Add the brandy and boil to reduce until almost dry. Add the white wine and continue to reduce. Add 1.75 litres (3 pints) of stock, bring to the simmer and continue to simmer for 20 minutes.

Add the rice and bring back to the simmer for 20–25 minutes. The rice should cook until overcooked to create a starch and thicken the soup. Check the soup for seasoning with salt, pepper and a pinch of cayenne pepper. The bisque can now be blitzed in a liquidizer, with the lobster shells, to cream the soup, then pushed through a fine sieve. You now have a good, rich lobster bisque. The soup should be reasonably thick, well coating the back of a spoon. If it's very thick, add some more stock until you have the right consistency.

Always when making soups taste for seasoning once finished. Add the cream, and a few drops of lemon juice or extra brandy will always lift the taste.

Variations

This recipe works well with crab and also prawns or shrimps. If you want to make a shrimp bisque, use either 450 g (1 lb) of good quality shrimps or 450 g (1 lb) of shrimp shells. The same applies to prawns.

If it's crab bisque you are making, just use the same preparation and cooking methods. Once the claws have been cracked and the meat removed, the flesh from the remaining two joints can be taken out with the back of a spoon. All the white meat should be kept to garnish the soup, and all the shell and brown meat can be broken and used for the soup. If you want to keep the brown meat, simply remove the central undershell and scrape out all of the inside.

OVERLEAF *Mussel Chowder in the foreground (see p.20),*
Gazpacho (see p.13) and
Gary making Cream of Onion Soup (see p.15).

Mussel Chowder

Chowder is an old dish that was (and still is) a complete meal made with mussels, onions, potatoes and pork all cooked together (see pp.18–19). It was originally made with cider or white wine but over the years milk and/or cream were added instead. This recipe has two stages: the first one tells you how to cook the mussels and the second is for the finished soup. Mussels, of course, can be bought already cooked. The vegetables and white wine are an optional extra which will give more flavour to the stock; you can just cook the mussels in the hot fish stock. If you are just using water, increase the quantity of mussels to 675 g (1½ lb).

SERVES 4

For the Mussels

1 carrot, roughly chopped
1 onion, roughly chopped
1 celery stick, roughly chopped
½ leek, roughly chopped
1 bay leaf
25 g (1 oz) unsalted butter

1 glass white wine
750 ml (1¼ pints) Fish Stock (see p.221)
   or water
450 g (1 lb) fresh mussels, washed and
   bearded

For the Chowder

50 g (2 oz) butter
4–6 rashers streaky bacon, cut into
   2.5 cm (1 in) pieces
2 large potatoes, cut into 2 cm (¾ in)
   dice
3–4 large onions, cut into 2 cm (¾ in)
   dice

2 celery sticks, cut into 2 cm (¾ in) dice
600 ml (1 pint) mussel stock, Fish Stock
   (see p.221) or water
300 ml (10 fl oz) hot milk
150 ml (5 fl oz) single cream
Salt and freshly ground black pepper

To cook the mussels, cook the vegetables with the bay leaf in a little butter without colour until just beginning to soften. Add the white wine and boil to reduce until almost dry. Add the stock and bring the liquor to the boil. Add the mussels to the boiling cooking liquor and cook for a few minutes until the shells open. Discard any that do not open. Drain off the mussels, reserving the strained cooking liquor.

Melt the butter in a hot pan and add the streaky bacon pieces immediately. The pan must be kept hot to fry the bacon, allowing it to become golden; this will bring out the flavour of the bacon. There may be some bacon residue sticking to the base of the pan. Don't worry about this; it will give a good flavour to the soup. Once the bacon is coloured, add the diced potatoes, onions and celery and cook, without colouring, for a few minutes, reducing the heat of the pan. Add the mussel or fish stock or water and bring to the simmer. Continue to simmer for about 20 minutes or until the potato is cooked but not breaking too much. The stock will have reduced a little, increasing the flavour. Add the hot milk and single cream and bring back to the simmer, checking the seasoning with salt and pepper. Add the mussels and warm for 1–2 minutes before serving.

Onion and Anchovy Pastry Pieces

These are lovely little appetizers: the strength of the anchovy contrasting with the rich sweetness of the onion on crisp puff pastry. To achieve the rich sweetness of the onions they must first be caramelized, a slow process but worth it.

SERVES 4

4–8 large onions, sliced	1 egg, beaten
1 tablespoon water	100 g (4 oz) tinned anchovy fillets,
Salt and freshly ground white pepper	drained
175 g (6 oz) Puff Pastry (see p.212)	Olive oil

Place the onions and water in a large pan and place over a very low heat and keep on a low heat for anything between 2 and 4 hours. This process allows all the natural juices and sugars from the onions to be released. Once the onions have really softened and broken down, the sugar content will slowly start to caramelize. The onions will start to change colour and are only ready at a deep golden stage. Season with salt and pepper.

Meanwhile, roll out the puff pastry very thinly and cut into 2.5 cm (1 in) wide strips. Rest it in the fridge for 30 minutes to prevent it from shrinking.

Pre-heat the oven to 220°C/425°F/gas 7 and grease a baking sheet.

Place the strips on the baking sheet and brush with beaten egg. Spoon some onions down the centre of the strips, leaving 3 mm (⅛ in) down each side. Lay the anchovy fillets head to tail down the centre of the onions. Bake in the pre-heated oven for 8–10 minutes until the pastry is golden and crispy. Sprinkle with olive oil and cut into 2.5 cm (1 in) squares. Serve at once.

Potato and Parsnip Crisps

We all like crisps with lots of different flavours (although some of them I'm not so sure about!), but you can't beat home-made salted crisps with no other tastes to spoil. If you're having a dinner party and want something to go with pre-dinner drinks, then have a go at these. The parsnip crisps are brilliant, just deep-fried slices of parsnip, as easy as that! They eat well dipped in Cranberry Sauce (see p.239).

Serves 4

2 large potatoes, peeled   Oil for deep-frying
2–3 large parsnips, peeled   Salt

Pre-heat a deep-fat frying pan to 180°C/350°F.

Shape the potatoes into neat cylinders, then slice them very, very thinly. Dry the slices on a cloth and fry a handful at a time until crisp and golden all the way through. Lift out and shake off any excess oil, sprinkle with salt and serve. The crisps will stay fresh and crisp for a few hours, or longer if kept in a sealed container. Always make sure you eat them within 24 hours.

For the parsnips, just slice very thinly lengthways and cook as for the potato crisps until golden all the way through. Lightly salt and serve. The parsnip crisps eat well dipped in cranberry sauce!

Duck Rillettes

Duck rillette is almost like a home-made coarse pâté. You can make it with pork or goose, as well.

Other flavours can be added to the duck before cooking to help flavour the cooking fat which will be used to hold the duck together. Orange peel can be left in (as for canard à l'orange*), or a clove of garlic, a bay leaf and sprig of fresh thyme. It's also possible to add some chicken or duck stock to this recipe for a moister flavour.*

Duck Rillettes are best served with slices of thick, hot toast.

SERVES 4

4 duck legs
2 teaspoons rock sea salt

900 g (2 lb) duck fat

To make the rillette, simply follow the recipe for Confit of Duck (see p.88), cooking for a minimum of 2 hours. The duck meat has to be very tender and on the point of being overcooked.

Once cooked and still warm, take the duck legs from the cooking fat and remove the skin. Take all the meat from the bone, then break down the duck flesh, pulling it apart with two forks so that the meat is shredded rather than making a purée. Once the duck is reasonably finely shredded, start to add some of the strained cooking fat. This will give the meat a coarse pâté texture. After 150 ml (5 fl oz) has been added, check the seasoning with salt and pepper; season generously as they will be served cold. The duck rillettes should be moist and rich to eat. More fat can be added to make the pâté even richer (300 ml (10 fl oz) would be the maximum for this quantity). Spoon the rillettes into individual ramekins or one larger bowl and set in the fridge.

Once set, spoon a little of the liquid fat on top of the moulds and allow to set. This will keep the rillettes fresh as long as they are chilled. I suggest, however, that you keep them no longer than a week. Because of the high fat content the pâté will set quite firm in the fridge so take out about an hour before eating to appreciate the full flavour.

Potted Salmon

This is a good summer dish which can be made and set in a serving dish and used as a starter or main course. Always be careful when cooking salmon as the fish is delicate. It needs very little cooking and should always be pink in the centre to keep it moist and succulent.

To make the clarified butter, simply melt 350 g (12 oz) of unsalted butter until it foams, then the foam dies. Don't allow it to brown. Remove from the heat and leave to stand until the milky residue sinks to the bottom. Strain off through muslin.

You can make the salmon pots a few days in advance, but always serve them at room temperature. This will allow the butter to become softer and a lot tastier.

SERVES 4

450 g (1 lb) salmon fillet	Freshly ground white pepper
300 ml (10 fl oz) clarified butter (see p.235)	1 tablespoon chopped fresh parsley
	1 tablespoon chopped fresh tarragon
2 shallots, finely chopped	A few salad leaves
1 small garlic clove, crushed	1 lemon, cut into wedges
½ teaspoon ground mace	Warm toast to serve
½ teaspoon salt	

Trim the salmon fillet and cut into 1 cm (½ in) cubes. Warm the clarified butter to simmering point and add the chopped shallots. Cook for a few minutes until the shallots have softened. Add the garlic, mace, salt and pepper. Carefully spoon the salmon into the butter and return to a *low* heat. The salmon can now only be stirred very carefully to avoid breaking. As soon as the salmon has a light opaque colour, after about 5–6 minutes, remove it from the heat and allow to cool. Add the chopped parsley and tarragon.

Spoon the salmon into individual 7.5 cm (3 in) serving moulds, making sure that the shallots and herbs are evenly distributed between the moulds. Top up with the remaining butter. You may find that you have some butter left. This can be used for cooking fish, or frozen until the next time. Cool and chill the moulds until set.

Remove from the fridge and allow to return to room temperature. Turn out the moulds on to plates and garnish with salad leaves and lemon. This dish also eats well with warm thick toast.

Mackerel Croquettes

These croquettes can be made with other fish: salmon, cod, prawns or shrimps. In this mackerel recipe, I've added one small fillet of smoked mackerel. This is not essential, but it does enhance the whole flavour of the fish without being overpowering.

SERVES 4–6

4 mackerel fillets, skinned
2 shallots or 1 small onion, finely chopped
Salt and freshly ground white pepper
1 glass white wine
1 bunch of spring onions, chopped
1 smoked mackerel fillet
225–350 g (8–12 oz) Mashed Potatoes (see p.133), without milk, butter or cream

Cayenne pepper
2 tablespoons plain flour
1 egg, beaten
100 g (4 oz) breadcrumbs
25 g (1 oz) unsalted butter and cooking oil or oil for deep-frying
1 lemon or lime, cut into wedges
1 quantity Lemon Butter Sauce (see p.228)

Pre-heat the oven to 200°C/400°F/gas 6 and butter a roasting tray.

To remove the central bones from the mackerel fillets, cut either side of the bones straight through the fish. This will leave eight strips of mackerel. Sit the fish on the tray with the chopped shallots, and season with salt and pepper. Add the white wine and cook in the pre-heated oven for about 6–8 minutes; the mackerel should only be just cooked. Drain off any excess liquor into a small pan, bring to the boil and boil to reduce by at least half. When the liquor has reduced, add the chopped spring onions and cook for 30–60 seconds until only just beginning to soften.

Flake the smoked and cooked mackerel fillets and add the spring onion reduction. Fold in 225 g (8 oz) of the mashed potatoes which will be enough to bind. The texture can be loosened by adding more potato. Season with salt and cayenne pepper. Shape into balls or croquettes about 6 × 2 cm (2½ × ¾ in). Leave to chill in the fridge.

Dust the croquettes lightly in flour, then pass through beaten egg. Roll in breadcrumbs and re-shape gently, if necessary, with a palette knife. To shallow-fry, heat the butter and oil over a medium heat and fry for 2–3 minutes until golden on all sides. To deep-fry, heat the fat to 150°C/300°F and fry until golden. Serve with lemon or lime wedges and lemon butter sauce.

Variations

Soured cream flavoured with fresh lime juice, salt and pepper makes a tasty dip.

Fillet of Mackerel with Caramelized Onions and Sweet Peppers

In this recipe, the mackerel is 'cooked' in a sousing liquor made with white wine, white wine vinegar and water and flavoured with pickling spices, star anise and herbs. The combination of the sharp, soused taste and the sweetness of the onions and peppers works really well. I like to present this dish on very thin short pastry discs. This gives the dish another texture, almost like eating an open flan.

SERVES 4

1 quantity Shortcrust Pastry (see p.211)	A few drops of balsamic vinegar
4 mackerel fillets, skinned and trimmed	2 teaspoons fresh chives, snipped
2 tablespoons Basic Vinaigrette (see p.241)	1 cm (½ in) long

For the Peppers and Onions

4 large onions, sliced	1 tablespoon olive oil
1 tablespoon water	Salt and freshly ground black pepper
1 large red pepper, cut into strips	

For the Sousing Liquor

2 teaspoons olive oil	1 star anise (optional)
½ onion, roughly chopped	2 teaspoons pickling spice
1 small carrot, roughly chopped	85 ml (3 fl oz) white wine
1 celery stick, roughly chopped	85 ml (3 fl oz) white wine vinegar
1 sprig of fresh thyme	450 ml (15 fl oz) water
1 sprig of fresh tarragon	A pinch of salt
1 bay leaf	Juice of ½ lemon

Pre-heat the oven to 190°C/375°F/gas 5.

Roll out the pastry very thinly, cut into 7.5–10 cm (3–4 in) discs and leave to rest in the fridge for 20 minutes. Bake in the pre-heated oven for about 10 minutes until cooked through and crisp.

To caramelize the onions, simply place them in a pan with a tablespoon of water and cook, uncovered, over a low heat for about 2 hours until all the natural juices and sugars from the onions begin to colour to a rich, golden brown. This can be done in advance.

Cook the red peppers in the olive oil for 2–3 minutes until softened. Add to the caramelized onions and season with salt and pepper.

Meanwhile, make the sousing liquor. Warm the olive oil and add the onion, carrot, celery, thyme, tarragon, bay leaf, star anise and pickling spice. Cook for a few minutes until the vegetables begin to soften. Add the white wine, wine vinegar and water with a pinch of salt and the lemon juice. Bring to the simmer and cook for 15–20 minutes. Strain.

Place the mackerel fillets in the warm sousing liquor and bring almost to the simmer. This will just warm them through, keeping the fish succulent and juicy.

Sweeten the dressing with a little balsamic vinegar and add the chives.

Spoon the warm onion and pepper mix on to the pastry discs and lay the mackerel fillets on top. Spoon the dressing over and around the mackerel.

Variations

If you haven't got enough time to make the caramelized onions, simply fry 2 or 3 sliced onions in butter until golden brown and almost burnt. This will give a more bittersweet taste that will become a lot sweeter when added to the red pepper.

Fillet of Mackerel with Caramelized Onions and Sweet Peppers.

Grilled Mackerel with Mussel Stew

You can leave out the first stage in cooking the mussel stew if you wish and simply cook the mussels in fish stock, but the pre-cooking does give a lot more flavour to the cooking liquor. Turn to p.30 to see the finished dish.

SERVES 4

4 mackerel fillets
25 g (1 oz) unsalted butter

Salt and freshly ground black pepper

For the Mussel Cooking Liquor

1 tablespoon unsalted butter
1 carrot, diced
1 onion, diced
1 celery stick, diced
1 bay leaf

1 sprig of fresh tarragon
300 ml (10 fl oz) dry white wine
600 ml (1 pint) Fish Stock (see p.221)
900 g (2 lb) fresh mussels, washed and
    bearded

For the Stew

2 tablespoons olive oil
100 g (4 oz) unsalted butter
2 large carrots, cut into 5 mm (¼ in) dice
2 onions, cut into 5 mm (¼ in) dice
3 celery sticks, cut into 5 mm (¼ in) dice
1 bouquet garni (a few fresh basil and
    tarragon leaves and 1 star anise tied
    in a muslin bag)

300 ml (10 fl oz) dry white wine
2 teaspoons Pesto Sauce (see p.235)
2 large tomatoes, skinned, seeded and
    diced
1 teaspoon chopped fresh parsley

Butter and season a baking tray.

Trim the mackerel fillets and remove all central bones. This can be done easily by cutting either side of the bones down to the skin but not cutting through. Pick from the head and pull out the central bones; they will come away from the skin in one piece. Place the fillets on the prepared tray skin-side up. Brush the skin with butter and season with salt and pepper, then place in the fridge.

To cook the mussel liquor, melt the butter in a pan and add the carrot, onion, celery, bay leaf and tarragon and cook gently, without colour, until softened. Add the white wine and boil until the liquid has almost evaporated. Add the stock and bring to a rapid simmer.

To clean the mussels, run under cold water and scrape until all grit and beard are removed. Discard any that are open and do not close when tapped sharply. Drain from the water and drop into the cooking liquor. Bring the liquid back to the boil, stirring frequently. As soon as the mussels begin to open, drain in a colander, reserving the stock. This should now be drained through a fine sieve. Pick the mussels from their shells and check that they are clean from all impurities. Discard any that have not opened.

Warm a pan and add the olive oil and 25 g (1 oz) of the butter. Add the diced vegetables with the bouquet garni. Cook without colouring until they begin to soften. Add the white wine and reduce until almost dry. Add enough of the mussel stock until the vegetables are covered; you may not need all of the stock so just add a little at a time. Bring to a simmer and cook until the vegetables are tender. This will take about 8–10 minutes.

Pre-heat the grill.

Cook the mackerel fillets under the pre-heated grill until the skin is crisp. The fish will only take between 4–6 minutes.

While the mackerel is cooking, whisk the remaining butter into the liquor and add some pesto sauce to taste, the diced tomatoes, chopped fresh parsley and, of course, the mussels. Warm through and spoon into large bowls, distributing the garnish equally. Sit the mackerel on top and serve.

ABOVE *Grilled Mackerel with Mussel Stew (see p.28).*

RIGHT *Seared Peppered Salmon (see p.32) and*
Cucumber Pickle (see p.244).

Seared Peppered Salmon

This dish has very few ingredients but the method and preparation give lots of texture and taste. It's like eating warm salmon gravad lax with a fiery bite from the pepper.

The salmon can just be sliced and eaten, but the raw black pepper is very strong. The purpose of the searing is to take away that rawness, create texture and give aroma and bite. I like to eat it with Cucumber Pickle (see p.244) – classic salmon and cucumber combination with a difference!

SERVES 4–6

450 g (1 lb) salmon fillet with skin	1 tablespoon caster sugar
1 tablespoon finely ground black pepper	Olive oil
1 tablespoon salt	Lemon or lime juice

Trim the salmon fillet and remove any bones. Along the fillet run several 'pin' bones; these can easily be removed with tweezers or small pliers. The black pepper must be finely ground. You can do this in a food processor or in a pepper mill. Shake the pepper through a sieve to leave you with a fine grind. Mix with the salt and sugar and sprinkle over the salmon so that it is covered in one layer of ground black pepper. Wrap the salmon in cling film and chill. The salmon will be 'cooked' by the salt and sugar mix. This curing process can take as little as 1–2 hours, but I like to make this in the morning for eating in the evening.

Remove the cling film and cut the salmon into 2–3 cm (¾–1¼ in) thick slices. Pre-heat a frying-pan and brush with olive oil. Make sure the pan is hot. Sit the salmon in the pan and sear for about 15–20 seconds on one side. Providing that the pan is hot, the salmon will be almost raw but just coloured, with very slightly burnt tinges burnt on the pepper. Serve the salmon as a starter with a squeeze of lemon or lime juice or try it sitting on the cucumber pickle.

Smoked Salmon and Asparagus with Poached Egg Hollandaise

Cold smoked salmon on warm toast with warm asparagus and a gently poached egg just breaking on top sounds delicious – and it is. Lots of traditional flavours working together. This dish can be even better. I like to top the poached egg with Hollandaise Sauce (see p.235). It eats beautifully and gives a good finish to the dish.

SERVES 4

12–16 medium asparagus spears	Horseradish sauce or cream
Salt	225 g (8 oz) sliced smoked salmon
25 g (1 oz) unsalted butter	4 poached eggs
4 thick slices wholemeal bread	1 quantity Hollandaise Sauce (see p.235)

The first job is to prepare and cook the asparagus. To be certain of them being tender, lightly peel them from half way down to the base of the spears and cut about 2.5 cm (1 in) off the root. The asparagus will now be deep green from the top, changing tones down to white.

Drop the asparagus into boiling salted water and keep on full heat for 2–3 minutes, then drain. The spears will still have a nice bite in them. If you are cooking the asparagus in advance, simply drop them into ice cold water to refresh them. To re-heat, just drop them back into hot water for 30–40 seconds, lift out, season with salt and pepper and brush with butter.

Toast the bread and spread with a thin layer of horseradish sauce or cream; the flavour works really well with smoked salmon. Cover the toast with the salmon and sit the asparagus tips on top. Sit the warm poached eggs on top and finish with hollandaise sauce.

Variations

Instead of the hollandaise, you can use some Basic Vinaigrette (see p.241) with snipped fresh chives and just spoon it over the egg.

Grilled Tuna with Salsa Dressing or Sauerkraut

As you can see in the title, there's already two options for the tuna in this recipe, both of which are excellent. This dish also eats well as a main course. The tuna is best cooked and served as a medium rare steak, still nice and pink in the centre, to help the taste and texture. The tuna can be grilled or pan-fried, and should be served warm with the cold salsa dressing (p.243) or with the warm sauerkraut (p.94 - half the recipe will be enough for 4-6 starter portions).

If fresh tuna is unavailable or hard to get hold of, then other fish can be used – salmon, red mullet, trout or more. Tinned tuna can also be used and broken down with a fork and then mixed with the salsa dressing, this eats very well with a salad or even just a sandwich filling. The sauerkraut will only really work with fresh tuna steaks. The sauerkraut version is best served warm on the plate topped with some salad leaves and then the tuna steak sat on top. A good basic dressing with chopped chives goes very well with this dish.

The salsa is best served just sat next to the tuna with some green leaves (see p.10).

SERVES 4–6

4 × 100–175 g (4–6 oz) tuna fillet steaks	Basic Vinaigrette (see p.241)
Olive oil	Salsa Dressing (see p.243)
Salt and freshly ground black pepper	OR
Green or mixed salad leaves	½ quantity Sauerkraut (see p.94)

To cook the tuna, lightly brush the fish with olive oil and season with salt and pepper. The fish can now either be grilled on a hot grill or barbecue or pan-fried in a hot frying-pan. If the thickness of the steaks is 1 cm (½ in) the fish will only take 1-2 minutes on each side before it is ready to serve.

Toss the salad leaves in a little vinaigrette and arrange on plates with the steak.

Now all you have to do is decide – salsa or sauerkraut!

Grilling the tuna steak.

Crab and Salmon Fritters

These are a wonderful savoury starter that can also be cooked for hot canapés. The crab and salmon go together very well but both could be substituted with chopped prawns and cod or lots of other combinations. Once cooked until golden and crispy, I like to serve them with a soured cream lemon or lime dip made by flavouring some soured cream with lemon or lime juice, salt and pepper. This recipe comes in two parts: the crab and salmon filling and the choux pastry to bind it.

SERVES 6–8

For the Pastry

150 ml (5 fl oz) water
50 g (2 oz) butter
100 g (4 oz) plain flour

2 eggs, beaten
A pinch of salt

For the Filling

225 g (8 oz) salmon fillet
Salt and freshly ground white pepper
1 glass white wine
15 g (½ oz) unsalted butter
2 teaspoons olive oil
1 green pepper, finely diced

1 red pepper, finely diced
½ bunch spring onions, finely diced
15 g (½ oz) root ginger, finely grated
225 g (8 oz) cooked white crab meat
1 teaspoon chopped fresh dill
Tabasco sauce

Pre-heat the oven to 200°C/400°F/gas 6 and grease and season a baking tray.

To make the pastry, bring the water and butter to the boil. Remove from the heat and add the flour. Return the pan to a moderate heat and cook, stirring vigorously, until the paste comes away from the sides of the pan. Leave to cool. Gradually beat the eggs into the dough with the salt, leaving you with a smooth choux pastry mix with a dropping consistency.

To cook the salmon, sit it in the baking tray and add the glass of white wine. Cover with foil and bake in the pre-heated oven for 10–15 minutes, depending on the thickness of the fish. To check the salmon, it should be just firming to the touch, cooked like a medium steak, still pink in the middle. Once cooked, allow to cool. Reserve any cooking liquor.

Melt the butter with the olive oil. When it begins to bubble, add the peppers, spring onions and ginger and cook for 1–2 minutes. Remove from the pan and allow to cool.

The crab meat can be bought cooked and prepared (it's also possible to buy it frozen). Break it down and checked through for any broken shell. Add the salmon, peppers and dill and season with salt, pepper and a few drops of Tabasco sauce. Bind together with the choux pastry.

Heat the deep-frying oil to 180°C/350°F. Spoon the fritter mix straight from the bowl into the fryer or on to a floured tray before cooking. This gives a rustic natural shape. Fry the fritters until golden brown and crispy. If they seem to be cooking too quickly, then turn the fryer down to 150°C/300°F.

Note

The fritters should be no bigger than a soup spoon size. This will ensure they cook evenly. For little tasters, the size of a teaspoon should be just right.

Crumbled Baked Sardine Fillets

This dish can only really be made with fresh sardines. Sardines are great for grilling whole on a barbecue or under the grill, but the small bones can often be too much hard work. So for this dish, ask your fishmonger to scale and fillet them for you. If they are from large sardines you will only need three or four fillets a portion as a starter. Some of the small bones within the fillets can be removed with a small knife or tweezers. Any remaining ones are quite edible as for tinned sardines. The 'crumbled' is a breadcrumb and fresh herb mix sprinkled on top and grilled. Once crumbled, the sardines can be served on a simple salad or just with a squeeze of lemon. The dressing is one I used in Rhodes Around Britain *in a skate recipe with potato, fennel and artichokes, but it goes equally well with this dish.*

SERVES 4

6–8 sardines, filleted
Mixed green salad leaves

Olive oil
A few drops of lemon juice

For the Crumble Topping

25 g (1 oz) unsalted butter
1 large shallot or ½ onion, finely
    chopped
4 slices white bread, crusts removed and
    crumbed

1 teaspoon chopped fresh parsley
½ teaspoon chopped fresh tarragon
½ teaspoon chopped fresh basil
Salt and freshly ground white pepper
Juice of ½ lemon

For the Anchovy Dip

6 tinned anchovy fillets, drained
1 egg
25 g (1 oz) capers
1 garlic clove, crushed
2.5 cm (1 in) root ginger, peeled and
    chopped
1 bunch of fresh basil leaves

Juice of 1 lemon
½ teaspoon chopped fresh thyme
A pinch of sugar
50 ml (2 fl oz) warm water
225 ml (7 ½ fl oz) olive oil
225 ml (7 ½ fl oz) groundnut oil

Pre-heat the grill and butter and season a tray.

To make the crumble topping, Melt the butter with the chopped shallot or onion and cook without colour for 1–2 minutes. Mix the breadcrumbs and chopped herbs and season with salt and pepper. Mix some of the shallot butter into the crumbs until a crumbly texture is formed; you may not need all the shallot mixture. Add a few drops of lemon juice to the mix.

Sit the sardine fillets skin-side up on the tray. Sprinkle the crumble crumbs on top of each fillet. Place the sardines under a hot grill. Once the crumbs have become golden brown and crispy the fillets will be cooked; it will take just a few minutes.

Meanwhile, to make the anchovy dip, place all the ingredients, except the oils, in a food processor and blitz to a paste. With the processor still running, slowly add the oil as you would for mayonnaise. Season the dressing with salt and pepper and push through a fine sieve. The dressing will have a mayonnaise sauce consistency with a hint of green from the basil and capers.

Toss the salad leaves in some olive oil with salt and pepper and a few drops of lemon juice.

Spoon the anchovy dip on to the plates, forming a circular pattern. Sit the salad leaves on the centre of the sauce and place the crumbled fillets on top of the lettuce. The dish is ready!

Grilled King Prawns with Warm Spicy Relish

This dish is great as a starter or main course. King prawns can be cooked loose or made into kebabs (about five prawns per portion as a main course, or three or four as a starter) and cook really well on the open grill or barbecue. That's the beauty of a dish like this: it has so many combinations and options. The prawns taste delicious with the spicy relish, or you can just serve them on their own, with a squeeze of lemon or with mayonnaise. Also, you don't have to use king prawns. Just ordinary fresh prawns (or even frozen!) will also eat really well with the warm relish. You can eat the whole lot cold, warm under the grill or toss in butter in a frying-pan. That's how simple and easy this dish can be.

This relish can be made several days in advance and kept chilled, then either served cold or simply re-heated. Oh, and by the way, the relish also eats well with other fish and also chicken, so have a go!

To save time, you can use a tin of chopped tomatoes for this recipe; it's never quite the same but it does work. You can simply drain off all liquid from the can and add the tomatoes to the mix, or you can boil the tomatoes to reduce all the excess liquid until thick and strong in flavour before adding this to the mixture.

SERVES 4–6

20 raw king prawns
Olive oil

Salt and freshly ground black pepper

For the Relish

8 plum or salad tomatoes
1 tablespoon olive oil
2 large red onions, finely chopped
1 garlic clove, crushed
2 green peppers, seeded and finely diced

2 fresh green chillies, very finely diced
1 teaspoon tomato purée
2 teaspoons demerara sugar
1½ tablespoons malt vinegar
Salt

Pre-heat a grill or barbecue.

If the prawns are whole including heads, then firstly remove the heads, then pick the shell from the tails, leaving the base of tail intact. The prawns can be placed on wooden skewers or left loose. Brush the prawns with olive oil and season with salt and pepper. The prawns will take about 1½–2 minutes per side on a hot open grill or barbecue, under a domestic oven grill or in a frying-pan.

To make the relish, remove the eyes from the tomatoes, then blanch them in boiling water for 8–10 seconds, then refresh in cold water and remove the skins. Quarter the tomatoes and remove all the seeds and water. Dice the flesh into 5 mm (¼ in) dice.

Warm the olive oil in a pan and cook the chopped red onions over a low heat for a few minutes until they begin to soften. Add the garlic, peppers and chillies, increasing the heat to medium. Continue to cook for a few minutes. Add the tomatoes and tomato purée and cook for about 6–8 minutes. As the tomatoes cook, all excess water will be released, creating a tomato sauce effect. However, this may seem a little too thin, so either continue to cook until a thicker tomato base is achieved or, and I think this is better, simply drain off all juices through a sieve and simmer the liquor on the stove until it begins to thicken, then remix with the other ingredients. You will now have a tasty warm chilli relish. To finish it off and give a spicy effect, mix together the demerara sugar and malt vinegar and bring to the boil. This mix will only take a couple of minutes to boil and reduce in volume. The consistency should be like a thick syrup. Add this to the relish a little at a time, tasting until a sweet and sour flavour is achieved. Season with salt and pepper.

Variations

If you are using straightforward, small, frozen peeled prawns, then why not mix some cold spicy relish with mayonnaise and turn the whole dish into a spicy prawn cocktail!

Griddled Scallops with Crispy Aubergines

This dish shows another taste alternative with basic ingredients. The sweetness of the scallops mixed with an almost bitter/burnt flavour of the frying works really well with the tomato and olive taste. For a quick salad dressing, just mix a few drops of balsamic vinegar with some olive oil and season with salt and pepper. Alternatively, a good extra-virgin olive oil would be enough on its own. Turn to p.11 to see the finished dish.

Serves 4

1 large aubergine	6–8 black olives, finely diced
2–3 tablespoons plain flour	Basic Vinaigrette (see p.241) or olive oil
1 teaspoon cayenne pepper	25 g (1 oz) unsalted butter
Salt and freshly ground white pepper	12 large scallops, cleaned and trimmed
Oil for deep-frying	Mixed green salad leaves such as rocket,
1 quantity Tomato Relish (see p.40)	curly endive, baby spinach

Split the aubergine lengthways and slice across thinly. Mix the plain flour with the cayenne pepper and a pinch of salt. Sprinkle the flour over the aubergines and lightly dust off any excess. These can now be fried in hot fat until golden and crispy. Drain off any excess fat and sprinkle with salt. The aubergines can be cooked before cooking the scallops and will stay crispy and warm before finishing the dish.

Warm the tomato relish, then mix the chopped black olives with a little vinaigrette or olive oil.

Heat a frying-pan until very hot but not burning, add a few drops of olive oil and a little butter. Sit the scallops in the pan, in batches if necessary, keeping the pan hot. If the pan is not hot enough, the scallops will simply begin to stew in their own juices which will spoil their taste and texture. Once they have coloured golden brown on both sides, turn them out, season with salt and pepper and repeat the same process if you are cooking in batches. This will only take 2–3 minutes.

Season the salad leaves and toss with a little olive oil. Spoon the warm tomato relish into the centre of the plate, making a circular platform for the scallops. Spoon the black olive dressing around. Sit the scallops on to the relish and place the salad leaves in the centre. To finish the dish, simply arrange the fried aubergines on top.

Spooning the black olives around the tomato relish
while the scallops cook on the griddle.

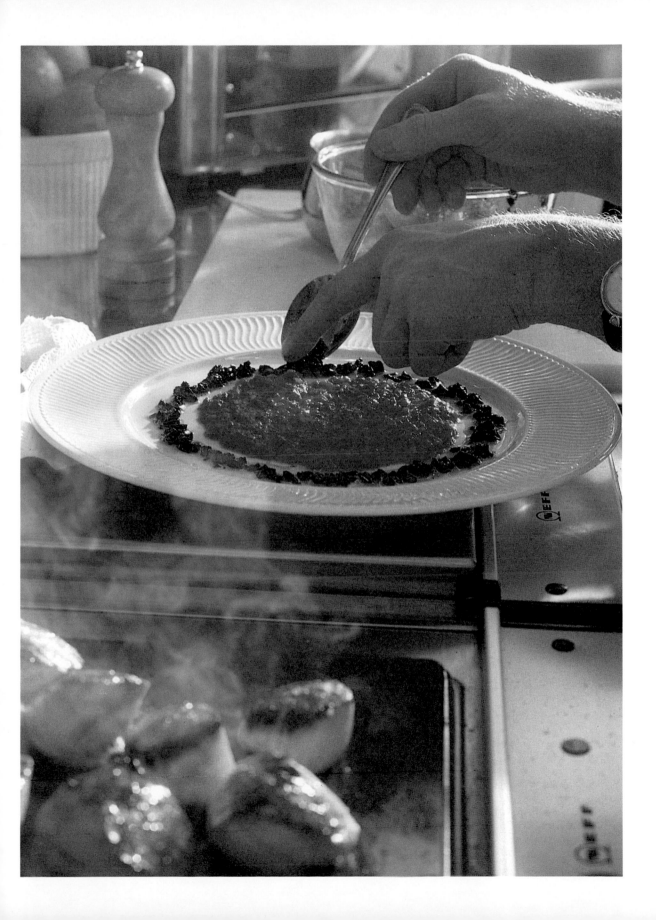

Fried Cockle Salad

Eating deep-fried cockles is delicious. They get really crispy and tasty. Just be careful not to fry too many at once otherwise you'll almost have a popcorn situation. So it's best to use a deep-fat fryer, or certainly a large pan with a lid.

The crispy cockles eat very well with Salsa Dressing (see p.243), although it is best to make the relish looser with more olive oil and lime juice, making it into more of a dressing.

You can buy cooked cockles in most fishmongers and supermarkets. If you buy live cockles, wash them well, removing any grit, then drop them into a pan of boiling water. The cockles will start to open after 30 seconds. Once they are open, drain off the water and leave the cockles to cool. Pick the cockles from their shells and leave to drain on a cloth.

Use whichever salad leaves you prefer. There's plenty of choice from lollo rosso and oakleaf to curly endive, rocket or lambs' lettuce.

SERVES 4

1 quantity Salsa Dressing (see p.243)	175–225 g (6–8 oz) fresh cooked cockles
2–3 tablespoons olive oil	2–3 tablespoons milk
Juice of ½ lime	2–3 tablespoons self-raising flour
Salt and freshly ground white pepper	Mixed salad leaves
Oil for deep-frying	A few drops of olive oil

Loosen the salsa relish recipe with some more olive oil and a few drops of extra lime juice. Check the dressing for seasoning with salt and pepper.

To cook the cockles, pre-heat the fat fryer to 180°C/350°F. Coat the cockles in milk, then roll lightly through the flour, shaking off any excess. Fry the cockles in the pre-heated oil for 1–2 minutes until golden and crispy. Lift them from the fryer and sprinkle with salt.

Spoon the relish on to the plates and scatter over the crispy cockles. Mix the salad leaves with a few drops of olive oil and season with salt and pepper. Sit the leaves in a small pile in the centre of the plate. The leaves should be standing high with the dressing and cockles being visible all around the plate.

Sautéed Scallop and Fennel Salad

Scallops are available fresh from many fishmongers, or you may find some good quality scallops frozen.

SERVES 4

4 fennel bulbs
Juice of 1 lemon
1 star anise (optional)
900 ml (1½ pints) water
Salt and freshly ground white pepper
50–75 g (2–3oz) unsalted butter

1 tablespoon olive oil
12 scallops, trimmed and roes removed
Green salad leaves
Basic Vinaigrette (see p.241)
1 tablespoon snipped fresh chives

Top and tail the fennel. Using a small knife, remove the core from the base of each fennel. Add the lemon juice and star anise to the water with a pinch of salt and bring to the boil. Add the fennel, cover and simmer over a medium heat for 15–20 minutes until just tender.

Pour off half of the cooking liquor and boil it to reduce to about 150 ml (5 fl oz). This will increase the flavour of the fennel. Add the butter to the liquor and whisk vigorously to make a butter sauce. For an even lighter and smoother sauce, use an electric hand blender to finish. This sauce can be kept warm and re-heated and blitzed before serving.

Slice the fennel 5 mm (¼ in) thick lengthways. Heat a frying-pan and add a teaspoon of olive oil to the pan. Fry the fennel slices on both sides until golden brown. Season with salt and pepper.

To cook the scallops, heat a frying-pan with a few drops of olive oil and a knob of butter. It is very important to cook scallops in a hot pan. This will colour and seal them quickly. If the pan is only warm, the scallops will begin to poach in their own juices, creating a different texture and taste. Once coloured and seasoned on both sides, the scallops are ready; this should only take 2–3 minutes depending on size.

To serve the dish, lay the fennel slices on the centre of a warmed serving plate and sit the scallops on top. Mix the salad leaves with a little vinaigrette and sit them in the centre of the scallops. Add the chives to the sauce and spoon around the plate.

Warm Smoked Eel and Broad Bean Broth on Mashed Potatoes

Smoked eel has a wonderful flavour. It's really good to use in a stew or simply cold with a horseradish sauce. The combination of flavours in this dish can work well together either for a cold or hot dish. This is a tasty hot version.

SERVES 4

450–675 g (1–1½ lb) smoked eel

For the Stock

1 onion, chopped
1 leek, chopped
2 celery sticks, chopped
1 bay leaf
50 g (2 oz) mushroom trimmings
  (optional)
1 sprig of fresh thyme

2 sprigs of fresh tarragon
A few black peppercorns
25 g (1 oz) unsalted butter
300 ml (10 fl oz) white wine
900 ml (1½ pints) Fish Stock (see p.221)
  or water

To Finish

350 g (12 oz) Mashed Potatoes
  (see p.133)
1 tablespoon finely chopped shallots
Juice of 1½ lemons
Salt and freshly ground black pepper

100 g (4 oz) unsalted butter
300 g (10 oz) broad beans, cooked and
  shelled
1 tablespoon snipped fresh chives

Fillet and skin the smoked eel, saving all the trimmings for the stock. Hopefully, your fishmonger will do this for you, but if not, simply cut off the head and position the knife against the top half of the central bone. Carefully cut along the bone, removing the fillet of fish. Turn the fish over and repeat the same process. Now the skin can be removed. Slide your finger or thumb under the skin at the head end and it should tear off all the way along. The fillets may need a little trimming down the sides to remove any excess skin. Turn the fillets on their back to show the centre. From the head end to half way down there will be some bones. Simply position the knife under these bones and cut away from the flesh. You now have two long, clean fillets of eel. Cut these into diagonal 2.5 cm (1 in) pieces and keep in the fridge.

To make the stock, place the chopped vegetables, herbs and peppercorns in a pan with the butter and cook without colour for 10 minutes. Add the chopped eel bones and trimmings and continue to cook for 5 minutes. Add the white wine and boil to reduce until almost dry. Add the stock or water. If you are using water ask your fishmonger to give you some fish bones to cook with the eel trimmings. Bring the stock to the simmer and cook for 20 minutes. Stain through a sieve. Re-boil the eel stock and reduce to 450–600 ml (15–20 fl oz) to increase the eel flavour.

Re-heat 300 ml (10 fl oz) of reduced eel stock. Warm the mashed potatoes, add the raw chopped shallot and juice of 1 lemon and season with salt and pepper. Add the butter to the eel stock and whisk into a light frothy broth; a hand blender can be used to help this. Add the broad beans and warm through. Drop the pieces of smoked eel into the liquor with the remaining lemon juice and the chives and continue to warm. Spoon or pipe the mashed potatoes into the centre of a bowl or plate and spoon over the eel and broad bean broth.

Fillets of Smoked Eel on a Warm Potato, Onion and Beetroot Salad

The potato, beetroot and onion salad eats very well with the smoked eel. This dressing also tastes good with the addition of 2 teaspoons of horseradish, but I'm keeping this fairly simple to make.

SERVES 4

1 smoked eel, filleted and skinned (see p.46)
225 g (8 oz) new potatoes, cooked
120–175 ml (4–6 fl oz) Basic Vinaigrette (see p.241)
100 g (4 oz) caramelized onion (see p.26)

225 g (8 oz) cooked beetroot
Salt and freshly ground black pepper
1 tablespoon chopped fresh parsley
Mixed salad leaves, such as rocket, pousses (baby spinach), curly endive

Cut the smoked eel into 5–7.5 cm (2–3 in) slices, allowing three or four slices per portion. While the new potatoes are still warm, leave the skin on and cut them in half. Add three-quarters of the dressing and the cooked onions and continue to warm in the pan. Add the beetroot, making sure that it's carefully mixed in and not colouring all the potatoes. Check for seasoning with salt and pepper. Add the chopped fresh parsley. Season the remaining dressing and add to the salad leaves. Divide the potato and beetroot salad between four plates. Sit the leaves on top of the salads and lay the smoked eel on top. Finish with the chopped fresh parsley dressing.

Smoked Eel and Broad Bean Salad

This is as simple as it sounds – very few ingredients but plenty of taste. It is a very basic salad that can take on so many more flavours. Sliced, cooked, peeled new potatoes can be warmed in the horseradish or mustard dressing and placed underneath the salad, and a hot poached egg can be popped on the top before finishing with the broad beans. Breaking the egg yolk over the smoked eel and salad and mixing it with warm new potatoes in a horseradish and mustard dressing – delicious!

SERVES 4

450 g (1 lb) smoked eel fillet, cut into 7.5 cm (3 in) strips

150 ml (5 fl oz) Basic Vinaigrette (see p.241)

Juice of ½ lemon

Salt and freshly ground black pepper

1 teaspoon horseradish sauce or grain mustard

275 g (10 oz) cooked and shelled broad beans

Mixed salad leaves

The smoked eel should be at room temperature. Mix 1 tablespoon of vinaigrette with a few drops of lemon juice and re-season with salt and pepper. This dressing will be used to flavour the salad leaves.

Warm the remaining dressing and flavour with the horseradish sauce or grain mustard. Both flavours work well with smoked eel. Add the broad beans to the dressing and warm through. Toss the salad leaves in the salad dressing with salt and pepper and arrange the leaves on plates. Sit the smoked eel fingers on top of the salad, slightly overlapping. Spoon the broad bean dressing over the eels and serve.

Note

Broad beans should be cooked in boiling, salted water until tender. This can take 6–12 minutes depending on the size of the bean. Refresh under iced water and shell. The beans will have a rich, deep green colour and can be kept in the fridge and used when required.

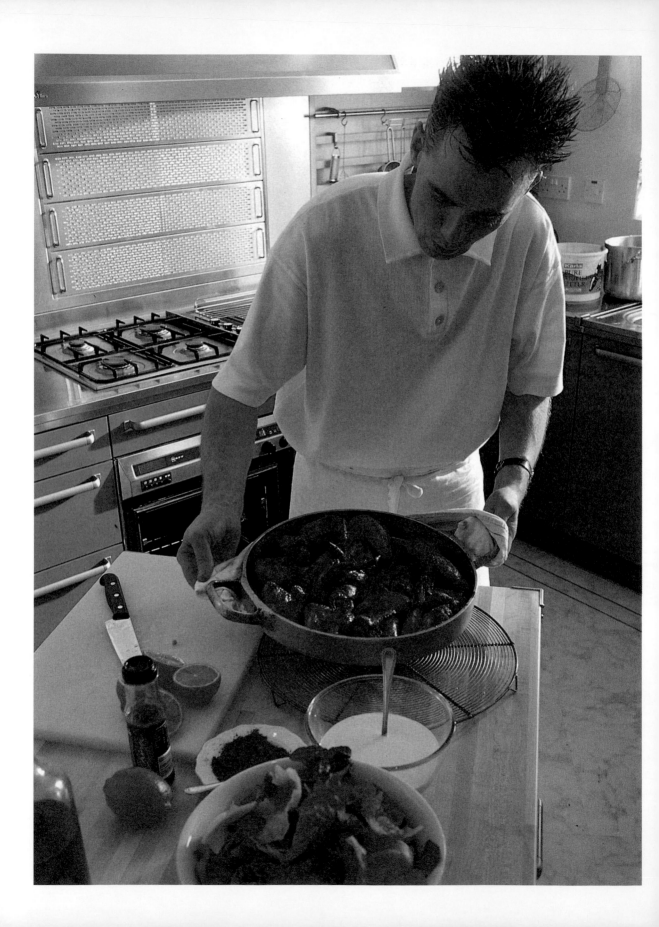

Chicken Wing Salad

If you have chicken wings left after preparing chicken breasts, this is a great way to use them. Barbecued chicken wings make a quick and easy snack, salad or lunch dish and are very moreish.

SERVES 4

900 g (2 lb) chicken wings
1 tablespoon paprika
Juice of 1–2 lemons

2 tablespoons soy sauce
Olive or cooking oil
Mixed salad leaves

Dust the chicken wings lightly with paprika. Add the lemon juice and soy sauce and toss together well. You can cook the wings now, but I prefer to leave them to take on the taste for anything from a few hours to a few days.

Lift the wings from the marinade. The best way to cook the wings is on an open barbecue. If you cannot do this, pre-heat the oven to 220°C/425°F/gas 7. Pre-heat a roasting tin on top of the stove with a little olive or cooking oil. Fry the wings until well coloured (even with a few burnt tinges), then transfer to the oven for 10–15 minutes.

Once the wings are cooked, pour over the marinade and bring to the boil. Remove from the heat and stir well. This will give the wings a paprika, lemon and soy glaze. Serve the wings on top of a mixed salad as a starter or in a big bowl for everyone to help themselves.

Variations

The wings also eat well with soured cream as a dip.

Spicy chicken wings for the Chicken Wing Salad.

Niçoise Salad

This country-style salad starter has over the years almost become a chefs' 'designer salad'. The tomatoes are laid at 12 o'clock, 3 o'clock, 6 o'oclock and 9 o'clock and all the other flavours follow suit at 10 minutes to and 10 minutes past! Chefs could argue all day over what should be included. Should there be tuna or anchovies or both?

Well, I'm going to give you my version, with the first five ingredients coming from the original recipe and the rest the optional extras. I include tuna fish, but it's going to be grilled fresh tuna fillet to sit on top of the finished salad. Of course this can be left out of the recipe completely or replaced with broken tuna fish tossed into the salad.

SERVES 4

12 very thin slices French bread
4 tablespoons olive oil or garlic butter
1 head of soft lettuce or mixed salad
    leaves
8 black olives, stoned and quartered
2 plum tomatoes, seeded and cut into
    6–8 wedges

1 teaspoon small capers
100 g (4 oz) fine beans, crisply cooked
4–8 tinned or marinated anchovy fillets
8 new potatoes, cooked and sliced
Salt and freshly ground black pepper
4 × 100 g (4 oz) tuna fillet steaks

For the Dressing

6–8 tablespoons olive oil
2 tablespoons tarragon vinegar
½ teaspoon Dijon mustard
Milled black peppercorns
A pinch of salt

½ small garlic clove, finely crushed
½ teaspoon snipped fresh chives
½ teaspoon chopped fresh tarragon
2 hard-boiled eggs, roughly chopped

To make the dressing, simply mix all the ingredients except the herbs and egg in a jar or bottle, only adding the fresh herbs just before finishing the salad. If the herbs are added too early the tarragon vinegar will discolour them.

Brush the bread with olive oil or garlic butter. Toast until golden and crisp on both sides. Separate the salad leaves and add the olives, tomatoes, capers, fine beans and anchovy fillets. Add the potato slices and season with salt and pepper.

Season the tuna with salt and pepper and start to grill or shallow-fry for about 1–1½ minutes on each side, keeping the tuna medium rare to medium.

While the tuna fish is cooking, mix the salad dressing with the chopped herbs and chopped hard-boiled egg. Pour some over the salad and toss together with the toasts. Divide between plates and sit the tuna on top.

Raw Fennel Salad

Fennel is a vegetable that is not used enough. It has the most wonderful aniseed flavour and can be eaten raw or cooked. To eat raw fennel, slice it very thinly otherwise it will be tough. All it needs then is a good marinade or dressing in which it should be served chilled. Eating a good, cold fennel salad with dressing is so refreshing and works all your taste buds. This can be eaten as a side dish to go with fish, or on its own.

Cooked fennel has many uses in salads, fish and meat dishes, or as a vegetable. It can also be served just with a dressing or grilled or shallow-fried with sauces and spices. I like it with hot Griddled Scallops (see p.42), Seared Peppered Salmon (see p.32) or grilled fresh tuna cooked on a barbecue or hot grill.

SERVES 4

2 fennel bulbs
7 tablespoons olive oil

Juice of 2 lemons
Salt and freshly ground white pepper

Trim the root and tops of the fennel and slice on a machine or cut very thinly with a sharp knife into rings. Mix together the olive oil and lemon juice and season with salt and pepper. Add to the fennel rings. The fennel will now taste crunchy with an acidic taste of lemon and rich olive oil.

Variations

It's also nice to turn this recipe into a full starter served with a tarragon mayonnaise. Just add chopped fresh tarragon and a few drops of tarragon vinegar to Mayonnaise (see p.242). Spoon the sauce into a bowl and sit some salad leaves on top, finishing with the fennel.

Caesar Salad

This salad was a great invention. Caesar Cardini, from Caesar's Palace in Los Angeles, found himself with some unexpected dinner guests and quickly came up with this dish. I'm not sure if this is the absolute original. I think plenty has been added and taken away, but it always stays similar and very tasty.

You'll notice that the egg should only be boiled for 1½ minutes. This helps the binding of the dressing without the whites being totally raw. If you are still worried about this, then simply use the yolk from one or two hard-boiled eggs; the dressing will still work. Tabasco sauce is very hot and strong, so a dash must literally be just one or two drops. Marinated anchovy fillets are bought soaked in a vinegar liquor, making them packed with flavour and taste.

SERVES 4

For the Salad

6 little gem or 2 cos lettuces
12 marinated or 8 tinned anchovy fillets
4 thick slices wholemeal bread

Olive oil
25 g (1 oz) Parmesan, grated
50 g (2 oz) Parmesan flakes

For the Dressing

15 g (½ oz) anchovy fillets, drained and
   chopped
2 teaspoons capers
2 teaspoons Worcestershire sauce
½ teaspoon Dijon mustard
A dash of Tabasco sauce
Juice of ½ lemon

½ garlic clove, crushed
2 tablespoons finely grated Parmesan
1 egg, boiled for 1½ minutes only
150–300 ml (5–10 fl oz) extra-virgin
   olive oil
Freshly ground black pepper

Break down the lettuces into separate leaves. Split the anchovy fillets into strips. Remove the crusts off the bread and cut into 1 cm (½ in) squares. These can be shallow-fried, toasted or (and this is what I do!) sprinkled with olive oil and baked in a pre-heated oven at 200°C/400°F/gas 6. Keep turning them every minute or so until golden brown and crunchy. Cooking them this way prevents them from becoming soaked in oil. While still hot, toss them in the grated Parmesan.

The quickest way to make the dressing is to place all the ingredients into a blender, using just 150 ml (5 fl oz) of oil to start with, and blitz until thick and creamy. Check for seasoning. Be careful of using any salt in this dressing because of the high salt content of the anchovies. The dressing can be pushed through a sieve or left rustic, which will give you more texture. If necessary, you can add a little more oil at a time. The consistency should be thick and emulsified, coating the back of a spoon.

To assemble the salad, toss the lettuce leaves in the dressing, making sure they are all coated. Add the anchovies, croûtons and half of the Parmesan flakes and divide between the salad bowls. Sprinkle with the remaining Parmesan and serve.

Caesar Salad.

Risotto

Risotto is a speciality rice dish from northern Italy and there is no other rice dish quite like it. The best rice all round to use (and the only one for this dish really) is arborio. This is an almost round rice that has an outer layer that creates a wonderful creamy texture as it cooks. It's the cooking method that creates this consistency: just adding a little hot stock at a time which, as it's braising on top of the stove, starts to break down the layers.

Risotto can be as basic and easy or as exciting and difficult as you wish. Probably the classic Italian risotto is Milanese, which is made with saffron and Parmesan; quite a simple dish that sparked off many variations.

All my risotto recipes are flexible; you can change the ingredients to suit yourself. One ingredient that is used in many Italian risottos is beef bone marrow. Added to the onions while they are softening in the butter and olive oil, this adds a richness to the dish which lifts the flavour and texture. It can be used in any of these risottos just adding 25-50 g (1–2 oz) per recipe. Risottos can also be lovely vegetarian dishes providing vegetable stock is used.

Here are the basic quantities for any risotto – the proportions of rice, stock, onions and butter are the same – a simple blueprint for making up your own.

225 g (8 oz) arborio rice

1.2 litres (2 pints) Vegetable Stock (see p.223), Chicken Stock (see p.222) or Fish Stock (see p.221)

100–175 g (4–6 oz) unsalted butter

2 onions, finely chopped

Finely grated Parmesan added at the end of cooking enriches all the flavours and makes the consistency even more creamy.

Mushroom Risotto with Crispy Black Pudding

Mushrooms and black pudding are a traditional British combination, usually served at breakfast. They work together very well in this recipe, contrasting the creaminess of the risotto with the crispy, rich black pudding. The best mushrooms to use in this recipe are the open cup or flat. These have an almost meaty texture and a much better flavour.

SERVES 4–8

100–175 g (4–6 oz) unsalted butter
1 tablespoon olive oil
2 onions, finely chopped
25–50 g (1–2 oz) bone marrow, chopped (optional)
1.2 litres (2 pints) Vegetable Stock (see p.223) or Chicken Stock (see p.222)
225–350 g (8–12 oz) open cup or flat mushrooms, sliced

225 g (8 oz) arborio rice
1 black pudding, cut into 1 cm (½ in) dice
1–2 tablespoons freshly grated Parmesan
Salt and freshly ground black pepper
Parmesan flakes

Melt the butter with the olive oil in a large pan. Add the chopped onions and chopped bone marrow, if using, and cook without colouring for 2–3 minutes. Meanwhile, bring the stock to the boil. Add the sliced mushrooms to the onions, increasing the heat of the pan. Allow the mushrooms to cook for 2–3 minutes. Add the rice and continue to cook over a medium heat for a further minute. Add the hot stock a ladle at a time, allowing it to become absorbed in the rice and evaporate before adding another ladle. Continue this process, stirring almost continuously to keep an even cooking. This will take 20–30 minutes. When the risotto is almost cooked, the black pudding can be either pan-fried until crispy or cooked under the grill.

Once the risotto is cooked, add some grated Parmesan and check the consistency is of a rich creamy texture. Season with salt and pepper and spoon on to a plate or into bowls. Sprinkle with Parmesan flakes, crispy black pudding and a few drops of olive oil.

ABOVE *Crab Risotto (see p.60).*

OPPOSITE *Checking the flavour of the risotto.*

Crab Risotto

Seafood risottos are really delightful to eat. In Italy, meat or fish are almost always included in the dish rather than served with it, making the risotto a complete meal in itself (see p.58).

For the maximum crab flavour, it's best to use fresh crab cooked in fish stock. This will leave you with a good crab stock to lift the flavour. If you are using fresh crab, follow the cooking method from the bisque recipe on p.16. Otherwise cooked white crab meat can be obtained from most fishmongers or supermarkets, either fresh or frozen.

I also like to serve the risotto finished with a border of crab bisque (see Lobster Bisque p.16). This is well worth the effort; it totally lifts the whole dish. But remember that tinned crab bisque is available – one or two tablespoons will be enough.

Serves 4–6

1.2 litres (2 pints) Fish Stock (see p.221)
100–175 g (4–6 oz) unsalted butter
1 tablespoon olive oil
2 onions, finely chopped
25-50 g (1–2 oz) bone marrow, chopped
  (optional)
225 g (8 oz) arborio rice

225 g (8 oz) white crab meat, shredded
Salt and freshly ground white pepper
1–2 tablespoons finely grated Parmesan
  (optional)
Crab Bisque (see p.16) or tinned (optional)
Parmesan flakes (optional)
Olive oil

Bring the fish or crab stock to the simmer. Melt 100 g (4 oz) of the butter with the olive oil, add the onions and cook for 3–4 minutes without colouring. As the onions begin to soften, add the bone marrow, if using. Add the rice and cook for 2–3 minutes. Now add two ladles of hot stock, keeping the rice over a medium heat. The hot stock will create a steam and immediately begin to evaporate. Because you only add a ladle at a time, the rice will absorb the stock without becoming totally encased. This is the process that helps cream the risotto. Continue to add the stock a little at a time until the rice is tender; this will take about 20 minutes. The finished texture of the rice should have the slightest bite.

Add the crab meat and the remaining butter and season with salt and pepper. I also like to add a little Parmesan to lift the taste. The consistency should not be at all stodgy but rich and creamy. Some crab bisque can be added to the finished risotto to improve the flavour and consistency even more; use a few spoonfuls.

The risotto is now ready to serve. If you are using crab bisque, spoon the risotto into bowls and pour some more bisque around. The risotto can also be garnished with Parmesan flakes and a trickle of olive oil.

Variations

This recipe can be used for lobster, prawn or shrimp risotto. Mussels also make a good risotto. Cook them first in fish stock, then use the resulting mussel stock for the risotto. Don't add the cooked mussels to the rice until the end otherwise they will be overcooked and tough.

Leek and Parmesan Risotto with a Warm Poached Egg

The traditional way to poach an egg is to bring a deep pan of water to a rolling boil. Add a generous quantity of wine or malt vinegar, then crack the egg into the water. Poach for about 3 minutes until the white has set. Remove from the pan and place in a bowl of cold water to stop the cooking or serve immediately.

SERVES 4

1.2 litres (2 pints) Vegetable Stock (see p.223) or Chicken Stock (see p.222)
450 g (1 lb) leeks, trimmed and sliced
175 g (6 oz) unsalted butter
2 onions, finely chopped
1 small garlic clove, crushed
225 g (8 oz) arborio rice

3–4 tablespoons grated Parmesan
Salt and freshly ground white pepper
4 poached eggs
2–3 tablespoons Basic Vinaigrette (see p.241) or seasoned olive oil
1 tablespoon snipped fresh chives
Fresh Parmesan flakes (optional)

Bring the stock to the boil and add the sliced leeks. Bring back to the boil and drain the leeks off, reserving the leeks and stock separately. Melt the butter in a large pan, add the onions and garlic and cook for a few minutes without colouring until softened. Add the rice and cook for a further minute. Start to add the hot stock a ladle at a time and cook over a medium heat, allowing the rice to absorb almost all the stock before adding more stock. Continue to add, cook and stir until the rice is softening but not getting to a purée creamed stage; this will take about 20 minutes.

Stir in the Parmesan. The more you add, the richer the taste will become. The Parmesan will also thicken the risotto so add more stock to give a loose consistency if necessary. Add the leeks, season with salt and pepper and warm through. Spoon into the bowls and sit a warm poached egg on top. Mix the dressing or olive oil with the chives and spoon a little over the eggs. Sprinkle with some Parmesan flakes to finish.

Main Courses

W ell, here we are, the course that we balance our menus around. That's really the best way of building a dinner party or restaurant menu. You first look at the main course and whichever one you choose will help determine your starter and pudding.

ABOVE *Roast Parsnip and Chestnut Crumble on Bubble and Squeak (see p.118).*
LEFT *Home-made Pork Pie (see p.92).*

I must admit if I'm cooking for myself and maybe a few friends I don't worry too much about balancing all the dishes; I tend just to cook what I feel like eating. However, balancing dishes is very important. Making sure that all the dishes aren't coated with cream sauces or too rich, for example, will give you a healthier and tastier meal.

The chapter has been broken down into smaller sections: Fish, Meat and Poultry, Vegetarian Dishes and Vegetables. Amongst these there are some more features of savoury crumbles and tarts to keep you busy!

Fish

I've kept this part of the chapter relatively short, because the majority of dishes in the Starters section are fish, all of which are suitable to serve as main courses as well.

Cooking with fish is so enjoyable, the first advantage being the variety available, all with their different textures, colours and flavours. The texture of the fish will also determine how it should be cooked: pan-fried, deep-fried, grilled, braised or stewed.

One of my favourite fish is cod (you can probably tell, I've featured four cod dishes in this chapter!). A fresh, thick cod fillet is built up of large white flakes, and when simply grilled or pan-fried with just a knob of butter and kept moist, the centre of the flakes become almost transparent and juicy.

When I ask for fillets, I do mean fillets. Your fishmonger should be able to help you out with this. A lot of cod, for instance, is sold as steaks cut straight through the bone. It looks very nice but can be difficult to handle when eating. On top of that, cutting straight through will break down the texture of the fish, loosing those lovely large flakes.

Skate is different altogether. This is normally sold on the bone and as skate wings. When cooking a skate wing dish, it's usually pan-fried and finished with nut brown butter, capers and parsley. Well in one or two of these skate dishes I'm using fillets. These are quite easy to cut away from the bone and when pan-fried golden brown and crispy can become part of a whole dish a lot easier to eat. Sitting the fillet on top of salads or pasta works really well and you certainly can't do that if it's a straight skate wing!

All the fish dishes in this chapter can be adapted to the fish you want to use. So instead of cod or skate, why not try the recipe with turbot, brill, halibut, salmon or even something else.

Roast Cod on Potatoes with Fried Anchovies

This has to be my favourite fish dish in the book (see pp.70–71) As with most of the recipes, another fish can be used or you can leave the fish out and serve the dish as a warm potato salad with crispy anchovies. Marinated anchovies are sold loosely, not in tins.

Because I'm roasting this cod, I want to keep the skin on. When shallow-fried then roasted, cod skin comes up very crisp and tasty; it's good enough to eat on its own!

SERVES 4

450 g (1 lb) new potatoes
Salt and freshly ground white pepper
150 ml (5 fl oz) Vierge Dressing (see p.243) or olive oil
Juice of 1 lemon
25 g (1 oz) unsalted butter
2 teaspoons cooking oil
4 × 175–225 g (6–8 oz) cod fillets
12 marinated anchovies
1 teaspoon self-raising flour
¼ teaspoon cayenne

2–3 tablespoons milk
Oil for deep-frying
1 tablespoon fine or chopped capers
2 shallots or ½ onion, very finely chopped
½ teaspoon chopped fresh parsley
1 teaspoon chopped fresh coriander
1 teaspoon chopped fresh tarragon
1 teaspoon chopped fresh basil
A few green salad leaves (optional)

Pre-heat the oven to 200°C/400°F/gas 6.

Cook the new potatoes, then peel off the skin. Cut into 5 mm (¼ in) slices while still warm, then season with salt and pepper. Add 1–2 tablespoons of dressing or olive oil and the juice of ½ lemon. Season again with salt and pepper and keep warm.

Melt the butter and oil in a hot pan. Season the cod with salt and pepper and place in the pan skin-side down. Cook until deep in colour, then turn over and finish cooking in the oven for 5–8 minutes, depending on the thickness of the cod.

Split the anchovies through the centre. Mix the flour with the cayenne and a pinch of salt. Dip the anchovies in the milk, then roll in the cayenne flour. Deep-fry in hot oil until very crispy. If you don't have a deep-fat fryer, cook them in about 5 mm (¼ in) of hot oil in a frying-pan, but don't let it get so hot so that it smokes, and keep turning the fish in the pan until they are crispy.

To finish the dish, warm the remaining dressing or oil and add the capers and shallots or onion with a squeeze of lemon juice and the herbs. Season with salt and pepper. The dressing should be served warm.

Spoon some potatoes on to plates and top with a few green salad leaves. Spoon the dressing all around and sit a few fried anchovy fillets on top of the dressing. Finish the dish with the roasted cod fillet on top with the crispy skin-side showing. Brush with a little butter to finish.

Fried Anchovies.

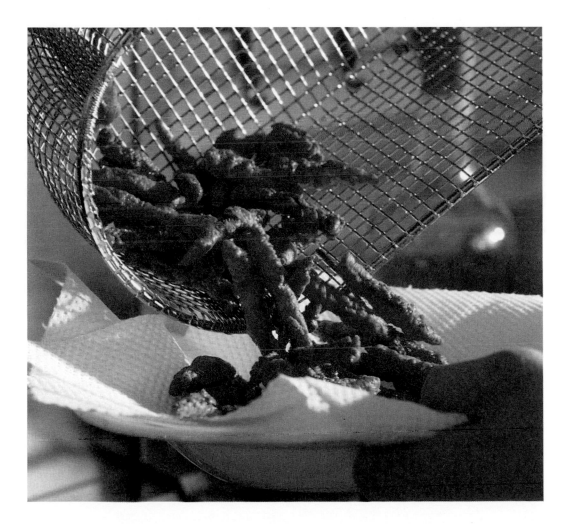

Pan-fried Cod on Fennel and Potato Salad with Tartare Dressing

Cod, chips and tartare sauce is probably Britain's most famous and classic fish dish, and cooked well with a good, crispy batter and a tartare made with fresh mayonnaise, you can't beat it (see overleaf). I decided to use nearly all of those tastes in this dish: the fresh cod, potatoes and tartare sauce flavour without the mayonnaise. To this I've added some fresh fennel which, with its slight aniseed flavour, really helps the potatoes and fish. You can, of course, leave out the fennel and I promise you'll still enjoy this lighter version of our old favourite.

Serves 4

4 × 175–225 g (6–8 oz) cod fillets
2 tablespoons plain flour

50 g (2 oz) unsalted butter
1 tablespoon olive oil

For the Dressing

2 teaspoons capers
2 teaspoons chopped cocktail gherkins
2 teaspoons chopped shallot or onion

½ bunch of fresh parsley
1–2 tablespoons olive oil
Salt and freshly ground black pepper

For the Fennel and Potatoes

2 large fennel bulbs
2 lemons
275 g (10 oz) new potatoes

50 ml (2 fl oz) Basic Vinaigrette
(see p.241)

To make the dressing, place the capers, gherkins and shallot or onion in a food processor and blitz until almost puréed. Add the parsley and 1 tablespoon of olive oil. Continue to blitz until the parsley is finely chopped. Season with salt and pepper. If the dressing is very thick, simply add more olive oil. This dressing keeps well for 24 hours in the fridge.

To cook the fennel, top and tail the bulbs and remove some of the core at the base. Bring about 1.2 litres (2 pints) of water to the boil (enough to cover the fennel) with the juice of 1 lemon and a pinch of salt. Place the fennel into the water and cover with a lid, bring back to the boil, then simmer until just tender; this will take 15–20 minutes. Leave to cool. Cut the fennel in half lengthways, then each half into 5–6 slices lengthways.

Meanwhile, boil the new potatoes until tender, then drain, peel off the skins and cut the potatoes in half. Mix the basic dressing with the juice of the remaining lemon and add to the new potatoes and fennel slices. Season with salt and pepper and bring up to the simmer.

To cook the cod, lightly flour and season each fillet and brush with butter on the skin side. Heat a frying-pan with a little olive oil. Lay the cod butter-side down into the pan and cook until golden brown. Turn the fish in the pan and continue to cook. The cod will take about 6–8 minutes to cook.

To serve, spoon the tartare dressing into bowls or plates and sit the fennel and potatoes on top. Finish by sitting the cod on to the garnish.

OVERLEAF *Clockwise, starting at the front:*
Deep-fried Cod in Batter (see p.72);
Pan-fried Cod on Pecorino Mashed Potatoes and Spinach (see p.73);
extra Fried Anchovies (see p.66);
Pan-fried Cod on Fennel and Potato Salad with Tartare Dressing (see p.68);
Roast Cod on Potatoes with Fried Anchovies (see p.66).

Deep-fried Cod in Batter

This must be the quickest batter to make. It's just lager and some salt and self-raising flour. The only secret is to make sure the batter is very thick, almost too thick. As the cod is cooking, the batter will soufflé, keeping it light and crisp (see preceding pages). If the batter is too thin, it tends to stick to the fish and become heavy. You can use the same recipe for any deep-fried fish, sausages or whatever. It also eats well with Tomato Sauce (see p.233).

Serves 4

450 g (1 lb) self-raising flour
Salt and freshly ground black pepper
4 × 175–225 g (6–8 oz) cod fillets,
    skinned and boned

600 ml (1 pint) lager
A pinch of salt
Oil for deep-frying

For the Tartare Sauce

300 ml (10 fl oz) Mayonnaise (see p.242)
25 g (1 oz) gherkins, chopped
25 g (1 oz) capers, chopped

25 g (1 oz) onion, finely chopped
2 teaspoons chopped fresh parsley
A squeeze of lemon juice

Season a spoonful of flour with salt and pepper. Lightly dust each fillet in the flour.

Whisk half the remaining flour into the lager with a pinch of salt, then gradually add the flour a spoonful at a time to make a thick batter. Dip the cod into the batter. Heat the oil to 180°C/350°F, then fry the cod until golden.

To make the sauce, mix all the ingredients together and season with lemon juice, salt and pepper. Serve with the crispy fried cod.

Pan-fried Cod on Pecorino Mashed Potatoes and Spinach

You don't have to stick to cod with this recipe: halibut, haddock, turbot or brill can all be used and taste just as good (see pp.70–71).

Pecorino is an Italian ewes' milk cheese with a similar texture to Parmesan. I like to use smoked Pecorino for extra taste. Pecorino cheeses were introduced to me by Giovanni, an Italian friend who lives in South Wales. Giovanni makes his own 'Pecorinos' with Welsh ewes' milk – and it works! The cheese is lovely. If you have trouble finding Pecorino, just use Parmesan.

All I do with this recipe is add grated smoked Pecorino to hot mashed potatoes to give you a delicious cheesey mash. Of course, you can use the cheesey mash with so many other things: top your shepherds' pie with it, make a cheesey champ (see p.134), or serve it with sausage and beans.

SERVES 4

1 tablespoon plain flour
Salt and freshly ground white pepper
4 × 175–225 g (6–8 oz) cod fillets, skinned
1 tablespoon cooking oil
100 g (4 oz) unsalted butter

3–4 tablespoons Fish Stock (see p.221) or water
900 g (2 lb) spinach, picked and washed
Juice of ½ lemon
450 g (1 lb) Mashed Potatoes (see p.133)
100–175 g (4–6 oz) Pecorino, grated

Lightly flour and season the cod with salt and pepper. Heat a frying-pan with the oil and 25 g (1 oz) of the butter. When the pan is hot and the butter bubbling, add the cod and cook for about 3–4 minutes on each side, keeping the pan hot, until the fish is golden brown. Always cook the presentation skin-side down first. When the fish colours, it will show every line of the fillet and also hold the fish together a lot better.

While the fish is cooking, bring the stock or water to the boil with 25 g (1 oz) of butter. Add the spinach leaves and stir for 2–3 minutes. The spinach will cook quickly and create a spinach liquor in the pan. Season with salt and pepper, drain off the spinach and re-boil the liquor. Whisk in the remaining butter to make a spinach butter sauce. Taste and adjust the seasoning if necessary and add the lemon juice to lift the flavour.

Warm the mashed potatoes with 100 g (4 oz) of cheese. Taste and add the remaining cheese, or more if you wish.

Spoon the potatoes on to plates and sit some spinach on top. Arrange the fish on top. You now have a tower of flavours. Pour the spinach butter sauce around and serve.

Fillet of Skate with Red Peppers, Potatoes, Capers and Bayonne Ham

Filleting skate is quite unusual – skate wings are normally cooked on the bone – but it really suits this dish. It's a simple recipe with not too many flavours, just enough to help each other. Bayonne is a cured ham usually made in Orthez near Béarn in south-west France. It has a similar texture to Parma ham but the flavours are different. Bayonne is usually lightly smoked to lift the taste. If you can't find any, substitute Parma ham. Cut the thin slices into 1 cm (½ in) strips ready to fry until crisp.

SERVES 4

2 red peppers
Juice of 1 lemon
6 tablespoons olive oil
Salt and freshly ground white pepper
225–350 g (8–12 oz) new potatoes,
    peeled, cooked and sliced
2 teaspoons fine capers

4 × 175 g (6 oz) skate fillets
1 tablespoon plain flour
25 g (1 oz) unsalted butter
4–6 slices Bayonne ham, cut into pieces
Mixed salad leaves
2 tablespoons Basic Vinaigrette (see
    p.241)

Core and halve the peppers lengthways, remove the seeds and cut into 1 cm (½ in) slices lengthways. Mix the lemon juice with 4 tablespoons of olive oil, season with salt and pepper, and pour over the potatoes. Fry the peppers in a little olive oil, colouring and softening slightly, then mix with the potatoes and capers.

Dust the skate with flour, brush with butter and season with salt and pepper. Pre-heat a frying-pan and brush with olive oil. Sit the fillets in the pan, presentation side down, and fry quickly for 2 minutes, then turn and cook for a further minute.

Meanwhile, heat another pan and fry the ham in virtually no fat, cooking and tossing until crisp.

Divide the potatoes and peppers between the plates. Toss the salad leaves in a little dressing and arrange on top. Sit the skate on the leaves and spoon the crisp ham over the top.

Note

Salad leaves are not essential for any of the fish dishes, but they always help the texture.

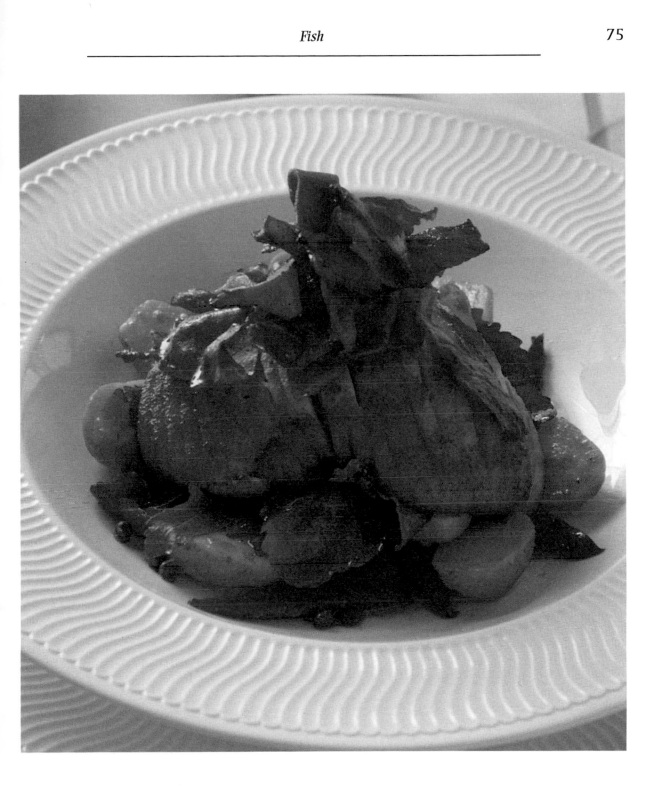

*Fillet of Skate with Red Peppers, Potatoes,
Capers and Bayonne Ham.*

Pan-fried Skate with Ratatouille Salad

The skate in this dish is also filleted and shallow-fried.

Serves 4

2 red peppers
1 green pepper
2 small courgettes
1 large onion, thickly sliced
2 tablespoons olive oil
50 g (2 oz) unsalted butter
2 large, flat mushrooms, sliced
Salt and freshly ground white pepper
1 tablespoon plain flour

4 × 175 g (6 oz) skate fillets
250 ml (8 fl oz) Basic Vinaigrette (see p.241)
6 fresh basil leaves (optional)
1–2 teaspoons Pesto Sauce (see p.235) (optional)
Green salad leaves
1 aubergine, sliced and fried (see p.42)

Core and halve the peppers lengthways, remove the seeds and cut into 1 cm (½ in) slices lengthways. Slice the courgettes at an angle to give oval slices. Fry the onion and peppers in a heavy-based pan in a little olive oil and butter until softened. Add the courgettes and cook for 1 minute then remove from the heat. Cook the mushrooms separately in a very hot pan in a little olive oil, then add to the other vegetables. Season with salt and pepper.

Lightly flour the skate fillets and brush with butter. Heat a frying-pan and brush with oil. Sit the fillets buttered-side down into the pan and fry quickly for 2 minutes on one side, then 1 minute on the other until golden brown.

Mix the vinaigrette with the basil leaves or pesto, if using, and use a little to dress the salad leaves. Add the ratatouille to the dressing and spoon on to plates. Sit the leaves on top and finish with the fish and aubergines.

Variations

Another skate dish that I enjoy is one that is cooked on the bone. The skate is shallow-fried in olive oil and butter for 3–4 minutes on each side until the flesh is crisp and golden brown. Arrange the skate on a plate and surround with some Lemon Butter Sauce (see p.228), finishing with some crunchy brown shrimps and parsley in nut brown butter.

The best shrimps to use are the small, brown variety. To pick them, simply pull off the heads and small tails and leave the rest of the shell on the tail itself. The shell is crispy without being too hard. To make the butter nut brown, heat a frying-pan and add some butter. It should be bubbling and beginning to colour almost immediately. When it's just turning brown but not burnt, add the shrimp tails, a squeeze of lemon juice and season with salt and pepper. Finish with chopped fresh parsley and spoon over the skate.

Sea Bass on Minestrone

This sauce is almost like a minestrone soup, with the flavour of all the vegetables cooked in a tomato liquor. The dish eats well with noodles or with the fish on mashed potatoes. Sea bass is not the only fish that can be used. Red mullet or most white fish will also eat well. A seafood minestrone of scallops, prawns, mussels and cockles is a real winner.

SERVES 4

50 g (2 oz) unsalted butter
1 tablespoon olive oil
2 carrots, diced
1 large onion, diced
2 celery sticks, diced
1 garlic clove, crushed
1 medium courgette, diced
½ leek, diced
2 glasses white wine
150 ml (5 fl oz) Fish Stock (see p.221)

150 ml (5 fl oz) Tomato Coulis (see p.232)
4 × 175–225 g (6–8 oz) sea bass fillets
2 tomatoes, skinned and diced
8–10 fresh basil leaves, cut into squares
12–15 fresh tarragon leaves, cut into squares
1–2 teaspoons Pesto Sauce (see p.235) (optional)

Melt half the butter with the olive oil, then add the carrots, onion, celery and garlic. Cook without colouring for a few minutes. Cook the courgette and leek separately in a knob of butter so that they retain their green colour. Once cooked, allow them to cool, then add them towards the end of cooking. Once the vegetables have softened, add the white wine and boil to reduce until almost dry. Add the stock and boil to reduce by half. Add the tomato coulis and simmer for 10–12 minutes until the sauce has a broth consistency.

Arrange the fish on a buttered and seasoned tray and cook under a hot grill for 5–10 minutes, leaving the skin golden and crispy.

While the fish is cooking, add the tomatoes, herbs, courgettes and leeks to the minestrone, bring to the simmer and add the remaining butter. Finish with the pesto sauce, if liked. Spoon the minestrone sauce into some bowls and sit the fish on top.

Variations

To make this into a more complete meal, cook some noodles and toss in butter. Sit the noodles in the centre of the bowls and spoon the sauce around. Arrange the fish on top.

Try serving the dish with mashed potatoes, leaving out the pesto sauce, and spooning some of the sauce on to the mash before sitting the fish on top and spooning the remaining sauce around.

Stuffed Herrings

This dish eats well on its own simply with a squeeze of lemon or served with a mustard cream sauce (see p.79).

SERVES 4

4 herrings, filleted   Pig's caul (optional)

For the Stuffing

4 medium slices white bread   ¼ teaspoon chopped fresh thyme
1 tablespoon melted butter   ½ teaspoon chopped fresh parsley
1 large onion, finely chopped   25 g (1 oz) bone marrow, finely diced
2 rashers smoked streaky bacon,   (optional)
    finely diced   2 tablespoons shredded suet
½ teaspoon chopped fresh sage   Salt and freshly ground black pepper

Pre-heat the oven to 200–220°C/400–425°F/gas 6–7.

To make the stuffing, remove the crusts from the sliced bread and crumb the slices. Melt the butter, add the chopped onion and cook without colouring for 2–3 minutes. Add the bacon and herbs and continue to cook for 2 minutes. Allow to cool. Mix with the breadcrumbs, diced bone marrow, if using, and suet. Season with salt and pepper. The texture of this stuffing should just hold and bind together if squeezed in your hand.

The herrings should be filleted and as many fine bones removed as possible. Lay out four fillets and divide and spread the stuffing over them. Cover with the other fillets. Before cooking, the fish can be wrapped in pig's caul or in a layer of buttered foil, then pan-fried in a little olive oil and butter until golden brown on both sides. Finish them in the pre-heated oven for a few minutes. Alternatively, if you have used foil, simply bake them in the oven for 12–15 minutes. Once cooked, the caul will be almost invisible. It is used only to hold the fillets together.

Herrings with Spring Onion and Bacon Potato Cakes

These herring fillets are grilled and arranged on top of potato cakes. They can then be served with a wedge of lemon or with a mustard cream sauce.

SERVES 4

8 herring fillets	4 Spring Onion Potato Cakes with bacon
Olive oil or unsalted butter	(see p.133)

For the Mustard Cream Sauce

50 g (2 oz) unsalted butter	A few tarragon leaves
1 shallot, chopped	2 glasses white wine
1 carrot, chopped	300 ml (10 fl oz) Fish Stock (see p.221)
1 celery stick, chopped	50–85 ml (2–3 fl oz) double cream
1 rasher of bacon, chopped	1–3 teaspoons grain mustard

Melt 15 g (½ oz) of butter and cook the vegetables, bacon and tarragon without colouring until they soften. Add the white wine and boil to reduce until almost dry. Add the stock and boil to reduce by half. Add the cream and cook for 8–10 minutes. Strain the sauce and whisk in the remaining butter. Add the mustard a little at a time until you have the right strength.

Meanwhile, brush the herrings with a little oil or butter and cook under a hot grill for 5–6 minutes.

Sit the potato cakes in the centre of the plates, spoon the sauce around and lay the herring fillets on top.

Variations

The potato cake works well using spinach instead of bacon and spring onions (see p.133). Cook 450 g (1 lb) of picked and washed spinach in 25 g (1 oz) of butter for a few minutes until tender, then drain, cool and chop. Add the spinach to the potato mix and proceed as for that recipe. They eat particularly well with fish dishes.

Cooked mushrooms, bacon, onion and many other ingredients can also be added to the potato cakes.

Fish on Spinach with a Cider and Mussel Sauce

I've just called this 'fish' because so many fish work well with this recipe: cod, halibut, sea bass, red mullet, turbot, brill – the list could go on. Make sure whichever fish you choose, it is well filleted with all bones removed. White fish should be skinned as well.

SERVES 4

4 × 175–225 g (6–8 oz) fish fillets
2 tablespoon plain flour
75 g (3 oz) unsalted butter

900 g (2 lb) fresh spinach, picked and washed

For the Mussel Cooking Liquor

15 g (½ oz) unsalted butter
1 onion, roughly chopped
1 carrot, roughly chopped
2 celery sticks, roughly chopped
½ leek, roughly chopped
1 bay leaf (optional)
1 sprig of fresh thyme

1 star anise (optional)
2 glasses dry white wine
600 ml (1 pint) Fish Stock (see p.221) or water
900 g (2 lb) fresh mussels, scrubbed and bearded

For the Cider Sauce

350 g (12 oz) shallots or onions, sliced into rings
25 g (1 oz) unsalted butter
A pinch of saffron (optional)

1–2 bottles dry cider
85–120 ml (3–4 fl oz) double cream
Salt and freshly ground white pepper

To cook the mussels, melt the butter and fry the vegetables, bay leaf, thyme and star anise, if using, for 8–10 minutes without colouring. Add the wine and boil to reduce until almost dry. Add the stock or water, bring to the boil and cook for a few minutes. Add the mussels and bring to the boil, stirring. Once the stock is boiling, the mussels will be opening and cooking. Drain and reserve the cooking liquor. Discard any mussels that have not opened and pick the rest from their shells. Keep them in a few spoonfuls of cooking liquor to keep them moist.

To make the cider sauce, soften the shallots in a knob of butter with the saffron, if using. Add the cider and boil to reduce by three-quarters. Add the mussel stock and continue to reduce by half. Add half the cream, bring to a simmer and simmer for a few minutes. Check for taste and consistency and season with salt and pepper. If the sauce is too thin, reduce a little more. Add a knob or two of butter to enrich the flavour.

The fish should be seasoned and lightly dusted in flour before being pan-fried, or just seasoned if being grilled. Cod will take 3–4 minutes on each side.

While the fish is cooking, melt the butter in a large pan and add the spinach. Cook and stir for 2–3 minutes until tender. Add the mussels to the fish sauce and warm through. Spoon the spinach on to plates and sit the fish on top. Spoon the sauce over the fish, forming a small pile of shallots on top of each fillet.

Poultry and Meat

In this section, I've tried to choose cuts of meat that I feel aren't used often enough, in restaurants or at home. These cuts have a lot more flavour and texture than many of the fine cuts such as fillet of beef. Given a slow cooking process, the wonderful textures are developed to the full. Braised ox cheeks are sensational, so is breast of lamb and haunch of venison. Pork belly is another winner. Left in a spicy marinade for 24 hours, then roasted and glazed with honey, it is transformed into something quite magical. I've also included roasted knuckles and explain how to make good pork scratchings. These again are cuts that we don't seem to use. How often do you make your own pork scratchings? Perhaps it's time you had a go.

Another dish I have included is Home-made Corned Beef. I always used to wonder how corned beef was made and how it got its texture (I'm still not quite sure how they manage to keep that deep red colour!). Well, after reading through several cookery books and plenty of trials I eventually finished with the recipe in this chapter. It is so simple and easy to make. Pork Pie is another homely favourite that we all buy in various sizes from supermarkets, and there are some pretty good ones on offer. But like anything else you can't beat home-made.

You'll also find a few duck dishes and, of course, chicken dishes, one of them with a Scottish theme served sitting on braised pearl barley, which normally features in Scotch broth.

So if you're 'scratching' for an idea to fill your 'belly' just 'knuckle' down and read this chapter!

TOP *Grilled Chicken Breast with Braised Pearl Barley, Lemon and Thyme (see p.84).*
BOTTOM *Grilled Chicken on Red Wine Onions and Mushrooms (see p.85).*

Grilled Chicken Breast with Braised Pearl Barley, Lemon and Thyme

This really is a simple dish, not too many ingredients but packed with textures and tastes (see preceding page). Instead of simmering the barley on the stove, it cooks evenly if you put in a pre-heated oven at 180°C/350°F/gas 4.

SERVES 4

1 large onion, finely chopped
175–225 g (6–8 oz) unsalted butter, softened but not melted
900 ml (1½ pints) Chicken Stock (see p.222)
1 leek, sliced or diced

100 g (4 oz) pearl barley
1 teaspoon chopped fresh thyme
Juice of 1–2 lemons
4 chicken breasts
Salt and freshly ground black pepper

To braise the barley, cook the chopped onion in 50 g (2 oz) of the butter, without colouring, until softened. Bring 600 ml (1 pint) of the chicken stock to the boil, add the leeks and cook for 30 seconds. Strain, reserving both stock and leeks. Add the pearl barley to the onions and cook for another 1–2 minutes. Add the stock and bring to the simmer. Cover with a lid and cook over a low heat, stirring continuously, until the barley becomes tender; this will take 30–40 minutes. Add more stock if the barley becomes dry. The remaining 300 ml (10 fl oz) of chicken stock can be boiled until reduced by half to leave you with a good, strong stock.

Mix 100–150 g (4–5 oz) of the butter with the thyme and lemon juice. (This can be made at any time and will keep in the fridge for as long as the butter will last.)

The chicken breasts eat very well if cooked on a grill pan or open barbecue. They can also be pan-fried or cooked under the grill. They will take about 15 minutes.

To finish the barley, add a knob of butter and the leeks and warm through. If there is still a lot of excess chicken stock, simply pour it off. Re-boil the reduced chicken stock, then gradually add and whisk in enough of the lemon and thyme butter until you have a smooth sauce consistency. Season with salt and pepper. Spoon the barley on to the centre of a warmed serving plate and pour the sauce around. Slice the chicken breast through the middle and place on top of the barley.

Grilled Chicken on Red Wine Onions and Mushrooms

This dish is very rich; the flavour of the red onions cooked in red wine eats beautifully (see p.83). Use flat or open cup mushrooms; both have a good flavour and texture. This mushroom and red wine garnish also works well with lamb and beef.

SERVES 4

50 g (2 oz) unsalted butter
8–10 large red onions, sliced
50 g (2 oz) demerara sugar
300 ml (10 fl oz) red wine vinegar
Salt and freshly ground black pepper
1 bottle red wine

2 tablespoons crème de cassis (optional)
8–12 flat or open cup mushrooms
4 chicken breasts
300 ml (½ pint) Red Wine Sauce (see p.230)

Pre-heat the oven to 200°C/400°F/gas 6.

Melt half the butter in a large pan, add the onions and cook for a few minutes without colouring until they begin to soften. Add the sugar and red wine vinegar and boil to reduce until almost dry. Season with salt and pepper. Add the wine and also reduce until almost dry. Season again with salt and pepper and stir in the crème de cassis, if using.

Remove the stalks from the mushrooms and tear off the outer skin from the mushrooms. This is not essential but makes them even more tender. Lay them upside down on a buttered and seasoned tray, brush with butter and season again. Cook under the grill for 4–6 minutes.

Meanwhile, cook the chicken on an open grill or on a grill plate, or just fry in a little butter until golden, then finish in the pre-heated oven for 8–10 minutes. Warm the red wine sauce.

To serve the dish, divide the onions between four bowls (there may well be enough for more!), then sit the mushrooms on top. Carve the chicken through the centre and arrange on top of the mushrooms. Pour the warm sauce around.

Variations

For a lighter sauce, take any of the red onion trimmings from slicing them and cook in a knob of butter for a few minutes until softened. Add 600 ml (1 pint) of red wine and reduce until almost dry. Add 450 ml (15 fl oz) of chicken stock and reduce by half. Strain through a sieve and whisk in 50–75 g (2–3 oz) of unsalted butter. This will give you a lighter red wine sauce that can be blitzed with a hand blender to make it even lighter!

Crispy Roast Duck Breasts with Parsnip Purée

The duck breasts I use for this recipe are called magrets. *This is a duck breast that has been completely removed from the bone and has no wing attached. This breast can then have the skin removed or left on. I prefer to leave the skin on, as this gives a crispy finish.* Magret *duck breasts usually come vacuum-packed from France and are ready to cook. If you can't get* magrets, *simply roast duck breasts still on the carcass, then remove them from the bone once cooked and rested.*

SERVES 4

4 *magret* duck breasts
1 tablespoon vegetable or olive oil
Salt and freshly ground black pepper
4 teaspoons clear honey

450 g (1 lb) parsnips
50 g (2 oz) unsalted butter
1 quantity Cranberry Gravy (see p.238)

Pre-heat the oven to 200°C/400°F/gas 6.

First score the fat on the duck breasts with a sharp knife all the way across (right to left) about 1–2 mm apart. The fat only needs to be scored and not cut through into the flesh. Pre-heat a roasting pan on top of the stove with the oil. Season the scored duck breasts with salt and pepper. Sit the breasts skin-side down into the pan. This will create some spitting from the pan as all water content from the fat will cook out. Once the breasts are cooking fast, turn the heat down to medium and continue to cook the breasts fat-side down until dark and almost burnt. The layer of skin will have cooked right down almost like a confit. Turn the breasts over and finish in the pre-heated oven for 6–10 minutes until the flesh is cooked to medium, depending on the thickness of the breast; a large, thick breast will take 8–10 minutes. Once cooked, the skin will be dark, rich and crispy, almost like duck crackling!

This can now be made even tastier if honey is spooned on top and glazed under the grill. Before serving the breasts, it's best to leave them to rest for 5–10 minutes as this will allow the meat to become more tender.

To make the parsnip purée, peel and split the parsnips lengthways into quarters, and cut out the woody centres. Boil in salted water for about 15 minutes until tender, drain and shake dry. Add the salt and pepper and butter and mash the parsnips. Push through a sieve to get a smooth-textured purée. Serve with the cranberry gravy.

The *magrets* can be left whole or sliced diagonally and arranged on a plate. Serve the parsnip purée separately or shape it between two large spoons to give an oval shape and serve on the plate with the duck. Pour some of the cranberry gravy on to the dish and serve.

Crispy Roast Duck Breasts with Parsnip Purée.

Confit of Duck

This was featured in Rhodes Around Britain. *It's a classic French dish that can also work with goose or pork. In the last book, the duck legs were steeped in a marinade for a few days. Well, this recipe is without the marinade and these duck legs will just be salted for 24 hours before cooking.*

SERVES 4

4 duck legs
2 teaspoons rock sea salt

900 g (2 lb) lard or goose fat, melted

Trim the legs of any remaining feather stalks and remove the knuckle on the underside of the thigh. The skin can also be scored around the top of the drumstick knuckle so this will shrink while cooking and reveal the bone. Salt the legs on the skin side and chill for 24 hours. This will draw any water from the fat and ensure that the skin is crisp when the legs are cooked.

Pre-heat the oven to 160°C/325°F/gas 3.

Sit the legs in a braising dish and cover with melted lard. Bring just to a light simmer, cover with a lid and cook in the oven for 1½–2 hours. To check the legs, remove one from the fat and push the skin side. When you feel the meat is starting to become tender and give, remove from the heat and leave to cool in the fat.

Transfer the legs to a clean dish and cover completely in fat. They will keep chilled almost indefinitely.

To roast the legs, pre-heat the oven to 200°C/400°F/gas 6. Remove the legs from the fat and cut off the end knuckle. Cook in the pre-heated oven for 15–20 minutes until crispy.

Confit of Duck with Orange Sauce and Buttered Spinach

This is a variation on the original confit (see p.88). When salting the duck legs, add the pared rind of one orange and leave it with the legs during the cooking stage. This will help infuse the orange taste. To add even more orange taste to the duck, finely grate the zest of an orange, add it to some clear honey and use to glaze the roasted duck confit and give a sharp orange flavour.

Serves 4

4 Confit of Duck legs (see p.88)

For the Orange Sauce

300 ml (½ pint) Red Wine Sauce (see p.230)

Pared rind of 1 orange
Juice of 1 orange

For the Buttered Spinach

900 g (2 lb) spinach, picked and washed
50 g (2 oz) unsalted butter

Salt and freshly ground black pepper

To make an orange sauce, start with a red wine sauce. During the cooking of the vegetables, add the orange rind and follow the recipe until the red wine has reduced in volume. Add the orange juice and boil until reduced by three-quarters. Continue with the recipe, adding the veal *jus* or alternative, and cook for 20–30 minutes, pushing the finished sauce through a sieve. The orange sauce is now ready and has a richness helped by the red wine.

To cook the spinach, make sure all excess water has been shaken off the leaves. Melt the butter in a hot pan. Once the butter begins to bubble, add the spinach and stir with a wooden spoon, keeping the pan at a high temperature. The spinach will cook very quickly. After 2–3 minutes, season the spinach with salt and pepper. Drain off any excess liquor and the spinach is ready.

To serve spinach with the duck it's nice to divide the spinach between individual plates or bowls and sit each glazed duck leg confit on top. Just finish by pouring the orange sauce around.

Peppered Confit of Duck with Peppercorn Sauce

Cook the duck legs as for the basic salted recipe (see p.88). Once cooked and removed from the fat, sprinkle finely crushed black peppercorns on top of each leg. The legs can now be roasted and glazed.

SERVES 4

4 Confit of Duck legs (see p.88)

For the Peppercorn Sauce

2 teaspoons green peppercorns, lightly crushed
2 shallots, finely chopped
25 g (1 oz) unsalted butter
50 ml (2 fl oz) brandy

1 glass dry white wine
300 ml (10 fl oz) Veal *Jus* (see p.224) or alternative (see p.226)
150 ml (5 fl oz) double cream

To make a peppercorn sauce, cook the peppercorns and shallots in the butter until just softened. Add the brandy and boil to reduce until almost dry. Add the white wine and boil to reduce until almost dry. Add the veal *jus* or alternative, bring the sauce to the simmer and cook gently for 20 minutes. Add the double cream (it will not curdle) and continue to cook and simmer for a few minutes. You should now have a good sauce consistency with a *café au lait* (milky coffee) colour.

Boiled Collar of Bacon on Mustard Mashed Potatoes with Chive Liquor

I enjoy boiled bacon dishes. The beauty of boiling meat is that it creates its own stock as it cooks, which then becomes the base for the sauce.

Mashed potatoes go well with this dish. I normally don't even tamper with mash, but mustard and bacon are good friends and using them to flavour the potatoes gives them a real bite. You can choose whatever mustard you prefer, but I recommend grain, Dijon or English. My favourite is Dijon mash; not too hot but packed with flavour.

The combination of mustard mashed potatoes and bacon works so well. The potatoes eat equally well with almost any form of pork – roast leg or loin, sausages, or braised belly are just a few.

SERVES 4–6

900 g–1.5 kg (2–3 lb) smoked bacon
    collar, rolled and rind removed
1 onion, roughly chopped
2 carrots, roughly chopped
2 celery sticks, roughly chopped
½ leek, roughly chopped
1 bay leaf
1.2–1.75 litres (2–3 pints) Chicken
    Stock (see p.222) or water

100 g (4 oz) unsalted butter
Salt and freshly ground white pepper
675–900 g (1½–2 lb) Mashed Potatoes
    (see p.133)
About 1 tablespoon Dijon mustard
1 tablespoon snipped fresh chives

Soak the bacon in water for 24 hours before cooking to reduce the salt content.

Sit the bacon in a pan with the vegetables and bay leaf. Cover with the stock or water. Bring to the simmer and continue to simmer for 1–1½ hours. Leave to rest in the liquor for 20–30 minutes.

Drain off 600 ml (1 pint) of the stock, bring to the boil and boil until reduced by half. Whisk in a spoonful of butter at a time to make a creamy sauce; you may find that 75 g (3 oz) is enough. You can use a hand blender to give a creamier consistency. Season with salt and pepper.

Add some mustard to the mashed potatoes a teaspoon at a time, tasting as you go until you have the mustard flavour you want. Spoon the potatoes on to plates. Add the chives to the liquor and spoon round the mash. Carve the bacon, two slices per portion, and arrange on top of the potatoes.

Home-made Pork Pie

A lot of dishes, like this one and the corned beef, sound hard work and you may think there is no point going to all that trouble when there are so many varieties available to buy. In fact, both recipes are very simple, and there's a great feeling of satisfaction when eating the home-made versions. They will never have the artificial pink colour that most bought varieties have. Your pork pie will have a natural colour with just a tinge of pink when finished (see p.62).

The meat I use for this recipe is belly pork, bought already skinned and boned. If you're buying from a butcher then try and get the pork coarsely minced. The pork pie filling must be made before the pastry as hot water crust must be moulded while still warm. The pork pie can be made as a raised pie or flan-style pie. The mould I am using is 18 cm (7 in) diameter by 7.5 cm (3 in) deep. If you don't have a deep pie mould or dish use a 25 cm (10 in) flan ring or mould and follow the same method, but cook for about 1–1½ hours.

To finish the pie, it's best to fill the mould with a jelly made by using a good Chicken Stock (see p.222) boiled to reduce from 1.5 litres (2½ pints) to 900 ml (1½ pints). Alternatively you can use a pork stock by cooking three or four pig's trotters in water for a few hours. This will create its own jelly that can be helped, if needed, with the addition of 15 g (½ oz) of gelatine per 600 ml (1 pint) of stock.

SERVES 8

25 g (1 oz) unsalted butter
2 onions, finely chopped
1 teaspoon chopped fresh sage
1 teaspoon chopped fresh thyme
1 level teaspoon ground mace
½ teaspoon dried English mustard
½ teaspoon dried mixed spice

900 g (2 lb) pork belly, coarsely minced
 or chopped
Salt and freshly ground white pepper
1 egg, beaten
900 ml–1.2 litres (1½–2 pints) jellied
 stock

For the Pastry

600 ml (1 pint) water
100 g (4 oz) lard

450 g (1 lb) plain flour

Melt the butter in a pan. Once the butter begins to bubble, add the chopped onions and cook for a few minutes, without colouring, until just softened. While the onions are still warm, add the sage, thyme, mace, mustard and mixed spice. Allow to cool. Mix the onions and spices with the minced pork, making sure the meat is not over-beaten as this will break down the fat content and texture. Season generously with salt and pepper. It's important to make sure the mix is highly seasoned at the raw stage, as serving it cold will reduce the strength of the seasoning. Leave the filling in the fridge.

Pre-heat the oven to 220°C/425°F/gas 7. Grease a pie mould and place it on a baking sheet.

Bring the water and lard to the boil. Sift the flour with a generous pinch of salt into a bowl, leaving a well in the centre. Pour in the boiling water and lard and stir in the flour to form a dough. Knead lightly by hand (the pastry will be very warm) to give a smooth dough. Keep a quarter of the pastry warm to one side, then work the rest of the pastry on a lightly floured table by hand or with a rolling pin until just under 5 mm (¼ in) thick. Sit the pastry into the mould and work by hand, starting from the centre and gently pushing out to make the pastry thinner and to fill the mould. The finished pastry should be about 3 mm (⅛ in) thick and 5 mm (¼ in) above the top of the mould.

Fill the mould with the pork filling, packing it in just above the top of the mould. Fold the pastry around the top on to the mix and brush with the beaten egg. Roll out the remaining pastry to the same thickness and sit on top of the pie, pressing the edges together and cutting off any excess. Using a small cylinder pastry cutter or piping nozzle, cut a hole in the centre and leave the cutter or nozzle sitting in the hole. The border of the pie can be pinched or pushed with a fork to give a simple patterned edge. Brush the pie with beaten egg.

Bake the pie immediately in the hot oven for 20 minutes, then reduce the oven temperature to 190°C/375°F/gas 5 and cook for a further 1½–2 hours (30 minutes less if you are using a shallow mould). During the first 20 minutes the pie may colour very quickly. Once it's reached golden stage cover lightly with tin foil, only covering the top and not the sides as this will slow down the cooking time.

Test whether the pie is ready either by feeling the filling through the hole in the centre – the mix should be firm to the touch – or inserting a knife into the filling. It should feel tender and the knife will still be clean. Remove the pie from the oven and leave to cool for 30 minutes.

During cooking, the pork filling will have shrunk a little, leaving a border to be filled with jelly. Using a funnel or jug, pour 300 ml (10 fl oz) of the jelly stock into the pie. It will be absorbed by the meat, giving it a moister finish. Leave the pie to finish cooling, by which time the stock will be almost at jelly stage. Pour in the remaining stock until filled and jellied. It's now best to keep the pie in the fridge. See, it was worth it!

Boiled Collar of Bacon with Home-made Sauerkraut

Sauerkraut is a warm pickled cabbage. I used to eat sauerkraut a lot when I lived in Amsterdam in the late 70s and also when visiting my brother who lived in Germany. We would always have grilled bratwurst sausage with sauerkraut in a roll. I think these were the German answer to hotdogs and ketchup!

Sauerkraut is often cooked with bacon to help the flavour. I decided to keep the sauerkraut 'vegetarian'. Serve it with the boiled bacon and mustard seed sauce.

Serves 4–6

900–1500 g (2-3 lb) bacon collar - boned, skinned, rolled and tied
1 onion, roughly chopped
2 carrots, roughly chopped
2 celery sticks, roughly chopped
1 bay leaf

Chicken Stock (see p. 222) or water to cover bacon
150 ml (5 fl oz) double cream
25 g (1 oz) unsalted butter
1–2 teaspoons mustard seed
Salt and freshly ground white pepper

For the Sauerkraut

1 medium white cabbage, finely shredded
150 ml (5 fl oz) white wine
150 ml (5 fl oz) white wine vinegar

Bouquet garni (2 teaspoons pickling spice, 2 teaspoons lightly crushed juniper berries, a pinch of thyme)
25 g (1 oz) unsalted butter
3 onions, sliced

To start the sauerkraut, place the shredded cabbage in a bowl with the wine and vinegar. Tie the bouquet garni ingredients in a square of muslin and add to the bowl. Leave to marinate for 48 hours, turning occasionally to make sure all the cabbage is marinated. This will give it a good pickly texture and taste.

Soak the bacon in water for 24 hours before boiling. Soaking the bacon releases excess salt content, leaving a better and less salty taste.

Once soaked, remove and wash the collar, and place in a pan with the vegetables, bay leaf and stock or water. Bring to the simmer and continue to simmer for 1-1½ hours. Once cooked, the bacon should be left to rest in the liquor for 20 minutes to relax the meat and make it more tender.

To make the mustard seed sauce, take 600 ml (1 pint) of the cooking liquor and boil to reduce by half. Add the cream and cook for 10 minutes. Add the butter and mustard seed to taste. Check for seasoning with salt and pepper.

To finish the sauerkraut, drain off the liquor and keep to one side. Melt the butter in a pan and add the sliced onions. Allow to cook on a medium heat with no browning until slightly softened. Add the white cabbage, bouquet garni and 2-3 tablespoons of the liquor and cover with a lid. Cook on a medium heat, stirring from time to time. As the cabbage is cooking the pickling liquor will start to evaporate. Add some more liquor a little at a time until the cabbage becomes tender. This will take about 20 minutes. The cabbage should be tender but still have a slight bite. Season with salt and pepper.

To serve the dish, spoon some sauerkraut on to plates. Remove the bacon from the liquor and carve, allowing either one thick or two thinner slices per person. Sit the bacon on top of the cabbage and spoon some liquor over to add some extra moisture to the meat. The dish can now be finished with either extra liquor or the mustard seed cream sauce.

*Boiled Collar of Bacon with Home-made Sauerkraut
and mustard seed sauce.*

Roast Leg of Pork

Roasting must be one of Britain's most popular cooking methods, especially on Sundays, and pork is a particular favourite. In fact it was one of the meats served at Christmas before turkeys were introduced from America. Roast pork and apple sauce is delicious if the pork has been cooked so that it stays succulent and the skin turns to crackling. You can also mix apple sauce with cranberry sauce to eat with pork (or as a dip for the crackling). When I'm cooking pork I like to sit the leg on pork bones (if you can get them) to protect the meat, or you can use halved onions. The quantity of pork here serves at least ten people but you can, of course, use a smaller cut to suit your own needs.

SERVES 10 or more

3.5–4.5 kg (8–10 lb) leg of pork	4 onions, halved
Lard or cooking oil	600 ml (1 pint) Veal *Jus* (see p.224) or
Salt	alternative (see p.226)
Pork bones (optional)	Salt and freshly ground black pepper

Pre-heat the oven to 200°C/400°F/gas 6–7.

To achieve a good, crisp crackling, the skin on the leg must be scored just deep enough to break through. Brush with lard or cooking oil and sprinkle fairly liberally with salt.

Sit the leg on a few pork bones in a roasting pan. Alternatively, sit the pork on halved onions with the skin left on, placing them face down. The onions not only protect the meat but also slowly cook, absorbing some of the pork juices. Leaving on the skins holds them together. Roast the pork for about 20–30 minutes by which time the pork will have started colouring and crisping. Once it has reached the golden stage, loosely sit a piece of foil on top to prevent it from becoming too dark; don't overtighten it or the leg will create steam underneath and you won't get a crispy crackling. Roast for a further 3 hours, then remove the foil and finish cooking for about 30 minutes until the meat is tender and the crackling has crisped even more. Allow the meat to rest for 20–30 minutes before removing the crackling and carving the meat. A leg of pork this size will always take at least 4 hours to cook.

Once the pork has cooked, pour off any excess fat and add some gravy to collect all the taste from the cooking juices. The onion flavour comes through to lift the gravy. Spoon the onions out of their skins, season with salt and pepper and serve as a vegetable to go with the pork; they are packed with flavour.

Pork Crackling and Scratchings

Roast pork is so good to eat, but I think the best bit is the crackling – good, crunchy, salted pork flavour.

To get good, crispy crackling, the skin has to be scored with a sharp knife just deep enough to break through. Brush the skin lightly with cooking oil or lard, then sprinkle liberally with salt before roasting. The salt will draw any water from the skin and leave a very crisp finish.

I also like to make crackling or scratchings without any meat attached (see overleaf). Ask the butcher for some pork rind, preferably from the loin, and cut off any excess fat underneath. Score and salt the skin and roast in a pre-heated oven at 200°C/400°F/gas 6. The rind will take 30–40 minutes to become crunchy.

To make scratchings, instead of scoring the rind, remove the fat and cut it into 5 mm (¼ in) strips, then sprinkle with salt. Bake in the pre-heated oven for about 30 minutes. It's nice to offer your own scratchings with pre-dinner drinks or use them in a starter for a meal. I like to make a pork scratching and apple salad. Simply quarter some apples and cut again into eight. Fry and toss them in butter, giving a little colour, for 2–3 minutes. Sit them around the plate with warm pork scratchings and mix some snipped fresh chives with Basic Vinaigrette (see p.241) to spoon over. Dress the centre of the plate with mixed salad leaves tossed in dressing.

At Christmas, if you've got some roast pork and crackling left over, use up the crackling in this salad. You can also spoon some Cranberry Sauce (see p.239) into the centre of the plate, dressing the salad leaves on top.

OPPOSITE *Home-made Pork Scratchings in the foreground, and Crackling (see p.97).*

RIGHT *Seared Spicy Pork Belly (see p.100) served with Fried Spinach, Mushrooms and Beansprouts (see p.144).*

BELOW *Hocks and Hands (see p.101).*

Seared Spicy Pork Belly

Pork belly is quite a cheap cut of meat and, I think, highly underrated. Belly slices are wonderful roasted or barbecued, they have a great balance of meat and pork fat content which helps them 'crisp up' during cooking (see preceding page). Well, for this recipe I'm not using the strips but instead squares of belly that have all bone and skin removed. It should be no problem to ask the butcher to cut some for you, but make sure they do remove all skin and bone. The squares you need should be about 7.5 cm (3 in). Teriyaki marinade is available in most large supermarkets; you'll find it near the soy sauce. The pork almost tastes Chinese; it has a good spicy flavour and eats very well with just buttered noodles or with Fried Spinach, Mushrooms and Beansprouts (see p.144).

SERVES 4

4 pork belly squares, prepared as above	4–5 tablespoons of Basic Vinaigrette (see p.241)
1 tablespoon olive oil	
4 teaspoons clear honey	4–6 spring onions

For the Spicy Marinade

150 ml (5 fl oz) teriyaki marinade	2 garlic cloves, sliced
85 ml (3 fl oz) soy sauce	50 g (2 oz) root ginger, finely diced or grated
1 teaspoon Tabasco sauce	
3 tablespoons Worcestershire sauce	

Score the pork belly squares diagonally on the fat side about 3 mm (⅛ in) deep. They should also be scored very lightly underneath. The pork is now ready for marinating.

To make the marinade, simply mix all the ingredients together. Reserve 3 tablespoons to use in the finished dressing, then pour the rest over the pork, turning from time to time. The pork only needs to marinate for 24 hours before cooking. It can, of course, be left longer but this will increase the taste of the spices which could become too strong.

Pre-heat the oven to 200°C/400°F/gas 6.

To cook the pork, heat the olive oil in a roasting pan and add the pork fat-side down over a medium heat. The fat will start to colour almost immediately, giving a rich roasted/seared colour. Continue to colour until quite dark. Turn the pork and cook in the pre-heated oven for about 15–20 minutes. The cooking time will really depend on the thickness of the belly.

Once cooked, spoon the honey on top and glaze under a hot grill. Remove the pork and leave to rest for a few minutes. Mix any excess honey in the pan with the reserved marinade and the vinaigrette dressing and strain through a sieve. Cut the spring onions into small, thin oval pieces. Slice the pork into thin slices and sit in the bowl. Spoon the marinade dressing over and sprinkle with the spring onions.

Knuckles and Hocks, Hands and Scrag Ends

Knuckle, hocks and hands of pork or lamb scrag ends are all 'rough' cuts of meat. Although cheap, they are are packed with flavour, especially when slow roasted and served with gravy (see p.99).

Any of these cuts can be roasted in a medium oven at about 180°C/350°F/gas 4 for 2–2½ hours.

Hand of pork (from the shoulder with the trotter removed) can be bought on or off the bone. Once scored and tied, it is ready to cook. If it's salted and slowly roasted, you will have some very crispy crackling and moist pork underneath. Sliced and served with mustard or apple sauce, it eats really well. It's a brilliant cut to roast and just sit and pick at, or break off crackling, tear the meat and eat it in a French stick sandwich with the bread soaking up all the juices. The same can be done with the other joints.

Scrag ends of lamb are normally casseroled, but a knuckle is for roasting and eats well if glazed with honey and mint.

These are cuts of meat we should use more often. If you have four knuckles of lamb roasted off for a Sunday lunch and you sit them in a bowl and plonk them on the table, I promise you everyone will be excited and delighted by the messy eating!

Breast of Lamb with a Mustard and Herb Crust

Breast of lamb is a cut of meat taken from the belly. It's quite cheap and is packed with flavour. When buying lamb breasts, make sure the lamb has been skinned, boned and any excess fat has been removed. One breast will give you enough for two portions. Once cut in two, roll the lamb lengthways and tie tightly. Lamb breasts are usually roasted or cut into chunks and braised. This dish holds several cooking methods: frying, braising and grilling. It's braised in a stock and can be cooked a few days in advance and kept in its jellied stock. You can add any lamb bones to the stock during cooking to increase the lamb flavour.

SERVES 4

4 portions of lamb breast, rolled and tied
2 tablespoons lamb fat or cooking oil
50 g (2 oz) unsalted butter
1 garlic clove, crushed
1 sprig of fresh thyme
1 sprig of fresh rosemary
A few fresh sage leaves
1 onion, diced
2 carrots, diced
2 celery sticks, diced

½ leek, diced
1.2–1.75 litres (2–3 pints) Chicken Stock (see p.222)
A few lamb bones (optional)
1 teaspoon chopped mixed thyme, sage and rosemary
1 quantity Basic Crumble Mix (see p.114)
2–4 teaspoons Dijon or grain mustard
150 ml (5 fl oz) double cream

Heat a frying-pan and colour the lamb breasts in the fat or oil. Melt half the butter in a braising pan and fry the garlic, herbs and vegetables slowly for a few minutes. Add the stock and lamb bones, if using. Bring to the simmer. Add the lamb breasts and simmer until tender; this will take about 2 hours.

Once cooked, the lamb can be left in the stock and jellied (to use later) or taken out of the stock and finished with the crust.

Add the chopped mixed herbs to the crumble mix and flavour with 1–2 teaspoons of mustard.

Cut the meat into 1 cm (½ in) slices and separate into portions. Push the slices together, just slightly parted at an angle. Top with the herb crust and crisp under a hot grill until golden brown.

To make the sauce, reduce some of the cooking liquor to about 300 ml (10 fl oz). Thicken with the remaining butter and add the double cream, cooking for 5–10 minutes, then add 1–2 teaspoons of mustard and serve.

Breast of Lamb with a Mustard and Herb Crust.

Roast Best End of Lamb with a Parsnip Crumble

The best end of lamb can be ordered from your butcher. If you ask for a pair of best ends and want them chined (split), this will leave you with two best ends, which are like two fillets of lamb with bones attached. If you cut between the bones, this gives you lamb cutlets, and although you can use cutlets for this recipe, I prefer to leave the meat on the bone or as whole fillets before roasting; this will give a totally different taste and texture to the meat. Ask for the lamb to be French-trimmed to the eye of the meat and all fat removed; this means that the bones are clean. You now have the two meat fillets with individual bones attached. Split both through the middle leaving four roasting joints with about three bones attached on each (any excess bones can be cut off).

Serves 4

2 best ends of lamb, split, French-trimmed and fat removed
Salt and freshly ground black pepper
1 tablespoon cooking fat

1 quantity Parsnip Crumble (see p.117)
300 ml (10 fl oz) Red Wine Sauce (see p.230)

Pre-heat the oven to 200°C/400°F/gas 6.

Season the meat with salt and pepper, then colour it in the cooking fat in a hot pan on top of the stove. Once coloured, transfer to a roasting tin in the pre-heated oven and roast until medium rare. This will take 8–10 minutes, longer if you prefer the lamb a little more cooked. To test the meat, simply press between thumb and forefinger; the meat should feel tender and just give when pressure is applied. The lamb should now be left to rest for about 10 minutes before carving and serving, as this will give the meat a softer texture.

Meanwhile, shape the crumbles in individual rings. Finish in the hot oven or under the grill until golden and crunchy.

Carve between the bones, giving three roasted cutlets per portion. Sit the lamb on top of the individual parsnip crumbles and pour the red wine sauce around.

Roast Best End of Lamb with a Leek and Mustard Crumble

Here is another way of serving the best end of lamb. It's simple to cook. Just follow the lamb preparation and cooking instructions on p.104.

Best ends of lamb also eat well and cook a little quicker if the meat is off the bone. Providing that the lamb is French-trimmed, you can simply cut the meat away from the bone, leaving lamb fillets. Once cooked, these can be sliced either across or lengthways.

The Leek and Mustard Crumble works very well as part of the main dish or as a separate vegetable accompaniment.

SERVES 4

2 best ends of lamb, split, French-trimmed and fat removed
1 quantity Leek and Mustard Crumble (see p.116)

300 ml (10 fl oz) Red Wine Sauce (see p.230)

Roast the lamb (see p.104) and prepare and cook the crumbles in individual rings (see p.119). Arrange the crumbles on a serving plate and sit the roast lamb on top. Pour the red wine sauce around.

Peppered Lamb Fillet with Mint and Caper Sauce

The pepper flavour works really well with the sweetness of lamb, without being overpowering. This dish is packed with lots of different flavours, all of which you can still identify and taste. I use a standard pepper mill to grind the peppercorns, then shake them through a sieve to keep out any large pieces. The lamb fillet I use is from the best end of lamb, which is the joint lamb cutlets come from. All I've done is take the meat completely off the bone.

You don't have to follow this recipe exactly. The same idea can be used for roasting a leg of lamb. Roll it in the pepper and roast it as normal. When the joint is carved, every slice will have a wonderful pepper taste. You can make the same sauce or just flavour your lamb gravy with mint and capers.

Spinach eats very well with this dish, as do Fondant Potatoes (see p.134), which help to mop up the sauce.

SERVES 4

2 fillets from best end of lamb	Salt and freshly ground black pepper
Black or white peppercorns, crushed and sieved	1 tablespoon cooking oil or fat

For the Sauce (serves 8–10)

1 large shallot or ½ onion, roughly chopped	2–3 glasses red wine
1 carrot, roughly chopped	600 ml (1 pint) Veal *Jus* (see p.224) or alternative (see p.226)
1 celery stick, roughly chopped	1 bay leaf
1 tablespoon unsalted butter	2 teaspoons fine capers
12 fresh mint leaves	

Pre-heat the oven to 220°C/425°F/gas 7.

To make the sauce, cook the vegetables and bay leaf in the butter until softened and lightly coloured. Add the mint and wine and boil to reduce by three-quarters. Add the *jus* or gravy, bring to the boil and simmer gently for 20 minutes. Season with salt and pepper and strain. The sauce should have a slight mint flavour. Add the capers just before serving.

Meanwhile, cut the fillets in half, giving you four individual portions. Roll them in the crushed peppercorns, shaking off any excess. Season with salt. Heat a roasting pan with the oil or fat and fry the lamb for 1–2 minutes, sealing and colouring all over. Finish the lamb in the pre-heated oven for about 6–8 minutes to cook the lamb to medium. If you want the meat rarer, cook for 5 minutes, or allow 10–12 minutes if you like it well done.

Always allow meat to rest for 5–10 minutes once it is cooked; this will make it more tender to eat. Carve the meat and serve it with the caper *jus*.

Variations

You can make the sauce without the vegetables, just by reducing the red wine with the mint, then adding the *jus*.

Peppered Lamb Fillet with Mint and Caper Sauce served with Fondant Potatoes (see p.134).

Stewed Venison with Vegetables in Red Wine

Venison for stewing should come from the haunch, or you can use neck. I like to cut the meat into large pieces rather than dice. It takes a little longer to cook but the texture and taste are better.

SERVES 4

900 g (2 lb) haunch of venison
1 tablespoon cooking fat or oil
450 g (1 lb) onions, sliced
1 sprig of fresh thyme
1 bay leaf
A few juniper berries, lightly crushed

A few black peppercorns, lightly crushed
1 bottle red wine
900 ml–1.2 litres (1½–2 pints) Veal *Jus* (p.224) or alternative (see p.226)
Salt and freshly ground black pepper

For the Garnish

225–275 g (8–10 oz) button onions
1 tablespoon cooking fat
3 carrots

4 celery sticks
6 flat or open cup mushrooms

Cut the venison into chunks and colour in the fat in a hot frying-pan until completely sealed; remove from the pan. Cook the onions with the thyme, bay leaf, juniper berries and peppercorns for a few minutes. Add half the red wine and boil to reduce until almost dry. Add the *jus* and venison, bring to the simmer, then cook gently for 1½–2 hours, skimming occasionally. Add a tablespoon or two of water if the sauce becomes too thick.

When the stew is almost ready, fry the onions until well coloured. While they are colouring, quarter the carrots lengthways, then cut at an angle into 2 cm (¾ in) pieces. Slice the celery and quarter the mushrooms. Remove the onions from the pan. Add the carrots and celery and colour lightly. Add them to the onions. Add the mushrooms to the pan and fry for a few minutes, then return all the vegetables to the pan and cover with the remaining wine. Boil to reduce until almost dry. The vegetables should now be cooked.

Remove the meat from the sauce and strain the sauce through a sieve. Return the meat to the sauce and check for seasoning with salt and pepper. Add the vegetables to the meat and serve the dish as a stew, or sit the meat in bowls and top with the braised vegetables with the sauce spooned over.

Variations

To enrich the stew, redcurrant jelly can be added to sweeten the sauce; or a spoonful of Dijon or English mustard or a dash of Worcestershire sauce or mushroom ketchup.

The dish can also be turned into a pie by spooning the stew into a pie dish and topping with Shortcrust Pastry (see p.211) or Puff Pastry (see p.212).

You can adapt the recipe to use pheasant, grouse or other game birds.

Another venison dish I enjoy is roasted loin cooked pink, then carved and set on top of a basic Bubble and Squeak (see p.118) or Beetroot Bubble and Squeak (see p.140). Pour some Red Wine Sauce (see p.230) around and the dish is ready.

Venison also eats well with Celeriac and Potato Dauphinoise (see p.136).

Venison Dumplings

You can make these dumplings to serve with the Stewed Venison (see p.108). The offal will give a good, strong, gamey flavour, but if you're not too keen on offal, replace it with 175 g (6 oz) finely chopped or minced black pudding. This will give a strong flavour and can be used in so many other stews or braised dishes, with pork, chicken, duck or lamb.

Serves 4

50 g (2 oz) venison heart, coarsely minced
50 g (2 oz) venison liver, coarsely minced
50 g (2 oz) venison kidney, coarsely minced
2 tablespoons finely chopped onion cooked in butter
½ teaspoon chopped fresh sage and thyme

100 g (4 oz) shredded suet
225 g (8 oz) self-raising flour
4–5 juniper berries, crushed
A pinch of salt
50–85 ml (2–3 fl oz) water
1 egg
300 ml (10 fl oz) Chicken Stock (see p.222) or water

Mix the offal with the chopped onions, herbs, suet, flour, juniper berries and salt. Mix with the water and egg to a reasonably firm dough. Roll into balls and poach in stock or water for 20 minutes. The dumplings can then be added to a stew.

Home-made Corned Beef

You may be surprised to find that this really is a simple recipe. It just needs a little advanced planning as the beef must be soaked for three days before cooking. Corned beef is readily available for everyone, but it's so good to eat it home-made. The texture is similar to a standard corned beef, but this recipe isn't quite as pink in colour. The pig's trotters are optional but will help to create a jelly in the cooking liquor.

Corned beef is lovely to eat with chutney for tea or supper, or to break into pieces to make corned beef hash, fried with onions and potatoes. Hash is good for a cooked breakfast or lunch/supper dish.

The recipe I'm giving is using 2.25 kg (5 lb) of beef. This can be cut down in half but any smaller quantities won't really give you the right balance of beef meat and fat.

SERVES 8

2.25 kg (5 lb) beef flank
1.75 litres (3 pints) cold water
75–100 g (3–4 oz) salt

2 pig's trotters (optional)
25 g (1 oz) gelatine leaves or powder
(optional)

Trim the beef flank of all visible sinews but leave it as a whole piece. Mix the water and 75 g (3 oz) of salt to create brine. To test the strength of the brine, sit a raw new potato in the water; the potato should float. If it won't float, simply add the remaining salt, or more if needed. Sit the beef in the brine and chill for 3 days.

Remove the meat from the brine and wash it, discarding the salt water. Sit the meat in a clean pan with the pig's trotters, if using. Top up with fresh water. Bring to the boil, then simmer for 2½–3 hours, skimming any impurities from the liquor.

Once cooked, remove the meat from the liquor. Drain the cooking liquor through a fine sieve and taste; it should have a good beef flavour. Discard the trotters. Bring the stock to the boil and boil to reduce in volume, and increase its flavour and jelly content. Test the stock/jelly by spooning on to a small plate and placing in the fridge. The jelly must set very firm to enable it to hold the beef together. If it doesn't set firm enough, then add some or all of the gelatine to the mix. Only about 600–900 ml (1–1½ pints) of finished jelly stock will be needed. Make sure you do test the stock/jelly first as the dish is better if only set using natural jellies.

While the beef is still warm, break it down into pieces. The meat will almost separate itself between sinew strips. Any excess sinew can be removed, but make sure that all fat content is kept. The meat can now be pushed through a large mincer plate (5–10 mm/ ¼–½ in) or chopped by hand with the fat. Mix the meat with 600 ml (1 pint) of reduced liquor and check the consistency. The meat should absorb the liquor and be left reasonably loose. If the mix is too firm, add another 300 ml (10 fl oz) of stock. Taste the corned beef before setting in a mould and correct the seasoning with salt and pepper. The mix can now be pressed firmly into a terrine mould or bowl and set in the fridge overnight.

Once set, turn out the corned beef and serve with a salad and pickle, fried for breakfast or turn it into a corned beef hash.

Home-made Corned Beef.

Ox Cheek Stew with Neeps and Tatties

Ox cheeks are an unusual cut of beef with a good, open texture which is ideal for braising or stewing as it enables the beef to absorb all the sauce and liquor. If you can't find a butcher to offer you the cheeks, then just use large pieces of chuck steak. This is similar in texture and will work well in this recipe.

SERVES 4–6

1.1–1.5 kg (2½–3 lb) ox cheeks, trimmed of all fat and sinew
Salt and freshly ground black pepper
2 tablespoons cooking fat
2 large onions, sliced
1 small garlic clove, crushed
1 sprig of fresh thyme

1 bay leaf
1 bottle red wine
900 ml–1.2 litres (1½–2 pints) Veal *Jus* (see p.224) or alternative (see p.226)
450 g (1 lb) shallots
2 tablespoons unsalted butter

For the Neeps and Tatties

450 g (1 lb) swedes
450 g (1 lb) potatoes

100 g (4 oz) unsalted butter

Season the ox cheeks with salt and pepper. Pre-heat a frying-pan and add a little cooking fat. Fry the cheeks until well coloured on all sides. Remove from the pan and drain off excess fat or liquor. Colour the sliced onions in a braising pan until well coloured. Add the garlic, thyme, bay leaf and half the red wine. Bring to the boil and boil to reduce until almost dry. Add the veal *jus* and ox cheeks and bring to the simmer. Braise the cheeks slowly for 1½–2 hours until tender.

While the cheeks are cooking, split the peeled shallots in half lengthways and cook in a very little butter until well coloured (almost burnt). Add the remaining red wine and reduce until almost dry.

Meanwhile, cook the swedes and potatoes separately in boiling salted water until tender. (I also like to add carrots to this recipe which gives a slightly sweeter flavour.) Drain and leave to dry for a few minutes. Lightly mash the vegetables or stir with a wooden spoon to give a coarse purée. If you prefer a smoother finish push the vegetables through a sieve. Add the butter and season with salt and pepper.

Once the cheeks are cooked, remove them from the sauce and drain the sauce through a sieve. Re-heat the cheeks in the finished sauce and spoon into serving bowls. The shallots can be mixed with the stew or sat on top to finish. Serve with the neeps and tatties.

Vegetarian Dishes

I often find that vegetarian dishes are either not given enough thought or far too much, and are totally overdone with too many garnishes. My feelings about all dishes are that nothing should be added unless it's going to enhance the flavours.

All our eating habits and moods change. Whenever I have a 'pub lunch' (and it's not often enough!) I always go for the vegetarian dish of the day. It's usually a vegetable cottage pie, pasta dish or quiche and I always enjoy it.

A quiche is easy and simple to make, so I decided to make a feature with vegetarian tarts all using the same base mixture. The scope is endless; so many different flavours can be added to give totally different results. Another dish that also has a lot of variety is a vegetarian crumble, these can be complete meals on their own or accompaniments to a main course dish.

Basic Crumble Mix

This recipe really couldn't be simpler. It's just two ingredients held together with butter and, of course, seasoned with salt and pepper. The nicest thing about it is that it lends itself to so many flavour combinations: from parsley and lemon to horseradish or mustard and herbs. If you are using additional flavours, add them before stirring in the shallot butter. All these flavours work well with fish, meat or vegetarian dishes.

It's best to use sliced bread that is 24 hours old, as this will firm the bread slightly and prevent the crumbs from becoming doughy.

SERVES 4

6–8 slices white bread
25–50 g (1–2 oz) unsalted butter, melted
2 large shallots or ½ onion, finely
    chopped

Salt and freshly ground black pepper

Remove and discard the crusts from the bread and cut into quarters. The quickest way to turn these slices into crumbs is to blitz in a food processor. If you don't have a food processor, simply push the slices through a metal sieve.

Melt the butter with the chopped shallots and bring to the simmer, remove from the heat and leave to cool.

Gradually spoon some of the shallot butter into the crumbs, mixing all the time. The mix will be ready when it holds once pressed together, but it should still stay free-flowing.

Use the crumble as directed in the following recipes.

Spinach and Horseradish Crumble

This crumble recipe has the sharp tang of horseradish which goes so well with the buttered spinach. I've used this with lots of dishes, especially roast meats, grilled herrings or salmon.

SERVES 4

1 quantity Basic Crumble Mix (see p.114)
2 tablespoons horseradish sauce
25–50 g (1–2 oz) unsalted butter

900 g (2 lb) fresh spinach, washed and picked
Salt and freshly ground white pepper
Freshly grated nutmeg (optional)

Follow the recipe for the basic crumble, only using a maximum of 25 g (1 oz) of butter. Mix the horseradish sauce with the crust mix and taste, adding a little more if you like a stronger taste.

Cook the spinach at the last moment for the maximum taste, and cook it quickly. Heat a large, shallow pan and add the butter. As soon as the butter is bubbling, add the spinach, increasing the heat. Stir lightly with a wooden spoon to ensure even cooking. The leaves will immediately start to break down and will be cooked within 1–2 minutes. Season with salt, pepper and nutmeg, if using. If the spinach has produced a lot of liquor, drain it into a small pan and boil to reduce, then return it to the spinach. Spoon the spinach into a buttered flameproof vegetable dish and cover with the horseradish crumble mix. Finish under the grill until golden brown.

Variations

Herbs can be added to the crumbs: parsley, tarragon, thyme or sage will all work well.

You can reserve the spinach liquor and blitz in a little butter with a hand blender to create a spinach butter sauce. This works well with grilled herrings.

It is best to make this dish at the last minute, but there is an alternative. Plunge the spinach into boiling salted water for about 1–2 minutes until just tender, then drain and refresh in ice-cold water. Squeeze any excess water from the spinach, add a knob of softened butter and season with salt, pepper and nutmeg. Spoon into a flameproof, microwave vegetable dish and cover with the crust mix. Before serving, re-heat the whole dish in the microwave, then colour and crisp under the grill.

Leek and Mustard Crumble on Cheesey Mashed Potatoes

This recipe can be adapted to so many dishes, plus it's a complete vegetarian meal on its own. You can even make it without the cheesey mashed potatoes and still have a great accompaniment to many simple meat or fish dishes.

Serves 4–6

100 g (4 oz) unsalted butter
2 onions, sliced
150 ml (5 fl oz) Vegetable Stock (see p.223)
450–675 g (1–1½ lb) leeks, split and sliced
2 teaspoons chopped fresh parsley
2 teaspoons chopped fresh tarragon

1 quantity Basic Crumble Mix (see p.114)
2 teaspoons grain mustard
450–675 g (1–1½ lb) Mashed Potatoes (see p.133)
100–225 g (4–8 oz) Cheddar, grated
Salt and freshly ground white pepper

Pre-heat the oven to 200°C/400°F/gas 6.

Melt 25 g (1 oz) of butter in a pan. When the butter begins to bubble, add the sliced onions and cook for a few minutes over a medium heat until slightly softened. Add the stock and bring to the boil. Add the leeks, return to the boil and cook for 30 seconds. Strain off the leeks and onions, keeping the stock. Boil the stock until reduced by half to increase its flavour.

To finish the crust mix, add the chopped parsley and tarragon to the mix, then add the grain mustard to taste.

Warm the mashed potatoes with 100 g (4 oz) of the grated Cheddar until melted. I prefer the cheese flavour to be stronger, so continue to stir in the cheese until you have the flavour you want. Check for seasoning with salt and pepper.

Spoon the mashed potatoes into a large vegetable dish. Warm the onions and leeks in a teaspoon of the vegetable liquor, then spoon over the potatoes, and finish with the mustard seed crumble mix. Finish in the pre-heated oven or under a hot grill for about 10 minutes until the crumble is golden and crunchy.

To make the sauce, re-heat the reduced vegetable liquor and vigorously whisk in the remaining butter to give an almost creamy consistency. If you have an electric hand blender, just blitz the liquor and butter together; this will really bind the sauce. Season with salt and pepper and serve with the crumble.

Variations

Try different cheeses instead of the Cheddar; a smoked cheese tastes good.

The filling can also be left to cool and chilled and either re-heated through in the oven or microwaved.

Parsnip Crumble

If you want to make this in individual portions, divide the parsnips between four or six 10 cm (4 in) buttered flan rings, pushing the parsnips in so they almost mould together.

SERVES 4–6

900 g (2 lb) parsnips
2 tablespoons unsalted butter or cooking fat
Salt and freshly ground black pepper

1 quantity Basic Crumble Mix (see p.114)
1 teaspoon chopped fresh thyme
1 teaspoon chopped fresh rosemary

Pre-heat the oven to 220°C/425°F/gas 7.

Peel and split the parsnips lengthways into quarters, and cut out the woody centres. To roast the parsnips, pre-heat a roasting tray on top of the stove with a little butter or cooking fat. Add the parsnips and colour until golden brown. Season with salt and pepper. Roast in the pre-heated oven for 15–20 minutes, turning occasionally for even colour and cooking. For this particular dish, the parsnips need to be slightly overcooked to help shape them into the moulds and also give the centre a purée texture while the outside remains crispy.

To make the crumble, add the herbs to the crumbs before moulding with the shallot/onion butter. Spoon the crumble over the top of the parsnips in a vegetable dish or individual rings and finish in the hot oven or under a hot grill until golden and crunchy.

Roast Parsnip and Chestnut Crumble on Bubble and Squeak

This dish makes a great alternative vegetarian Christmas lunch that includes all those familiar traditional flavours (see p.63). It can be eaten on its own, or you can use this recipe as your total accompaniment to roast turkey. It can also be made any time of the year (perhaps leaving out the chestnuts!).

You can buy cooked chestnuts in tins or frozen. If you are using fresh chestnuts in shell, you will need about 225 g (8 oz). Pre-heat the grill. Pierce the chestnuts once with a knife, then grill for about 15 minutes until the skins split. Leave to cool, then peel and chop roughly.

This dish eats very well with cranberry sauce, especially my recipe flavoured with orange and port (see p.239).

I like to make this in individual moulds, but if you don't have them, don't worry. It works just as well and looks really tasty in a large vegetable dish. Just make the bubble and squeak in the traditional way in a large frying-pan, colouring on both sides, and then spooning into the vegetable dish in the same way.

If you have decided to make this in advance and have chilled it before finishing with the crumble, then it's best to re-heat in the oven for 30 minutes before adding the crumble. Return the dish to the oven or grill until it turns golden brown.

SERVES 4

For the Parsnips

15 g (½ oz) unsalted butter
2 tablespoons cooking oil
1.1 kg (2½ lb) peeled parsnips, split into quarters lengthways and cored

Salt and freshly ground black pepper
1 tablespoon clear honey (optional)

For the Bubble and Squeak

675 g (1½ lb) Brussels sprouts
50 g (2 oz) unsalted butter
2 large onions, thinly sliced

675 g (1½ lb) Mashed Potatoes (see p.133), made without milk or cream

For the Crumble

25 g (1 oz) unsalted butter
1 large onion, finely chopped
100–175 g (4–6 oz) cooked chestnuts,
    chopped (optional)
2 tablespoons chopped fresh parsley
2 tablespoons chopped fresh sage

1 tablespoon chopped fresh thyme
175 g (6 oz) fresh white breadcrumbs

Watercress sprigs to garnish
1 quantity Vegetable Butter Sauce (see
    p.228) to serve

Pre-heat the oven to 200°C/400°F/gas 6 and grease a baking sheet.

Heat the butter and oil in a roasting pan on top of the stove, add the parsnips and fry on a medium heat, turning the parsnips until golden. Season with salt and pepper, then transfer to the pre-heated oven and roast for 15–20 minutes. The parsnips will now be deep golden brown and crispy, but almost overcooked and soft inside. While still hot, lightly toss in the honey, if using.

To make the bubble and squeak, cook the sprouts in boiling salted water until tender. Cool and refresh in cold water. Once cold, halve lengthways and slice. In a small pan, melt 25 g (1 oz) of butter and gently cook the onions for 4–5 minutes until softened. Leave to cool. Mix the onions with the sprouts, then add the mashed potatoes a spoonful at a time until a firm texture is achieved. Season with salt and pepper.

If you wish to make these into individual crumbles, grease four to six 10 cm (4 in) pastry cutters and divide the mix between them. Heat the remaining butter in a frying-pan and place the squeaks, still in the cutters, into the pan and fry until golden brown underneath; this will take 4–5 minutes. Once ready, place the moulds on the greased baking sheet, cooked side down. Spoon the cooked parsnips on top of the bubble and squeak, lightly pressing down. You can leave the recipe to cool then chill at this stage and finish before serving.

To make the crumble (almost a Christmas stuffing), heat the butter in a small pan and cook the onion over a medium heat for 2–3 minutes. In a large bowl mix the chestnuts, if using, chopped herbs and crumbs and season with salt and pepper. Add the onion and butter and mix together.

Sprinkle the crumble mix on top of the warm bubble and squeak and parsnips and place in the pre-heated oven for 10–12 minutes (double the time if it has been chilled). The dish should now be hot all the way through and can be finished under a hot grill until golden and crunchy. Remove the rings, arrange the bubble and squeak on plates, garnish with watercress and serve with the vegetable butter sauce.

Savoury Tarts

I could make this almost a separate chapter; the combinations go on and on. These tarts make perfect vegetarian dishes as well as just good starters, main courses or snacks. They have a different texture to traditional quiche lorraine and are very easy to make. You can make this in one large flan ring or as individual tartlets.

The basic tart mix is made up of eggs, cream and cheese. I am using grated, fresh Parmesan to give a good, strong flavour and a smooth consistency. Other cheese can be used, from Cheddar and Gruyère to a smoked cheese – Italian Pecorino works well. When cooking the tart mix, it's important not to let it boil or this will scramble the eggs.

You can use puff or shortcrust pastry for your tarts, both of which are available at most supermarkets. I prefer puff pastry as it gives a lighter, cleaner finish. Turn to p.212 for details on how to make and blind bake puff pastry cases.

Basic Tart Mix

This recipe has almost unlimited combinations. It also has to be one of the quickest and easiest tart mixes to make. The quantity of this basic recipe can easily be adjusted, it really depends on what the filling is going to be. This amount will be enough for six 10 cm (4 in) individual or one 25 cm (10 in) case.

SERVES 6

300 ml (10 fl oz) double cream	2 eggs, beaten
2 heaped tablespoons freshly grated Parmesan	Salt and freshly ground black pepper

Beat the cream, Parmesan and eggs and season with salt and pepper. The mix is now ready to use.

Almost any filling can be bound and finished with this mix, but all the fillings must be previously cooked or blanched before adding to the Parmesan cream. The filling can then be warmed until it thickens, making sure it does not boil as this will scramble the eggs. The mixture can then be spooned into tart cases and cooked in the oven until set, or chilled to be used later.

Onion and Mushroom Tart with a Parsley Garlic Crust

This tart cooks almost like a crumble with the garlic and parsley crust (see overleaf). It eats very well with a tomato salad or Tomato and Mustard Seed Salad (see p.126).

SERVES 6

25 g (1 oz) unsalted butter
1 tablespoon olive oil
4 onions, sliced
225 g (8 oz) button mushrooms, sliced
Salt and freshly ground black pepper
1 quantity Basic Tart Mix (see p.120)

6 × 10 cm (4 in) or 1 × 25 cm (10 in) Puff Pastry cases, blind baked (see p.212)
½ quantity Basic Crumble Mix (see p.114)
2 tablespoons chopped fresh parsley
1 large garlic clove

Pre-heat the oven to 200°C/400°F/gas 6.

Melt the butter with the olive oil, add the sliced onions and cook over a moderate heat for 2–3 minutes. Add the button mushrooms, increasing the heat, and cook for a further 2–3 minutes. Season with salt and pepper. Add the basic tart mix and cook without boiling for 15–20 minutes. The filling is now ready to use, or it can also be cooled and kept chilled for a few days.

Spoon the mix into the cooked pastry cases and finish in the pre-heated oven for 15–20 minutes. One large flan will need 30–35 minutes.

While the tart is cooking, start to make the crumble topping. Add the crushed garlic to the shallots in the original recipe and cook in the butter. Add the chopped parsley to the breadcrumbs and finish as per recipe.

Once the flans are cooked, sprinkle the parsley and garlic crust on top, covering the flan completely. Finish slowly under a grill until golden and crispy.

Clockwise, starting top left: Onion and Mushroom Tart with a Parsley Garlic Crust (see above); Parsley, Shallot and Onion Tart with Tomato and Mustard Seed Salad (see p.126); Ratatouille Tart with Crispy Aubergine and Tomato Dressing (see p.127); Wild Mushroom Tart (see p.125); Provençale Tart (see p.124).

Provençale Tart

This is similar to the Ratatouille Tart (see p.127), using onions, courgettes, red and green peppers, but they both eat very differently with different textures, tastes and sauces. You can make the filling in advance and keep in the fridge for a few days. The tart eats very well with a pesto mayonnaise sauce (see preceding pages).

SERVES 6

25 g (1 oz) unsalted butter
2 onions, sliced
1 large red pepper, sliced
1 large green pepper, sliced
1 garlic clove, crushed
Salt and freshly ground black pepper
1 quantity Basic Tart Mix (see p.120)

2 courgettes, sliced
1–2 tablespoons olive oil
4–5 plum or salad tomatoes, sliced
6 × 10 cm (4 in) or 1 × 25 cm (10 in) Puff Pastry cases, baked blind (see p.212)

For the Sauce

1 tablespoon Pesto Sauce (see p.235)   150 ml (5 fl oz) Mayonnaise (see p.242)

Pre-heat the oven to 200°C/400°F/gas 6.

Melt the butter in a pan and add the onions, peppers and garlic. Season with salt and pepper and cook for 4–5 minutes over a moderate heat until the vegetables begin to soften. Add the basic tart mix and warm through gently until the mix thickens; this will take 15–20 minutes. Do not allow the mix to boil.

Fry the courgette slices in a hot frying-pan in a little olive oil for 20–30 seconds, giving the courgettes some colour. Spoon the filling into the tartlet case or cases, then decorate the top of the flans with slices of courgettes and tomato, making two alternating lines of each. Cook in the pre-heated oven for 15–20 minutes for individual tarts or 30–35 minutes for one flan until it sets to the touch. If the mix has been kept chilled it will take an extra 8–10 minutes to cook.

Mix the pesto with the mayonnaise and check seasoning with salt and pepper. Spoon the mixture on to the centre of the plates or bowls and sit the tart on top. Finish with a trickle of olive oil.

Note

The quantity of pesto to mayonnaise is only a guideline – more pesto can be added for a stronger taste. Shop-bought pesto and mayonnaise can be used.

Wild Mushroom Tart

Wild mushrooms are becoming increasingly readily available in our grocers and supermarkets. The variety also seems to be growing. Oyster mushrooms, ceps, trompettes de la mort *and chanterelles can all be used in this tart, as a mixture or just using one type.*

If you can't find fresh wild mushrooms, you should have no problems locating some dried wild mushrooms. These just have to be soaked in cold water until they soften, then you can use them as the fresh ones. Keep the soaking water, sieve it to remove any impurities, then boil it until reduced. This reduced liquor will increase the wild mushroom flavours.

The tart eats very well with a green salad and a dressing made with olive oil and chopped black olives and chives (see pp.122–23).

SERVES 6

100–150 g (4–6 oz) open cup or flat mushrooms, sliced
175 g (6 oz) fresh wild mushrooms OR 100 g (4 oz) soaked dried wild mushrooms
25 g (1 oz) unsalted butter
2 tablespoons olive oil
2 large onions, sliced
1 small garlic clove
1 quantity Basic Tart Mix (see p.120)
6 × 10 cm (4 in) or 1 × 25 (10 in) Puff Pastry cases, blind baked (see p.212),

Pre-heat the oven to 200°C/400°F/gas 6.

Fresh wild mushrooms must be washed and cleaned. If you are using oyster mushrooms, these can be torn by hand into strips. Any large mushrooms should be trimmed and sliced. If you are using dried mushrooms, soak them in water until soft, then drain.

Melt the butter with 1 tablespoon of olive oil in a large pan. Add the onions and cook for a few minutes without colouring. Add the garlic and mushrooms. Increase the heat and stir for a few minutes. If some liquor has been formed from the mushrooms with the onions, drain off any excess liquid to a separate pan and boil until reduced.

Add the mushroom and onion mix to the basic tart mix with any reduced liquor. Warm and thicken the tart mix for 15–20 minutes over a low heat, without overheating or boiling. Spoon the mix into the pastry rings and finish in the pre-heated oven for 20 minutes for individual tarts or 30–35 minutes for one flan. Once cooked and just set, brush with the remaining olive oil and serve.

Parsley, Shallot and Onion Tart with Tomato and Mustard Seed Salad

Continental flatleaf parsley has more flavour than ordinary parsley. It looks similar to fresh coriander. If you can't find any, just use ordinary parsley. You can make one tart or six individual ones (see pp.122–23).

SERVES 6

6 x 10 cm (4 in) or 1 × 25 cm (10 in) Puff Pastry cases, blind baked (see p.212)
1 large bunch of flatleaf parsley
1 tablespoon olive oil
25 g (1 oz) unsalted butter

3 large onions, sliced
225 g (8 oz) shallots, sliced
1 garlic clove, crushed
1 quantity Basic Tart Mix (see p.120)
Salt and freshly ground white pepper

For the Salad

6 ripe plum or salad tomatoes
1 teaspoon grain mustard or to taste

4 tablespoons Basic Vinaigrette (see p.241)
1 teaspoon snipped fresh chives

Pre-heat the oven to 200°C/400°F/gas 6.

Pick the flatleaf parsley from the stalks and blanch in boiling salted water for 45 seconds. Drain and refresh with cold water. Squeeze out any excess water from the parsley and lightly chop.

To cook the onions and shallots, warm the olive oil and butter until the butter begins to bubble. Add the onions, shallots and garlic and cook over a moderate heat without colouring until softened. Remove from the heat and allow to cool. Once cooled, mix with the chopped parsley and the basic tart mix. Season with salt and pepper. Warm the tart mix through gently until thickened.

Spoon the tart mix into the pastry cases and bake in the pre-heated oven for 30–35 minutes for one flan or 15–20 minutes for individual tarts.

To make the salad, eye the tomatoes and cut into eight pieces. Season with salt and pepper. Add the mustard to the vinaigrette, then add the snipped chives. Mix the dressing with the salad and serve with the warm tart.

Ratatouille Tart with Crispy Aubergine and Tomato Dressing

We all like ratatouille; it has that Italian theme and is packed with different flavours. Well I've taken all these flavours and put them into a tart case bound with my basic tart mix (see pp.122–23). One of the most exciting tastes in this dish is the aubergines. They eat like home-made aubergine crisps!

SERVES 6

3 tablespoons olive oil
25 g (1 oz) unsalted butter
2 onions, sliced
1 garlic clove, crushed
Salt and freshly ground black pepper
1 large red pepper, seeded and thinly sliced
1 large green pepper, seeded and thinly sliced
1 quantity Basic Tart Mix (see p.120)

2 courgettes
6 × 10 cm (4 in) or 1 × 25 cm (10 in) Puff Pastry cases, blind baked (see p.212)
1 large aubergine
100 g (4 oz) plain flour
1 teaspoon cayenne pepper
Oil for deep-frying
1 quantity Tomato Dressing (see p.233)

Pre-heat the oven to 200°C/400°F/gas 6.

Heat a large pan and add 1 tablespoon of oil and the butter. When the butter starts to bubble, add the onions and crushed garlic, season with salt and pepper and cook for a few minutes until softened. Remove the onions from the pan and add a dash more olive oil to the pan. Allow the oil to heat, then fry the peppers, seasoned, until lightly coloured. Return the onions to the pan, add the basic tart mix and thicken on the stove for about 15–20 minutes over a low heat. Do not allow to boil.

Split the courgettes lengthways and cut into thin slices. Quickly shallow fry in a little oil in a hot pan until golden; about 1–2 minutes. These can now be added to the mix.

Spoon the mixture into the flan cases and finish in the pre-heated oven for 15–20 minutes for individual tarts or 30–35 minutes for one flan. The tart should only be set to the touch. If the mix has been chilled, it will take a further 8–10 minutes to cook.

Split the aubergine lengthways, then cut across into thin slices. Mix together the flour and cayenne pepper with a pinch of salt. Dust the aubergine, then fry in hot deep oil until golden and crispy.

Place the tart in the centre of a serving plate and spoon some tomato dressing around. Sit the aubergine crisps on top of the tart and serve.

Stuffed Mushrooms

Stuffed mushrooms can be made so many different ways, with a range of fillings, toppings and textures. They work very well as vegetarian starters or main courses, or you can use prawns, mussels, bacon or other fish or meat ingredients. Rather than give you a basic recipe, I thought I would just share a few ideas.

I like to use large, flat mushrooms which have a good meaty texture and taste. It's best to half cook them before adding any filling. They can then be stuffed, topped and baked. I always half-cook the mushrooms on a seasoned and buttered tray under the grill with a trickle of olive oil.

My favourite filling is cooked spinach. You can flavour this with garlic, leeks or even crispy smoked bacon pieces, then top the spinach with either a herb crust (see p.121) or thick slices of grated Cheddar or Gruyère. Bake the mushrooms in a pre-heated oven at 200°C/400°F/gas 6, then finish under the grill. These eat very well as a starter.

Other good fillings are a small, diced ratatouille finished with Parmesan or Stilton and spinach or just Stilton and breadcrumbs, leeks with mustard and Cheddar, or sliced tomatoes topped with Welsh rarebit mix (from Rhodes Around Britain*).*

Turn to p.130 to see how good they look.

Vegetarian Stir-fry

This really is tasty to eat as a starter or main course. It also works well with some other fish or meat dishes.

SERVES 4

2 onions, sliced
2 tablespoons olive oil
50 g (2 oz) unsalted butter
225 g (8 oz) beansprouts, blanched in boiling water
225 g (8 oz) cup mushrooms, sliced
450 g (1 lb) spinach, washed and torn
175 g (6 oz) cooked fine spaghetti/noodles

1 tablespoon clear honey
2 tablespoons Spicy Marinade (see p.100)
Juice of 1 lime
Salt and freshly ground black pepper
6 spring onions, diagonally sliced

The first thing is to start to cook the onions in a wok with the oil and butter for a couple of minutes. Add the blanched beansprouts and sliced mushrooms and continue to cook over a moderate heat for 2 minutes. Add the spinach and cook for a minute until just wilted. Add the cooked spaghetti or noodles and cook for a further 2 minutes. Add the honey, marinade and lime juice. Check for seasoning with salt and pepper, divide between four bowls and spoon over the liquor. Finish with the sliced spring onions.

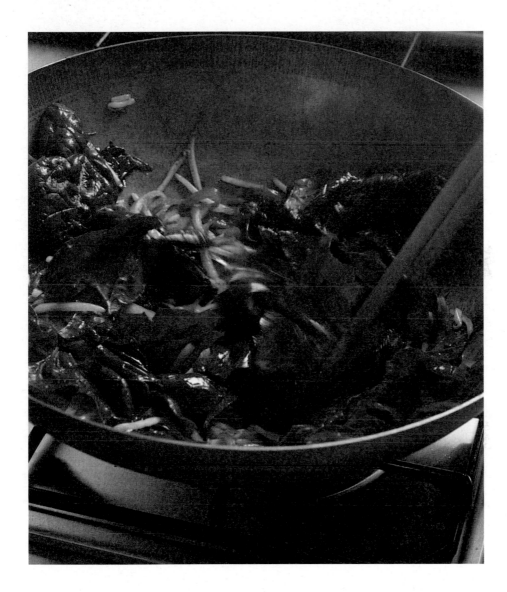

ABOVE *Making the Vegetarian Stir-fry (see p.129).*

OPPOSITE *In the foreground are mushrooms stuffed with spinach with a herb crust and behind are mushrooms stuffed with ratatouille (see p.128).*

Vegetables

Some of these recipes will tell you how to get the maximum flavour from a bowl of sliced carrots, peas or beans.

There's all sorts of potato dishes, including one of my favourites, Irish Champ – lovely mashed buttery potatoes with spring onions. I've also included a shocking pink recipe, Beetroot Bubble and Squeak. It's not just the colour that shocks, it's the flavour, too. The Beetroot Fritters are crispy and golden, the Spring Onion Potato Cakes are full of textures and as for the stir-fry – you won't believe how quick and easy it is.

Mashed Potatoes

I find Maris Piper are one of the best varieties for making mashed potatoes – then all you need to add is a little care.

SERVES 4–6

900 g (2 lb) potatoes, quartered
Salt and freshly ground white pepper
100 g (4 oz) unsalted butter

120 ml (4 fl oz) double cream or milk
Freshly grated nutmeg

Boil the potatoes in salted water until tender, about 20–25 minutes depending on size. Drain off all the water and replace the lid. Shake the pan vigorously which will start to break the potatoes. Add the butter and cream or milk a little at a time, while mashing the potatoes. Season with salt, pepper and nutmeg. The potatoes will be light, fluffy and creamy.

Spring Onion Potato Cakes

This is a basic recipe which can be developed to suit so many other dishes. I like to add diced, smoked bacon which goes well with the spring onions, and I serve this with a grilled herring dish (see p.79). It's also good to keep this a vegetarian dish so why not just add grated cheese and onion and serve with a good tomato salad.

SERVES 4

25 g (1 oz) unsalted butter
1 large bunch of spring onions, finely
    diced
350 g (12 oz) Mashed Potatoes (see
    p.133), made without cream or milk

2 tablespoons olive oil
2 egg yolks
Salt and freshly ground white pepper
3 tablespoons plain flour

Melt half the butter and fry the spring onions quickly. While the mashed potatoes are still warm, add the olive oil, egg yolks and spring onions and season with salt and pepper. Fold in the flour. The mix can now be divided into four discs about 1–2 cm (½–¾ in) thick and pan-fried in the remaining butter and a little extra olive oil. The cakes will take about 3–4 minutes on either side.

It is always best to pan-fry the cakes as soon as the mix is ready. This will prevent it from becoming soggy. Once cooked, the cakes can be kept and chilled, then baked through in the oven when needed. However, to eat them at their best, eat as soon as cooked.

Fondant Potatoes

These are potatoes that traditionally are shaped into barrels and then braised in chicken stock until all the stock has reduced and been absorbed. The potato is then packed with flavour. Well, I'm not changing this recipe too much, except the potatoes don't need to be shaped, they are just peeled and halved (see p.107).

SERVES 4

2 large baking potatoes, peeled and halved lengthways
600 ml (1 pint) Chicken Stock (see p.222) or Vegetable Stock (see p.223)
Salt
25 g (1 oz) unsalted butter

Pre-heat the oven to 200°C/400°F/gas 6.

Sit the potatoes in a small, buttered baking tray or flameproof dish. Pour in the stock, filling just three-quarters up the sides of the potatoes. Brush the potatoes with butter and lightly season with salt. Bring the stock to the simmer on top of the stove, then transfer to the pre-heated oven for 30–40 minutes. During this time the potatoes will be absorbing the stock. If the stock becomes almost dry, simply check the potatoes with a knife; they may be ready. If not, just add a little more stock, about 5 mm (¼ in) and continue to cook.

For the last 10 minutes of cooking time, brush the potatoes with butter to help give them a nice golden colour. They can also be finished under a hot grill.

Champ

I'm not quite sure if champ comes from Scotland or Ireland. I first experienced it in Northern Ireland, but have read in several books that it was first made in Scotland. It's one of those recipes that everybody believes their way is the only way to make it. Well, I'm not going to say that this is the way; I'll sit on the fence and just give you my version of champ!

The dish can be eaten on its own or just as a potato dish with boiled ham or bacon. I normally serve it with a boiled bacon collar, just spooned over with its cooking liquor and served with English mustard.

SERVES 4

150 ml (5 fl oz) milk
225 g (8 oz) spring onions, sliced
450–675 g (1–1½ lb) Mashed Potatoes
 (see p.133), made without cream or
 butter

Salt and freshly ground white pepper
A pinch of freshly grated nutmeg
 (optional)
100–175 g (4–6 oz) unsalted butter

Bring the milk to the simmer with the spring onions. Add this to the mashed potatoes and season with salt and pepper. I like to add a pinch of nutmeg. Add half the butter to give a creamier texture. Spoon the potatoes into a bowl and make a well in the middle. The remaining butter can now be sat in the centre. The champ is ready.

Variations

You can substitute chives, nettles, onions or even peas for the spring onions. You can also make red champ with pieces of cooked beetroot added to the potatoes.

Champ.

Celeriac and Potato Dauphinoise

This is a French potato dish that has undergone one or two changes. The flavours are lovely and this eats well with most of the main courses.

SERVES 4

2 large onions, sliced
50 g (2 oz) unsalted butter
600 ml (1 pint) double cream
1 garlic clove, crushed

Salt and freshly ground black pepper
450 g (1 lb) potatoes, thinly sliced
1 large celeriac, peeled and thinly sliced

Pre-heat the oven to 180–190°C/350–375°F/gas 4–5.

Cook the onions in half of the butter for 2–3 minutes without colouring, then allow to cool. Bring the cream to the boil with the crushed garlic and remaining butter and season with salt and pepper. Arrange the onions, potatoes and celeriac in layers in a large ovenproof dish, making sure the potatoes are on the top and bottom. Overlap the top layer of potatoes to give a neater finish. Pour over the cream, making sure the potatoes are covered. Bake in the pre-heated oven for 45–60 minutes until the vegetables are tender and have absorbed the cream. Test the vegetables by piercing with a knife. Cover with foil if the potatoes are browning too quickly. Once cooked, finish, if necessary, under a hot grill for that golden colour.

Variations

For a creamier texture, sit the dish in a roasting tray filled with hot water to come three-quarters of the way up the dish, cover with foil and bake in the oven for 1–1¼ hours, finishing under the grill.

This dish eats well without the celeriac as a straightforward Dauphinoise Potato. I also like to run anchovy fillets through the centre of the potatoes to add another taste.

Boulangère Potatoes

This is another potato dish with the potatoes simply sliced with onions and cooked in the oven in stock. It is a classic French recipe that is served in restaurants all over Britain, traditionally with roast best ends or legs of lamb.

SERVES 4

25–50 g (1–2 oz) unsalted butter
2 onions, sliced
675 g (1½ lb) potatoes, thinly sliced
Salt and freshly ground white pepper

450 ml (15 fl oz) Chicken Stock (see p.222) or Vegetable Stock (see p.223), warm

Pre-heat the oven to 230°C/450°F/gas 8.

Melt a little of the butter and fry the onions until softened. Reserve some good round potato slices to arrange on the top of the dish, then mix the remainder with the cooked onions and season with salt and pepper. Place the mixture in an ovenproof vegetable dish and cover with the reserved potato slices, overlapping them across the top. Pour over the warm stock and dot with the remaining butter. Cook in the pre-heated oven for 20 minutes until the potatoes begin to colour. Reduce the oven temperature to 200°C/400°F/gas 6 and cook for a further 40–50 minutes, pressing down the potatoes with a spatula occasionally for more even cooking. By the end of cooking, the potatoes will have absorbed the stock and should be golden and crispy on top. To finish, just sit the potatoes under the grill to achieve that extra rich colour.

Variations

There are a good many variations you can try. Add some strips of smoked bacon; sliced leeks; truffles (very nice – expensive, too!); sliced celeriac; sage and thyme – or just use your imagination!

Beetroot Fritters

These fritters eat very well with a classic accompaniment of just salt and vinegar, and also eat well if just dipped in soured cream or yoghurt and chives. They make a good alternative vegetable dish or can be used as a vegetarian starter (using the right beer).

To cook beetroot, plunge it into boiling salted water then return to the boil. The cooking time depends on age and size. Don't test them with a fork or they will bleed. Lift one out of the water after 30 minutes and try to pull back the skin with your thumb. If the skin comes off easily, the beetroot is cooked. If not, continue to test every 5–10 minutes. Once cooked, drain and leave to cool, then peel, cut in half and cut into 2 cm (¾ in) wedges. You can serve them as they are with some salad dressing or vinegar, sugar and a little water mixed together and poured over, or you can try this!

Serves 4

450 g (1 lb) self-raising flour
Salt
300 ml (10 fl oz) lager
Oil for deep-frying

12 beetroot wedges
Salt and freshly ground black pepper
Malt vinegar (optional)

Mix the flour and salt into the lager until you have a smooth, thick batter with almost a glue-like consistency. Pre-heat a deep frying-pan to 180°C/350°F. Season the beetroot wedges and dust with flour. Coat with batter. Drop into the hot fat and fry for a few minutes until crisp and golden. Remove and salt lightly. Sprinkle with vinegar before serving, if liked.

Variations

Parsnips also work well in this recipe. Peel and quarter the parsnips lengthways, cut the root from the centre and blanch the parsnips in boiling salted water for 2–3 minutes. Drain, cool and pat dry. Lightly flour, coat with batter and cook in the same way, then salt lightly before serving.

Beetroot Fritters.

Beetroot Bubble and Squeak

Bubble and squeak is traditionally made using potatoes, onions and Brussels sprouts, the name coming from the noise it makes while cooking. I get the occasional mad idea of what variations can be made to the dish – here's one that actually works. It goes well with venison, pheasant, pigeon or just about any game. It also eats well with most meats, making a roast leg of pork or lamb, for example, just that bit more interesting. Top it with spinach and a crumble mix to make a complete vegetarian dish.

SERVES 4

2 large onions, sliced
50 g (2 oz) unsalted butter
225 g (8 oz) beetroot, cooked and grated
175 g (6 oz) Mashed Potatoes (see
 p.133), made without milk or cream

Salt and freshly ground white pepper
1 tablespoon plain flour

Cook the onions in half the butter for a few minutes until softened but not coloured. Leave to cool.

Mix the beetroot with the potatoes, add the onions and season with salt and pepper. Stir well. The mix will be a shocking pink colour. It can now be fried as one large cake (the classic bubble) or shaped into small cakes. Pre-heat a frying-pan. Dust the bubble cakes with a little flour and fry in the remaining butter over a medium heat for about 4–5 minutes until golden brown on each side.

Variations

This can become a black pudding and beetroot cake by dicing and frying some black pudding and bacon (or pieces of sausage) and adding it to the mix before frying it. Serve it with a fried egg on top and grilled tomatoes.

Try making potato and onion bubble, top it with slices of corned beef, then thick slices of tomato, season and dot with butter then pop under the grill. If you're feeling really mad, top the lot with slices of Cheddar and let it melt over the bubble!

Glazed Carrots

Cooking carrots has become a very standard job. While they are a useful everyday vegetable, they are great to flavour so many things and I like cooking them this way to make them really tasty and exciting to eat.

SERVES 4

450 g (1 lb) carrots
A pinch of salt
Water

1 teaspoon caster sugar
25–50 g (1–2 oz) unsalted butter
Salt and freshly ground black pepper

The carrots can just be sliced into rings for this recipe, but I like to split them lengthways, twice if they are thick, then cut them at an angle into 1 cm (½ in) pieces. This gives more substance and texture to the vegetable. Place the carrots in a pan with a pinch of salt. Literally just cover, and only just, with water. Add the sugar and butter. Bring the water to the boil, then simmer until the carrots are just tender but still with a slight bite. The cooking time will be determined by how you have sliced them; 8–15 minutes. Drain the liquor into another pan and boil to reduce until 5–6 tablespoons are left. In the reduction process, the butter and sugar content will thicken the liquor, giving you a glaze. Add a little more butter if you want to thicken it a little more. Add the carrots to the pan and re-heat in the glaze. This will give them a wonderful, appetizing shine. Check the seasoning and serve.

Green Beans and Runner Beans

Green beans, known as haricots verts *in the catering industry, must be the most popular vegetable in restaurants; what we consider a first-class vegetable. They need minimum preparation – just top and tail them – and cook quickly. You can even buy them ready trimmed in most supermarkets!*

Another advantage is that you can cook them hours in advance, refresh them in iced water, then re-heat them later when you are ready to eat.

The secret to keeping good colour on any green vegetable is to make sure the water is salted and boiling rapidly before you add the vegetables, don't use a lid, and don't cook too many at once. For home cooking, it's best to cook only 450 g (1 lb) at a time. This is plenty for four to six portions.

To cook beans or any green vegetables, have a large pan three-quarters full of boiling water with a good pinch of salt. Drop in the beans and return the water to the boil. If the beans are extra fine they will be just about cooked; if just fine, cook for 30–45 seconds once the water has re-boiled. Check the beans during cooking; they should always have a good bite in them. Drain the beans and toss them in a knob of butter, seasoning with salt and a good twist of pepper.

The exception to this method is spinach, which is best cooked from raw in melted butter. It will cook and create all its own juices.

Runner beans are another favourite. To prepare these, just top and tail them, pulling away the sinewy string on either side. Cut the beans at an angle into thin 5–7.5 cm (2–3 in) strips. This way, the beans are cooked as soon as the water returns to the boil. If you prefer large pieces, cut them into 2.5 cm (1 in) diamonds; these will take 1–2 minutes.

When cut into strips, runner beans leave lots of room for extra tastes. I like to mix them with sliced onions cooked until golden in butter with strips of smoked bacon.

A selection of fresh runner beans,
green beans and carrots.

Fresh Peas

Fresh peas are lovely to eat, providing they are properly cooked. Remember, don't try to cook too many at once, and don't cover the pan.

Once the peas have been shelled, bring a large pan of salted water to the boil. Drop in the peas, return the water to the boil and boil for 15–20 minutes, keeping the water boiling all the time. If the peas are not tender by that time, just keep boiling until they are ready. Drain off the peas, toss in butter and season with salt and pepper. Peas also eat well mixed with Glazed Carrots (see p.141); this then becomes a Flemish-style dish. Of course, you could substitute frozen peas.

This is a classic French dish called petits pois à la française. *It is almost braised peas with onions and lettuce, with the liquor thickend with a little flour. Well, I've changed it slightly and this is what I do.*

SERVES 4

50 g (2 oz) unsalted butter
2 onions, sliced
4 rashers smoked streaky bacon, rinded and cut into strips

50–85 ml (2–3 fl oz) Chicken Stock (see p.222) or Vegetable Stock (see p.223)
Salt and freshly ground black pepper
450 g (1 lb) peas, cooked

Melt 25 g (1 oz) of butter and cook the onions and bacon until slightly softened. Add the stock and bring to the boil. Add the remaining butter and season with salt and pepper. Quickly re-heat the peas for 30 seconds in a pan of boiling water, then drain off. Toss the peas in the reduced bacon and onion liquor and serve.

Fried Spinach, Mushrooms and Beansprouts

This eats well on its own but is even better with the Seared Spicy Pork Belly (see p.100).

SERVES 4

750–900 g (1½–2 lb) spinach
1–2 tablespoons olive oil
25 g (1 oz) unsalted butter
225 g (8 oz) cup mushrooms, sliced

225 g (8 oz) beansprouts, blanched in hot water
Salt and freshly ground black pepper
Juice of 1 lime

First remove the stalks from the spinach and tear the leaves carefully into small pieces. Wash the leaves and leave to dry.

Heat a wok or frying-pan and add the olive oil and butter. Add the mushrooms and toss for 30 seconds. Add the beansprouts and continue to cook for 2 minutes. Add the spinach and continue to stir for 30 seconds. Add the seasoning and lime juice and cook for about 30 seconds more until the vegetables are just tender.

Braised Lentils

Braised lentils can be used in so many dishes – fish or meat – and is perfect as an accompaniment to a main course or as a vegetable dish in its own right.

SERVES 4

50 g (2 oz) unsalted butter
1 carrot, finely diced
1 small onion, finely diced
2 celery sticks, finely diced
225 g (8 oz) lentils

1 piece of bacon trimming (optional)
900 ml (1½ pints) Vegetable Stock (see p.223) or Chicken Stock (see p.222)
Salt and freshly ground black pepper

Pre-heat the oven to 200°C/400°F/gas 6.

Melt the butter in a flameproof casserole and fry the finely diced vegetables for a few minutes. Add the lentils and bacon, if using, and fry for a further minute. Add about 600 ml (1 pint) of the stock, making sure the lentils are just covered with stock, and bring to a simmer. Cover with a lid and cook in the pre-heated oven for 30–40 minutes, stirring occasionally, until the lentils are tender. As the lentils cook, they will tenderize as they absorb the stock. You may need to add a little more stock during cooking.

You can serve the lentils straight away, or they can be cooled and chilled. They will keep in the fridge for two to three days and can be re-heated in a spoonful of stock or water with a knob of butter.

Variations

This recipe can also be made into lentil soup by doubling the quantity of stock. Bacon is a good flavouring for lentils, so try adding a small dice or piece of bacon during cooking. If you've had a boiled bacon collar dish for lunch or dinner one day, then make sure that you keep all the stock it cooked in and dice any left-over bacon. With some chopped vegetables, you'll have an almost instant lentil and bacon soup to put together.

Puddings

This is a very full chapter: lots of puddings with lots of features, recipes for different kinds of biscuits, chocolate puddings, steamed sponges and, of course, a whole section of home-made ice-creams.

The ice-cream feature runs from a straight Vanilla Ice-cream to Honey and Whisky Ice-cream and even a Black Forest Arctic Roll!

ABOVE *Knickerbockerglory (see p.204)*.
LEFT *Adding the honey to Griddled Honey Apples (see p.166)*.

Ice-cream recipes could be endless. The ones I have included are all personal favourites that have simple alternative methods for those in a hurry. You could almost make them all using a bought vanilla ice-cream, then stirring in the other flavourings.

There's also some simple tart recipes, including Treacle Tart and one of my favourites from 'school dinner' days, Gypsy Tart.

Pineapple Fritters

This recipe uses the same cider batter I used for Apple Fritters in Rhodes Around Britain. *That's the beauty of cooking, so many flavours help each other. With these I like to serve Coconut Ice-cream (see p.195) and Rum Custard Sauce (see p.215). It's almost like eating a hot Piña Colada cocktail! The fritters also eat well with clotted cream and Chocolate Sauce (see p.216). If you don't fancy either of these serving ideas, just pour over fresh cream.*

SERVES 4

1 small, ripe pineapple
300 ml (10 fl oz) sweet cider
100 g (4 oz) plain flour plus a little extra
    for coating

25 g (1 oz) caster sugar
Vegetable oil for deep-frying

Cut the outside skin from the pineapple, then split it into quarters. Remove the central core from all four pieces. Each quarter can now be cut into three leaving you with twelve large chunks.

To make the batter, mix together the cider, flour and sugar. Heat the oil to about 180°C/350°F. Lightly flour the pineapple chunks, then dip them into the batter and deep-fry for about 5 minutes until crispy and golden. You may need to do this in batches.

Pineapple and Almond Tart

This tart eats really well sitting on a rich Chocolate Sauce (see p.216) and topped with Coconut Ice-cream (see p.195). All those flavours work so well with pineapple. The pineapple should be fresh and ripe. This will be a deep yellow colour with a moist sweet taste. If you find the pineapple to be firm and opaque in colour, the fruit will need to be poached in some Stock Syrup (see p.217) until tender. This dish can also be made using a good quality tinned pineapple. You can make this pudding with lots of different fruits from apple and blackberry to raspberry, pear or peach. All these fruits work with different ice-creams and sauces.

Serves 6–8

225 g (8 oz) Shortcrust Pastry (see p.211)
½ fresh pineapple, peeled

2 tablespoons pineapple jam (optional)
1 quantity Almond Paste (see p.213)
Icing sugar, sifted

Pre-heat the oven to 190°C/375°F/gas 5 and grease a 25 cm (10 in) flan ring.

Roll out the pastry, use to line the flan ring and leave to rest in the fridge. Cut the pineapple into 2 cm (¾ in) cubes. For extra pineapple taste, spread some pineapple jam on to the pastry base first before spooning in the almond paste and smoothing over.

Push the pineapple cubes into the almond paste. During the cooking of this tart the almond paste will become liquid and flood the tart case. As the paste cooks it will develop a moist sponge texture. Bake the tart in the pre-heated oven. The tart will take between 45–60 minutes. The almond paste will rise slightly.

To give an extra finish and glaze to the tart, sprinkle liberally with icing sugar and glaze under the grill.

Note

For a different finish to the dish, liberally scatter diced fresh pineapple over the top of the tart 10 minutes before it is completely cooked and return it to the oven. The tart can still be finished with the icing sugar glazed under the grill, giving a slight burnt tinge to the pineapple.

Apricot and Almond Tart

For this recipe I'm using a large 28 cm (11 in) diameter x 4 cm (1½ in) deep flan ring which really does make a large pudding. The recipe can easily be cut down by half and a smaller 18 cm (7 in) flan ring can be used. You can use whichever stock syrup you prefer for this recipe.

The flan eats well hot or cold and goes well with clotted cream, custard or ice-cream and is a great alternative for Christmas when served with Christmas Pudding Ice-cream (see p.194).

SERVES 6–8

20 dried, ready-soaked stoned apricots
300 ml (10 fl oz) Stock Syrup (see p.217)
225 g (8 oz) Shortcrust Pastry (see p.211)

4 tablespoons apricot jam
1 quantity Almond Paste (see p.213)
Icing sugar, sifted

Pre-heat the oven to 190°C/375°F/gas 5. Butter and lightly flour a 28 cm (11 in) flan ring.

Split the apricots through the middle, leaving circular discs of fruit. Warm the stock syrup with the fruits and then leave to cool. These can be prepared and chilled days in advance or left until the last minute and drained off before using. The stock will still keep in the fridge. This process softens the apricots even more and leaves them tender.

Roll out the pastry and use to line the flan case. Heat the jam and reduce by half. Spread the jam over the pastry base, then place 20 apricot pieces evenly over the jam. Spoon over the almond paste, leaving a smooth finish on top, and filling to about three-quarters of the way up to allow for it to rise during cooking. Bake in the pre-heated oven for 45 minutes. Remove from the oven and arrange the remaining apricots on top in a circular pattern. (If you put them on before cooking, they sink into the almond paste as it warms and loosens.) Return to the oven for a further 10–20 minutes until golden brown and just firming to the touch.

Sprinkle the flan liberally with icing sugar and glaze under a hot grill, allowing the sugar to caramelize and almost burn in places for a bitter sweet taste.

Apricot and Almond Tart.

Chocolate and Pear Brûlée

Chocolate and pears are a classic combination; the flavours work so well together. The texture of the brûlée has an almost chocolate-toffee consistency which can become more toffee-ish if you use extra chocolate.

I like to eat crème brûlées at room temperature so the consistency is similar to egg custard. However, this pudding can also be eaten chilled.

SERVES 4

8 egg yolks
50 g (2 oz) caster sugar
600 ml (1 pint) double cream
100 g (4 oz) or more good quality plain
   chocolate, grated

4–6 Poached Pear halves (see p.181) or
   tinned pear halves
100 g (4 oz) icing sugar, sifted

Pre-heat the oven to 160–180°C/325–350°F/gas 3–4.

Beat the egg yolks and sugar together in a bowl. Bring the cream to the boil and whisk it into the egg yolk mix. Sit the bowl over a pan of hot water and heat until the custard thickens, stirring all the time; it should have the consistency of double cream. Add the grated chocolate and stir until melted. The mix should now be tasted. If the chocolate flavour is not strong enough, simply keep adding, stirring and tasting until you have the right flavour. Divide the chocolate custard between individual ramekins and sit them in a roasting tray. Fill the tray with hot water to come three-quarters up the sides of the moulds. Finish in the pre-heated oven for 20–30 minutes until the mix thickens and sets. Check the brûlées by removing a ramekin from the tray and shaking gently. The brûlée should be only slightly runny in the centre. If the mix is still too liquid, return to the oven and check after a further 5 minutes. Once cooked, remove from the oven and tray and allow to cool to room temperature.

To finish the dish, cut the pears lengthways into slices and arrange overlapping on top of each pudding. Sprinkle liberally with icing sugar and glaze under a hot grill until you have a golden crisp sugar topping. To achieve a good glaze the icing sugar may have to be applied two or three times.

Variations

It's also possible to slice a quarter of a pear per pudding, then dice the remaining fruit and place it in the bottom of the ramekins before adding the brûlée.

Steamed Sponge Pudding

These puddings are real homely classics – just the sort of pudding to finish your meal, especially for a Sunday lunch. Steamed sponges seem to be playing a big part in The Great British Revival. In fact, steamed lemon sponge was one of the, if not the, first pudding that I made. The sponge can be so light and fluffy to eat and will take on so many other flavours, many of which I am featuring here.

To make it a lot easier to turn out the puddings, use plastic moulds which hold up very well to steaming, and when lightly pressed the sponge should fall out easily. You can use 150 ml (5 fl oz) individual moulds or a 900 ml (1½ pint) mould.

SERVES 4–6

100 g (4 oz) unsalted butter
150 g (5 oz) caster sugar
2 eggs
1 egg yolk
200 g (7 oz) self-raising flour

1–2 drops of milk, if needed
Lightly butter and flour 4 × 150 ml
(5 fl oz) moulds or one 900 ml
(1½ pint) pudding basin.

Beat the butter and sugar together until almost white in colour and the sugar has dissolved. This is easily achieved in an electric mixer. It does, however, take a little while to cream to this stage. Beat in one egg at a time, making sure after each egg is added that the mix is beaten until completely mixed and fluffy again. Once both eggs have been added, continue with the same process for the egg yolk. Most recipes will tell you now to fold in the flour slowly and carefully. Well, I want you to do almost the opposite. Add the flour and beat until all the flour has completely creamed into the mix but do not over-work. Add the milk if needed.

Spoon in the mixture, filling each mould one three-quarters full. Cover the moulds with lightly buttered squares of tin foil, just lightly folding the foil over the rims so the sponge can rise and push up the foil during cooking. Steam the sponges over boiling water, allowing 35–40 minutes for individual puddings or 1¼ – 1½ hours for the larger mould. Top up the boiling water as necessary during cooking.

Golden Syrup Sponge

Golden syrup sponge is always a favourite - just add a generous spoon of syrup to the sponge mixture and sit some more in the base of each mould and then steam. Pour a little more syrup on top before serving (see overleaf).

Steamed Lemon Sponge with Lemon Curd Ice-cream and Lemon Custard Sauce

This sponge eats beautifully with lemon curd ice-cream and lemon custard sauce (see preceding pages). If you feel this is all a bit too strong, simply serve the pudding with one or the other and some whipped or pouring double cream.

SERVES 4–6

1 Steamed Sponge Pudding recipe
   (see p.153)
Finely grated zest of 1 lemon
Juice of 1 lemon

A little milk
Lemon Curd Ice-cream (see p.197)
Lemon Custard Sauce (see p.215)

Add the lemon zest to the butter and sugar mixture in the basic sponge method, then continue to make the sponge until the flour has been added and mixed. Fold in the lemon juice and a little milk, if necessary. Because the zest was in at the beginning the flavour will become more powerful and strong. The sponges can now be steamed in the usual way (see p.153).

PRECEDING PAGES *Clockwise, starting top left:*
Steamed Chocolate Sponge (see p.160); Golden Syrup Sponge (see p.153);
Steamed Lemon Sponge with Lemon Curd Ice-cream
and Lemon Custard Sauce (see above);
Steamed Apricot Sponge with Apricot Sauce (see p.159);
and Steamed Orange Sponge with Hot Orange Sauce
and Marmalade Ice-cream (see p.158).

Steamed Lemon and Rhubarb Sponge

Using the redcurrant jelly with the rhubarb is an optional extra that helps enrich the liquor and juices from the sugared rhubarb. If eaten cold, the mixture will almost set to jam. The beauty of the recipe is that so many other flavours work with it. A little ginger may be added, or you can use other fruits such as blackberries or blueberries. The rhubarb recipe can also be cooked a little more and then puréed and turned into a sorbet or ice-cream (see p.189).

You can make individual puddings or one large one. The flavours of the rhubarb and lemon work really well together, and you can serve the dessert with pouring cream, Lemon Custard (see p.215) or even Vanilla Ice-cream (see p.190).

SERVES 4–6

450 g (1 lb) fresh rhubarb
25 g (1 oz) unsalted butter
225 g (8 oz) caster sugar

1 tablespoon of redcurrant jelly
  (optional)
1 Steamed Lemon Sponge (see p.156)

Peel any coarse skin from the rhubarb stalks; young, tender rhubarb will not need to be peeled. Cut the rhubarb into 2 cm (¾ in) pieces. Melt the butter in a pan until it begins to bubble. Add the rhubarb and stir gently for 1–2 minutes. Add the sugar and bring to the simmer. As the rhubarb is warming it will also be cooking. When it becomes tender, after about 4–5 minutes depending on size and ripeness, remove from the heat. Stir in the redcurrant jelly, if using. Allow the rhubarb mix to cool.

Butter and flour one large mould or individual moulds. Spoon 4–5 tablespoons of the rhubarb into the large mould or 1 tablespoon into the individual moulds, cover with the lemon sponge mix and finish and cook in the usual way (see page 153).

When the sponges are cooked, re-heat the remaining rhubarb. Turn out the puddings and spoon some more fruit over the top.

Steamed Orange Sponge with Hot Orange Sauce and Marmalade Ice-cream

This pudding gives us three different orange flavours from bitter to sweet, and also three different textures (see pp.154–55). It has to be my favourite steamed sponge. The whole dish is packed with orange flavour.

SERVES 4–6

100 g (4 oz) unsalted butter	Finely grated zest of 1 orange
150 g (5 oz) caster sugar	200 g (7 oz) self-raising flour
2 eggs	Juice of 2–3 oranges, boiled to reduce by
1 egg yolk	two-thirds then cooled

For the Sauce

600 ml (1 pint) fresh orange juice	Marmalade Ice-cream to serve
25–50 g (1–2 oz) caster sugar	(see p.198)
1 teaspoon arrowroot or cornflour	A few fresh mint sprigs
1 tablespoon cold water	

To make the sponge, cream the butter and sugar together. Mix the eggs and egg yolk together and beat into the butter and sugar mix. Add the orange zest and fold in the flour. Add the orange juice, making sure it is cold.

Line six 150 ml (5 fl oz) moulds or one 900 ml (1½ pint) mould with butter and flour. Spoon in the sponge mix to fill three-quarters of the way up the mould and cover with buttered paper or tin foil. Steam individual puddings for about 35-40 minutes or larger puddings for 1¼–1½ hours.

Meanwhile, make the orange sauce. Boil the orange juice until reduced by half, then add the sugar to taste (start with a tablespoon and add until you have the sweetness you want). Mix the arrowroot or cornflour with the water then whisk a few drops at a time into the simmering juice until you have a good sauce/coating consistency. Allow to cook for 3–4 minutes.

Once the pudding is cooked, just turn out and serve with a spoonful of marmalade ice-cream, some hot orange sauce and a sprig of mint.

Variations

This is a recipe for a basic orange sauce. To change the flavour, some grated zest can be added or a little Cointreau, Grand Marnier or brandy can be added to lift the taste.

Steamed Apricot Sponge with Apricot Sauce

This recipe has many alternatives – you can use dried or tinned apricots, or even apricot jam. This, of course, makes it quite a rich pudding that is packed with flavour.

When buying dried apricots it's best to select 'ready-to-eat' or no-soak ones that are available in almost all supermarkets. They still have about 25 per cent moisture left in them, which leaves them soft and almost toffee-like to eat straight from the packet. Also for this recipe choose the apricots which are still orange in colour. The texture of this dish is lovely to eat. You have good soft apricots on top of a light fluffy sponge with the rich sauce. The best accompaniment is simply clotted cream and apricot sauce.

SERVES 4–6

12–16 ready-to-eat dried apricots
1 × 425 g (15 oz) tin halved apricots in syrup
1 Steamed Sponge Pudding recipe (see p.153)

1 tablespoon apricot jam
Icing sugar, sifted

It's best to start this recipe either in the morning or day before to achieve the best flavour from the apricots. To give them more moisture and flavour they should be soaked in some syrup, and with this recipe you don't even have to make it. Just open the tinned apricots and pour off and keep the syrup. Warm the syrup and add the dried apricots. Leave them to stand for a few hours. The apricots should be a little softer and more juicy.

Grease and flour six 150 ml (5 fl oz) moulds or one 900 ml (1½ pint) mould.

You can now place three halves of apricot per portion, without syrup, into the bottom of the individual or large pudding moulds. If you have soaked some extra, then simply chop them up and mix into the basic sponge mix. Spoon the mix on top and steam as for the basic recipe (see p.153).

To make the apricot sauce, blend the tinned apricots to a purée. Warm in a pan with the apricot jam, then add enough of the remaining syrup until you have a good sauce consistency. The sauce may taste a little sharp. To help this, just add some icing sugar a pinch at a time until you have the right sweetness. Push the sauce through a sieve and it is ready.

Once the sponge is cooked, turn out on to a plate and spoon the warm sauce over.

Steamed Chocolate Sponge

Along with steamed jam sponge, this has to be a children's favourite. In fact, I think it's a favourite for everyone (see pp.154–55). One of the pleasures of cooking is never allowing recipes to be over-strict. This pudding can have so many different textures and tastes added from walnuts and almonds to dates and orange zest – and many more.

There are two or three sauces which go very well with this pudding. Try Chocolate Sauce (see p.216), Coffee Custard Sauce (see p.215) or Pecan Nut Sauce (see p.168). It's all very rich but very tasty!

SERVES 4–6

1 Steamed Sponge Pudding recipe (see p.153), omitting 50 g (2 oz) of the self-raising flour	50 g (2 oz) cocoa 50–100 g (2–4 oz) good quality plain chocolate, grated

Simply follow the basic sponge recipe mixing the cocoa with remaining self-raising flour. Stir the grated chocolate into the mix to lift the flavour and texture.

To cook this pudding, only steam for 35 minutes if using individual moulds or for 1½ hours in a large mould. This leaves it slightly softer in the centre. Turn out and serve with the sauce of your choice. I also like to finish the dish with either grated chocolate or chocolate shavings.

Cloutie Dumpling

I ate this recipe for pudding when I visited Alan Craigie at the Creel Restaurant in the Orkneys while filming Rhodes Around Britain. *It was delicious. What did surprise me was that I had also eaten it that morning with my cooked breakfast! Now that's what I call variety.*

Cloutie dumpling is a Scottish speciality. Cloutie comes from the word 'clout' meaning cloth, which is what the dumpling is wrapped in before boiling. I would describe it as a light Christmas dumpling. For me, it ate best as a pudding with lots of thick cream.

If you have any left over, just cut it into slices and shallow fry in butter for breakfast the next day.

SERVES 4–6

175 g (6 oz) self-raising flour
175 g (6 oz) brown breadcrumbs
175 g (6 oz) shredded suet
100 g (4 oz) currants
175 g (6 oz) raisins
175 g (6 oz) sultanas
1 teaspoon bicarbonate of soda

A good pinch of ground ginger
A good pinch of freshly grated nutmeg
A good pinch of ground cinnamon
100 g (4 oz) soft dark brown sugar
2 tablespoons golden syrup or treacle
250 ml (8 fl oz) milk

Simply mix all the ingedients together. Boil a large cloth then dust with flour. Place the mix in the cloth, then pull the cloth around, making a ball shape. Boil in a pan of water for 2–2½ hours, topping up as necessary, then unwrap, slice and serve with cream.

Blackberry Jam Tart

I used to love jam tarts as a child: just sweet pastry tartlet moulds filled with jam. I thought they were really delicious. Well, this recipe is for a jam tart with a difference. I have always felt that a jam tart needed another texture, so read on and you'll see exactly what I mean!

For this recipe I'm going to use four individual tartlet cases, but a 28 cm (11 in) flan case will be fine. If you use a large flan case, the pastry can be left raw before adding the almond mix then all baked at the same time, in which case it will need 1–1¼ hours.

The jam tart eats well just with thick or clotted cream. I also like to serve home-made Custard Sauce (see p.215) either cold or warm, or sometimes flavoured with calvados.

SERVES 4–6

175–225 g (6–8 oz) Puff Pastry (see p.212)	175 g (6 oz) ground almonds
	40 g (1½ oz) plain flour
175 g (6 oz) unsalted butter	3 eggs, size 2
175 g (6 oz) caster sugar	225 g (8 oz) Blackberry Jam (see p.210)

Pre-heat the oven to 180°C/350°F/gas 4.

Roll out the pastry thinly and line the flan cases, leaving any excess pastry hanging over the edge of the rings. This will prevent the pastry from shrinking back into the mould during baking. Leave to rest for 20 minutes. Line the pastry with greaseproof paper and fill with baking beans or rice and bake in the pre-heated oven for 15–20 minutes until the pastry is cooked and set. Remove the paper and beans and cut off any excess pastry hanging over the flan cases. To do this, simply take a sharp knife, position it at the top of the tart ring and cut all the pastry away. By cutting this way the pastry will be neatly flush with the tart case.

You can, of course, make the filling in a food mixer or processor. Beat the butter and sugar together until well creamed. Fold in the almonds and flour. Beat in one egg at a time, making sure they are well mixed in. Spoon the almond filling into the flan case, leaving it about 2 mm from the top. (If you find you have some mix left over, then simply chill it and it will keep for up to one week.) Bake the tarts in the pre-heated oven, allowing 30–35 minutes for the small tarts or 45–60 minutes for a large flan case. When cooked, the tarts will be firm to the touch and a knife inserted in the centre will come out almost clean.

Once cooked the almond sponge mix should have risen slightly. This can simply be sliced off the top to expose the sponge. While the tart is still warm, spoon some of the jam over the tarts until just covered. Return to the oven for 1–2 minutes by which time the jam will be making its way through the sponge. To serve, simply remove the flan case and eat either hot or cold.

Variations

We all know what a great combination blackberry and apple is. If you really want to make this different and give other tastes then simply add some grated apple to the almond mix, or place poached apples or pears in the pastry cases before spooning on the mix. This gives you different textures as well as tastes.

Treacle Tart

This is a very quick and easy recipe. It has, like so many other recipes, many alternatives. Half a teaspoon of ground ginger works very well, so does the addition of a little grated orange zest, or you can enrich the whole recipe with the addition of a few tablespoons of double cream and one or two eggs. You can eat it on its own or with clotted or pouring cream.

SERVES 4

1 quantity Sweet Pastry (see p.211)
50 g (2 oz) unsalted butter
10 tablespoons golden syrup

225 g (8 oz) fresh breadcrumbs
Finely grated zest and juice of 1 lemon

Pre-heat the oven to 200°C/400°F/gas 6.

Roll out the pastry and use to line a 23 cm (9 in) flan ring. Cover with greaseproof paper and baking beans or rice and bake in the pre-heated oven for 10–15 minutes until set. Remove the paper and beans. Reduce the oven temperature to 180°C/350°F/gas 4.

Melt the butter and syrup together. Add the breadcrumbs and lemon juice and zest. Pour the mix into the pastry case and bake in the oven for 20 minutes. If the treacle filling is bubbling, then remove from the oven. If it is not quite at that stage, cook for a further 5–10 minutes. When the treacle is at the bubbling/sizzling stage, remove the tart from the oven and allow to settle. The tart can be eaten warm or cold.

Gypsy Tart

This is a recipe I had been searching for for years. It's a pudding I remember from school days and it was my favourite. When I found somebody who knew the dish and was given the recipe I couldn't believe how simple it is – and it still tastes great.

SERVES 6

225 g (8 oz) Shortcrust Pastry   1 × 400 g (14 oz) tin evaporated milk
   (see p.211)   350 g (12 oz) dark muscovado sugar

Pre-heat the oven to 200°C/400°F/gas 6.

Roll out the pastry and use to line a 25 cm (10 in) flan ring. Line with greaseproof paper and baking beans and bake in the pre-heated oven for 15–20 minutes until cooked. Leave to cool.

Whisk the evaporated milk and sugar together for 10–15 minutes until light and fluffy. The mix should be coffee coloured. Pour the mix into the pastry case and bake in the oven for 10 minutes. The gypsy tart will now have a slightly sticky surface but will not set completely until it has been left to cool. Serve cold. I told you this recipe was easy!

Toffee

This really is amazing. When I show people the results, most just can't believe it. As you can see you don't need a lot of ingredients! The toffee is great for so many things: crumbles, creams, ice-creams and sauces. You'll find some of the recipes in the book.

MAKES 400 g (14 oz)

1 × 400 g (14 oz) tin condensed milk

All you have to do is place the tin of condensed milk (totally unopened) into a pan and cover with cold water, making sure the tin is completely covered. Bring to the boil and continue to simmer for 3 hours (no less!). Leave to cool down in the pan. The toffee is now made and can be kept chilled in the unopened can until the date runs out.

Toffee Cream

The standard proportions for this recipe are one tin of Toffee to 450 ml (15 fl oz) of cream, but this makes a lot of cream, so it is best to make it in a smaller quantity.

SERVES 4

200 g (7 oz) Toffee (see p.164) 250 ml (8 fl oz) double or single cream

Stir the toffee in a bowl to loosen. If you're looking for a thick pouring cream, then simply add all the cream and whisk in until well mixed (single cream works well for this). If you want a thick and light cream, then use double cream, just adding a quarter of the cream and whisking until thickened, then adding another quarter, and so on until everything is mixed. The toffee cream may still seem to be a little soft, so it's best to make this 1–2 hours before you need it and then chill it in the fridge. This will give the cream a totally new texture and, when spooned on to the plate, it will hold its shape.

Griddled Honey Apples with Toffee Cream

This must be the easiest and quickest apple pudding there is, so if you're ever stuck and time is running out, have a go! It's great to eat with the toffee cream but also works really well with just pouring cream or Vanilla Ice-cream (see p.190).

To speed up the glazing of the top, I use a gas gun, which works really well to caramelize sugar. However, please don't use one of these unless you're very familiar with them.

SERVES 2

3 apples, peeled and cored
15 g (½ oz) unsalted butter
4 teaspoons clear honey

2–3 tablespoons icing sugar, sifted
Toffee Cream (see p.165) to serve
2 sprigs of fresh mint (optional)

Slice the apples across through the middle to give six thick apple rings in total. Warm a frying-pan and add the butter. Sit the apples middle-side down into the pan and fry until the apples become a rich brown with tinges of burnt around the edges to give a bitter-sweet apple taste. Turn the apples and continue to cook over a medium heat for 1–2 minutes (or you can place them in a medium oven for 1–2 minutes until the apples become just tender).

Spoon the honey on top of the apples. Spoon the icing sugar into a teastrainer and sprinkle well over the top. Finish under a hot grill until the sugar becomes crispy. To increase the crunchy topping, just sprinkle more icing sugar on top and re-glaze.

To serve the apples, sit three pieces on to each plate and serve with thick toffee cream and a sprig of mint.

Griddled Honey Apples with Toffee Cream.

Chocolate Fudge Cake with Pecan Nut Sauce

This pudding is rich, sticky and very tasty. You won't be able to eat it too often but every now and again it's a wonderful treat. This makes quite a large cake but it is worth the effort. It keeps brilliantly for days in the fridge and can be simply microwaved a portion at a time or as a whole pudding. To serve the pudding just pour the pecan sauce over each slice.

Serves 8

6 eggs
350 g (12 oz) caster sugar
A few drops vanilla essence
225 g (8 oz) good quality plain chocolate

225 g (8 oz) unsalted butter
100 g (4 oz) ground almonds
150 g (5 oz) fresh white breadcrumbs

For the Pecan Nut Sauce

175 g (6 oz) soft brown sugar
100 g (4 oz) unsalted butter

85 ml (3 fl oz) double cream
25–50 g (1–2 oz) pecan nuts, chopped

Pre-heat the oven to 180°C/350°C/gas 4 and grease a 20 × 25 cm (8 × 10 in) baking tray. The baking tray needs to be at least 2.5 cm (1 in) deep to achieve the right texture.

Whisk together the eggs, sugar and vanilla essence until the mixture forms stiff peaks (sabayon stage). Melt the chocolate with the butter in a bowl over warm water. Pour on to the egg and sugar mixture and then fold in the ground almonds and breadcrumbs. The mix will be very loose, almost liquid. Pour the mix into the prepared baking tray and bake in the pre-heated oven for 50–60 minutes. The texture of the pudding should be cooked but almost stodgy and moist. The pudding should be left to rest for 10 minutes before serving.

To make the sauce, place the sugar, butter and cream in a saucepan and bring to the boil. Simmer the sauce until the sugar has dissolved. Stir in the pecan nuts. The sauce is now ready.

Chocolate Mousse

This is a rich and light chocolate mousse which can be served in glasses or moulds. It can also be layered between chocolate sponge (see p.160) in a terrine mould or round cake tin.

SERVES 8

150 g (5 oz) good quality plain chocolate
275 g (10 oz) unsalted butter, diced
150 g (5 oz) cocoa

300 ml (10 fl oz) double cream
200 g (7 oz) caster sugar
6 eggs, separated

Chop the chocolate and melt it slowly in a bowl over a pan of hot water. Add the butter and let it melt in the warmth of the chocolate. Add the cocoa and whisk in until the mix is smooth. Whisk the double cream until it forms soft peaks, then reserve in the fridge. Whisk half the sugar with all the yolks until pale and fluffy. Whisk the remaining sugar and egg whites together until they form stiff peaks.

Fold the chocolate mix with the egg yolks and sugar, add the meringue mix and lastly fold in the cream. The mousse can now be set in glasses or moulds and needs half a day minimum to set.

Variations

If you wish to make this into a chocolate mousse cake or terrine, simply cut the sponge to fit the mould, layer it with the mousse and set in the fridge. The sponge can now be finished with the chocolate coating recipe on page 172 to make a really spectacular cake.

Irish Chocolate Coffee Cake

This recipe was given to me by a close friend, Gabrielle, who produces Rhodes Around Britain. *We often have different ideas about cooking and filming, but one thing is for sure, we both want the same results, and with this dish she won. It eats and keeps beautifully, especially when flavoured with good Irish whiskey!*

MAKES 1 × 20 cm (8 in) cake

175 g (6 oz) good quality plain chocolate
4–6 tablespoons strong black coffee
2–4 tablespoons Irish whiskey
75 g (3 oz) caster sugar
100 g (4 oz) unsalted butter at room
    temperature

3 eggs, separated
A pinch of salt
50 g (2 oz) ground almonds
A few drops of almond essence
50 g (2 oz) plain flour, sifted

For the Icing

100 g (4 oz) good quality plain chocolate
2 tablespoons whiskey or strong coffee

100 g (4 oz) unsalted butter

Pre-heat the oven to 180°C/350°F/gas 4. Butter and flour a 20 cm (8 in) cake dish.

Melt the chocolate, coffee and whiskey in a bowl over a pan of simmering water, then cool to room temperature. Reserve a tablespoon of sugar, then cream together the remaining sugar with the butter until you have a pale yellow, fluffy mixture. Beat in the egg yolks until well blended. Whisk the egg whites and salt until soft peaks form. Sprinkle on the tablespoon of caster sugar and beat until stiff peaks form. With a rubber spatula, blend the melted chocolate into the butter and sugar mixture, then stir in the ground almonds and essence. Fold in a quarter of the egg whites, sift in a quarter of the flour, then continue folding and sifting alternately until everything is blended. Turn the mixture into the prepared cake dish, pushing the mixture up to the rim with the spatula. Bake in middle of the pre-heated oven for about 25–30 minutes. The cake is done when it has puffed, and a skewer pushed into the middle comes out clean. Allow the cake to cool. It must be thoroughly cold to be iced.

To make the icing, melt the chocolate and whiskey or coffee in a bowl over a pan of simmering water until you have a smooth cream. Remove the bowl from the heat and beat in the butter a tablespoon at a time. Stand the bowl over cold water and beat until the chocolate mixture is cool and of spreading consistency. Spread it over the cake and serve with Cheesecake Cream (see p.180).

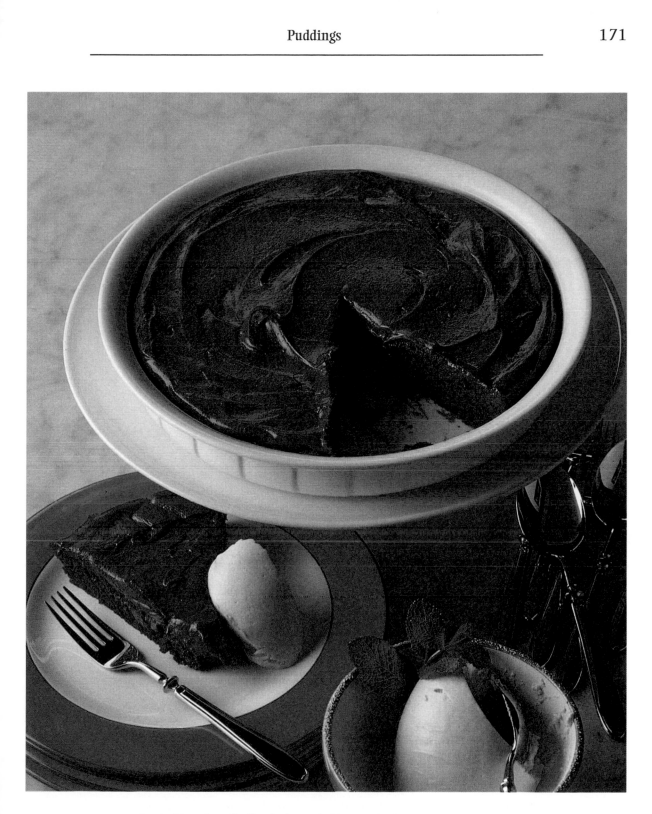

Irish Chocolate Coffee Cake with Cheesecake Cream (see p.180).

Chocolate Terrine

This is the sort of pudding for a special dinner party. It's rich in texture and taste and eats like a chocolate dream. One of the big advantages of making this dish is that it freezes so well and doesn't spoil. So if you've got a party coming up, make this now and just pop it in the freezer ready for the big day. The best size terrine mould to use is a Le Creuset 29 x 9 cm (11½ x 3½ in). The terrine mould is lined with a chocolate sponge, filled with a chocolate mousse and then coated with more chocolate.

SERVES 12

For the Sponge

225 g (8 oz) caster sugar
5 eggs, separated

100 g (4 oz) cocoa

For the Mousse

150 g (6 oz) good quality plain chocolate
175 g (6 oz) unsalted butter
75 g (3 oz) cocoa

300 ml (10 fl oz) double cream
4 eggs, separated
175 g (6 oz) caster sugar

For the Chocolate Coating

120 ml (4 fl oz) milk
65 ml (2½ fl oz) double cream

275 g (10 oz) good quality plain
chocolate, chopped
65 g (2½ oz) unsalted butter, chopped

Pre-heat the oven to 160°C/325°F/gas 3 and butter and line a 40 × 30 cm (16 × 12 in) baking tray. Line a 29 × 9 cm (11½ × 3½ in) terrine with greaseproof paper or cling film.

To make the sponge, mix half the sugar with the egg yolks and whisk until pale and fluffy. Whisk the egg whites until they form soft peaks, then add the remaining sugar and continue to whisk to a stiff meringue. Fold the cocoa into the egg yolk mix, then whisk in a quarter of the meringue mix. Carefully and lightly fold in the remaining meringue. Spread the mix in the prepared tin. Bake in the pre-heated oven for about 20–30 minutes. Leave to cool.

To make the mousse, melt the chocolate with the butter in a bowl over a pan of warm water until it binds to a thick cream consistency. Add the cocoa and beat until completely smooth and cooled. Whisk the cream until it forms soft peaks, then chill. Whisk the egg yolks with half the sugar until white and fluffy. Fold into the chocolate mix. Whisk the egg whites with the remaining sugar to meringue stage, then fold into the chocolate mix. Now fold in the whipped cream.

Cut the cold sponge into four, making sure you measure from the mould, then line the base and sides, saving one piece for the top. Pour the chocolate mousse into the mould, then place the remaining piece of sponge on top. Chill for for 2–3 hours or freeze.

The chocolate coating finishes and really lifts the pudding. Bring the milk and cream to the boil, then pour on to the chocolate and butter. Stir until melted and blended. Cool until thick and at room temperature. To cover the terrine, remove from the fridge or freezer, spoon some on top and spread on until completely covered. Return to the fridge or freezer until set.

To finish, turn out the terrine on to a small board or tray, then spoon over the remaining chocolate coating and spread evenly over the sponge. The terrine will, of course, no longer fit in the mould and so can be kept chilled or frozen on the tray or board. Once the coating has completely set, just cover with cling film.

The terrine will make at least 12 portions. However, the finished dish can be cut into 4 and then frozen so that it can be eaten whenever you like.

Variations

This pudding can be made a lot easier by simply sitting half the sponge into a lined flan case and then pouring the mousse on top and finishing with another layer of sponge. This can then be set in a fridge or freezer. Remove the flan ring and lining and finish with the chocolate coating. It will look like a rich chocolate cake but is in fact a rich chocolate mousse.

This chocolate pudding eats very well with either Orange Custard Sauce (see p.215) or Coffee Custard Sauce (see p.215).

OVERLEAF *Clockwise, starting from the left:*
Basic Tuile Biscuits (see p.176); Gingerbread Biscuits (see p.179);
Brandy Snap Biscuits (see p.176); Chocolate Brownies (see p.178);
and Shortbread Biscuits (see p.177).

Basic Tuile Biscuits

This is a very basic tuile biscuit recipe (see preceding pages). They eat very well with ice-creams and make good baskets to sit the ice-cream in. This mix keeps for up to a week if kept chilled. You can also change the flavour by adding the finely grated zest of 1 lemon or 1 orange (or both) or a little desiccated coconut.

SERVES 4

120 g (4½ oz) unsalted butter	3 egg whites
150 g (5 oz) icing sugar, sifted	120 g (4½ oz) plain flour

Soften the butter and add the icing sugar, beating until white. Add the egg whites and fold in the flour. The mix is ready and should now be chilled to set.

Pre-heat the oven to 180°C/350°F/gas 4 and butter a baking sheet.

Spread the mix very thinly into 13 cm (5 in) discs. This can be made easy by cutting a 13 cm (5 in) circle from a thin plastic ice-cream tub lid, then just placing it on the tray and spreading the mix in, keeping level with the lid. Bake the tuiles in the pre-heated oven for 5–6 minutes until totally golden brown. Remove from the tray while still hot and place over a tin can or mould to shape the basket.

Variations

If you wish to serve these as biscuits to go with your coffee or serve separately with ice-creams, then simply make 6 cm (2½ in) discs and bake them the same way. To shape them, take the centre roll from cling film or tin foil and cut it lengthways to give two semi-circular halves. Sit the warm biscuits into the mould to set.

Brandy Snap Biscuits

Brandy snap biscuits are easy to make and can be made into various shapes and sizes (see preceding pages). I like to serve them with sorbets and ice-creams. If you roll this mix into balls the size of a 2p piece and push them on to a buttered tray, the mix will spread to give you a disc big enough to place over or in a cup to make a basket for your ice-creams. But always make sure that you keep a good distance between each one on the tray or you'll have just one large tray of brandy snap!

100 g (4 oz) unsalted butter	100 g (4 oz) plain flour
100 g (4 oz) caster sugar	A pinch of ground ginger
100 g (4 oz) golden syrup	A pinch of ground cinnamon

Place the butter, sugar and syrup in a pan and heat gently to dissolve. Remove from heat. Mix the flour with the ginger and cinnamon, then beat into the sugar mixture. Leave to cool.

Pre-heat the oven to 180°C/350°F/gas 4 and grease two baking sheets.

Roll the mixture into balls the size of a 2p piece and place well spaced out on the prepared trays. Bake in the pre-heated oven for 7–10 minutes until golden brown with a perforated texture. Leave to cool slightly for a minute before removing from the tray and moulding over a tea cup or round the handle of a wooden spoon. If the snaps cool before you can finish shaping them all, just pop them back in the oven to warm slightly.

Shortbread Biscuits

This recipe works best if piped on to a greased baking tray.

225 g (8 oz) unsalted butter	450 g (1 lb) plain flour
75 g (3 oz) caster sugar	15 g (½ oz) cornflour

Pre-heat the oven to 180°C/350°F/gas 4 and grease and line a baking sheet.

Cream together the butter and sugar until the sugar has dissolved into the fat. Sift the flour and cornflour together and work into the butter mix. Pipe the mix on to the baking sheet and bake in the pre-heated oven for 20 minutes until golden brown. Leave to cool on a wire rack. The biscuits eat very well when sprinkled with caster sugar.

Variations

Lightly roll the shortbread mix about 1–2 cm (½–¾ in) thick and 20 cm (8 in) in diameter and place it in a flan ring. Mark it into eight pieces and prick all over with a fork before cooking. It will take about 30–35 minutes. Turn to pp.174-75 for a photograph.

Chocolate Brownies

Here are two alternative chocolate brownie recipes (see pp.174–75). The first is very rich and tasty and can be used as petits fours or as a biscuit to go with ice-cream. Remember that when melting butter or chocolate, don't let it heat above room temperature.

SERVES 4

300 g (10 oz) caster sugar	225 g (8 oz) good quality plain chocolate
4 eggs	100 g (4 oz) hazel or pecan nuts,
225 g (8 oz) unsalted butter	chopped
75 g (3 oz) cocoa	100 g (4 oz) white chocolate, cut into
75 g (3 oz) plain flour	1 cm (½ in) chunks

Pre-heat the oven to 180–200°C/350–400°F/gas 4–6 and lightly grease a 20 cm (8 in) tin.

Beat together the sugar and eggs, making sure the sugar has completely dissolved. Melt the butter and whisk into the eggs. Sieve together the cocoa and flour and add to the butter and egg mix. Melt the chocolate in a bowl over a pan of warm water, then stir in. Add the chopped nuts and white chocolate. Turn the mix into the prepared tin and bake in the pre-heated oven for 30-40 minutes. Leave to cool, then cut into wedges or squares.

Quick Chocolate 'Brownies'

This recipe is even simpler and quicker to make than the one above, and it also goes well with ice-creams.

SERVES 4

200 g (7 oz) unsalted butter	175 g (6 oz) plain flour
50 g (2 oz) caster sugar	1 teaspoon of baking powder
1 teaspoon vanilla essence	50 g (2 oz) cornflakes, crushed
50 g (2 oz) chopped dates (Medjools are	25 g (1 oz) cocoa
best)	

Pre-heat the oven to 180–200°C/350–400°F/gas 4–6 and grease a 20 cm (8 in) tin.

Cream the butter and sugar together. Add all the other ingredients. Spoon the mixture into the prepared tin and bake in the pre-heated oven for 25–30 minutes.

Gingerbread Biscuits

These biscuits taste delicious if you add some chopped pecan nuts or dates – or both (see pp.174–75). If you are using dates or nuts, simply stir them in with the evaporated milk.

MAKES about 20

225 g (8 oz) plain flour
¼ teaspoon salt
2 teaspoons bicarbonate of soda
1 heaped teaspoon ground ginger
½ teaspoon cinnamon

50 g (2 oz) unsalted butter
100 g (4 oz) soft brown sugar
100 g (4 oz) golden syrup
1 tablespoon evaporated milk

Pre-heat the oven to180–200°C/350–400°F/gas 4–6 and grease two baking sheets.

Sift together the flour, salt, soda and spices. Heat the butter, sugar and syrup until dissolved. Leave to cool. Once cooled, mix into the dry ingredients with the evaporated milk to make a dough. Chill for 30 minutes.

Roll out the biscuit dough to about 5 mm (¼ in) thick and cut into fingers, circles or even gingerbread men! Place on the baking sheets, allowing a little space to spread. Bake in the pre-heated oven for 10–15 minutes.

Keeping an eye on the kitchen.

Cheesecake Cream

I like to serve this cheesecake recipe just as a cream. Of course, it can be spread on to a digestive biscuit base and covered with a fruit topping for a classic cheesecake. Using this recipe as a cream gives it many more options, from serving with summer fruits, poached fruits, chocolate cake (especially the one on p.170) or even ice-cream and raspberry sauce. It also eats very well if flavoured with honey and a drop of Irish whiskey. The other bonus is that it's quick and easy to make. The following quantities can be halved to make less.

SERVES 6–8

50 g (2 oz) caster sugar	600 ml (1 pint) double cream, lightly
450 g (1 lb) full fat soft cream cheese	whipped

Beat the caster sugar into the cream cheese until the sugar has dissolved and creamed. Fold in the lightly whipped cream. It is important that the cream is only lightly whipped. This will prevent the cream from becoming over-beaten and separating when mixing with the cream cheese. Place the cheesecake in a suitable bowl or dish and set in the fridge for about an hour.

Once the cream has set, it can be served in the bowl or shaped between two spoons to serve on the plate.

Variations

Lots of other flavours can be added to this mix. One of my favourites is toffee. To make a toffee cream, simply add a tin of toffee (see p.164) to the cream cheese mix before folding in the whipped cream.

To make a chocolate version, melt 100–225 g (4–8 oz) of good quality plain chocolate, only allowing the chocolate to reach room temperature. The cream cheese must also be at room temperature and not chilled as this would set the cream when added. Simply mix the chocolate with the cream cheese and sugar, then fold in the whipped cream and set in the fridge. The 100 g (4 oz) is the minimum quantity of chocolate; your taste will determine the rest, but the more chocolate you add, the firmer the cream will be.

Poached Pears

This is an easy recipe to follow using simple quantities of two parts water to one part sugar, for example, 600 ml (1 pint) of water to 225 g (8 oz) of caster sugar. The best pears to use are Williams which have a good sweet taste and texture (see overleaf).

The pears can be used for many dishes like the Chocolate and Pear Brûlée (see p.152). They can also be made into a French classic, Poire Belle Hélène, which is poached pear with Vanilla Ice-cream (see p.190) and Chocolate Sauce (see p.216). This dish eats and looks very good if served in a Tuile Biscuit basket (see p.176). You could also use some poached pear in a knickerbockerglory glass layered with Vanilla Ice-cream (see p.190), pecan nuts, Chocolate Sauce (see p.216) and finished with Toffee Cream (see p.165). Now that is a rich pudding!

SERVES 6

6 pears
½ lemon
1 vanilla pod or cinnamon stick
   (optional)

1.2 litres (2 pints) water
450 g (1 lb) caster sugar

Peel the pears, then cut them in half. Remove the core either with a Parisienne scoop cutter or sharp knife. Also remove the vein of stalk running from the centre to the top of the pear by cutting diagonally either side of the vein. The pears can now be lightly rubbed with the lemon to prevent discoloration. Sit the pears in a pan with the lemon and vanilla or cinnamon if using, and cover with the water and caster sugar. Cover with greaseproof paper and bring to the boil. Simmer for a few minutes, then remove from the heat, leaving the pears to cool in the syrup.

The pears can now be kept chilled in the syrup with the lemon and vanilla or cinnamon in an airtight container until ready to be used.

ABOVE *Poached Pears (see p.181) and Poached Peaches (see p.184).*

OPPOSITE *Peach Melba (see p.185).*

Poached Peaches

Before poaching the peaches, they should be skinned. This is achieved by lightly scoring the peach skin all the way around the fruit with a sharp knife. Plunge the fruits into boiling water for a few seconds and then into cold water. This method is called blanching – very similar to skinning a tomato. The skin will now peel off.

These peaches eat very well as almost a pudding on their own or halved and used in a great Auguste Escoffier classic – Peach Melba (see preceding pages).

SERVES 4

4–8 peaches, skinned	300 ml (10 fl oz) water
½ lemon	300 ml (10 fl oz) white wine
½ cinnamon stick (optional)	225 g (8 oz) caster sugar

Sit the skinned peaches into a pan with the lemon and cinnamon stick, if using. Pour the water and white wine on top and add the sugar. If you find this is not enough you can add either half or the same quantities again. Cover with some greaseproof paper and bring to the boil. Simmer the peaches for 4–5 minutes (3–4 minutes if they are very ripe and soft), then leave to cool in the syrup. The peaches are now ready and can be used straight away (even while still warm) or chilled. If you wish to keep them for some time then seal them in airtight jars.

When cooking the fruits if you have any problems keeping them submerged in the syrup, simply sit a plate on top to hold them in place.

Peach Melba

I like to serve Peach Melba in tuile baskets (see p.176). It's simply vanilla ice-cream (see p.190) topped with poached peaches and then finished with Melba Sauce. I also like to add whipped cream flavoured with fresh vanilla and sprinkled with toasted almonds, but this isn't essential. The Melba Sauce can be spooned on to the plate and the finished basket placed on top (see p.182).

Melba Sauce

Melba sauce, of course, is the sauce that goes with peach melba. There are many ways of making this raspberry sauce. This particular recipe gives a good balance of fruitiness to sweetness, but if you want a really quick version then simply boil 225 g (8 oz) of raspberry jam with 5 tablespoons of water and then strain through a sieve; or mix 225 g (8 oz) of fresh raspberries with 100 g (4 oz) of icing sugar, push through a sieve and add a squeeze of lemon juice. Well, there's two recipes. Now here's mine.

SERVES 4

225 g (8 oz) frozen raspberries, thawed   225 g (8 oz) raspberry jam
150 g (5 oz) caster sugar

Heat the raspberries with 50 g (2 oz) of the sugar until dissolved, then bring to the simmer. Push through a sieve to make a raspberry purée. Mix the purée with the remaining sugar and the jam and bring to the boil. Simmer for 3–4 minutes, then strain through a sieve. The sauce is ready and can be eaten hot or cold with many puddings.

Iced Cranachan Parfait

This is a Scottish recipe which is traditionally served at Halloween with soft red berries. It can also be made into an ice-cream by replacing the cream with Vanilla Ice-cream (see p.190), but this recipe is an iced terrine which eats well with a drizzle of honey, or Melba Sauce (see p.185) and fresh raspberries.

This recipe is for a 25 cm (10 in) terrine mould, but you can halve the quantities and use four individual ramekins.

SERVES 4

225 g (8 oz) caster sugar
8 egg yolks
600 ml (1 pint) double cream
4 teaspoons clear honey

175–225 g (6–8 oz) oatmeal, toasted
Whisky to taste (optional)
Clear honey to serve

Whisk the egg yolks and sugar until pale and the mixture trails off the whisk in thick ribbons. (This is easier if you place the bowl over a pan of warm water.) Pour on the cream and continue to whisk (cold) until the cream begins to thicken. Fold in the honey, toasted oatmeal and whisky to taste. Pour into the terrine or individual moulds and freeze until firm.

The cranachan can now be sliced and served.

Iced Chocolate Parfait

Sweet parfaits are like freezing a sweet sabayon. They take on a light ice-cream texture. The quantities here will fill a 25 cm (10 in) terrine mould, or you can use individual ramekins. The ingredients may look a little costly, but remember there are quite a lot of portions in a terrine – or you can simply make half the recipe. Serve the parfait as it is or with the rich Chocolate Sauce (see p.216), Orange Custard Sauce (see p.215) or Coffee Custard Sauce (see p.215). Of course, if you really want to finish this pudding with a little extra, then cover it with Chocolate Coating (see p.172). This gives the parfait a lovely finish and another texture.

SERVES 8

7 egg yolks
100 g (4 oz) caster sugar

175 g (6 oz) good quality plain chocolate
600 ml (1 pint) double cream

Line a 25 cm (10 in) terrine with cling film.

Whisk the egg yolks and sugar in a bowl over warm water until thick and at least doubled in volume. Melt the chocolate in a bowl over a pan of hot water, then mix with the yolks and sugar. Pour on the double cream and whisk until a soft peak is reached. The parfait is ready to freeze in the terrine or in individual moulds.

Note

The double cream can be whisked separately to soft peaks and then lightly folded with the chocolate mix.

Fresh Fruit Salad

Fresh fruit salad has endless combinations. It's basically prepared fruits all mixed together. The recipe here for fruit salad is just to give you an idea and a basic recipe to work from. Some fruits have a coarser texture and eat a lot better if just lightly softened in Stock Syrup (see p.217). Or you can try using Poached Peaches (see p.184) or Poached Pears (see p.181).

Any soft red fruits should always be added just before serving to prevent them colouring the other fruits.

One particular favourite of mine is summer fruit salad which is just poached blackberries, blueberries, redcurrants, blackcurrants, tayberries, strawberries and raspberries in a warm Stock Syrup (see p.217). The flavours and colours together are fantastic.

And here's just one more extra flavour. Use scissors to cut some thin strips of mint leaves and add them to the syrup. You get a lovely sweet mint flavour with every bite!

Of course, the best accompaniment to fresh fruit salad is simply pouring cream or even home-made Vanilla Ice-cream (see p.190).

SERVES 4

2 apples, peeled and cored	½ Ogen or Galia melon
50–75 g (2–3 oz) fresh pineapple chunks	1 large orange, segmented
300 ml (10 fl oz) Stock Syrup (either recipe) (see p.217)	2 kiwis, peeled and cut into 8 pieces each
2 plums, each cut into 8 segments	12 strawberries or raspberries
1 mango	1 banana, sliced

Cut the apples into 12 segments and mix them with the pineapple chunks. Bring the stock syrup to the boil and pour on to the apple and pineapple. While the syrup is still warm, add the plums. The mix should now be left to cool to room temperature.

Peel the mango, then cut it in half, removing the stone. Cut the mango into chunks. Repeat the same cutting process for the melon. Add the mango, melon, orange and kiwi to the other fruits in the syrup.

The fruit salad is now ready. The strawberries, raspberries and banana should not be added until the salad is about to be served.

Ice-creams

These recipes could just go on and on – there are so many different ice-creams and sorbets. They all eat well as puddings on their own or as accompaniments for other dishes.

Most of these recipes are derivatives of a basic vanilla ice-cream. In the vanilla recipe, a vanilla pod is used. This gives the ice-cream a real vanilla taste and when split and scraped leaves a black speckled finish to the cream. This can be substituted by using a few drops of strong vanilla essence or if you keep some caster sugar in an airtight container with a vanilla pod the vanilla aroma and flavour will stay with the sugar.

In most of the other ice-cream recipes, I suggest that you leave out the vanilla. The quantity of ingredients given in the basic vanilla recipe can, of course, be halved and all the other recipes can follow suit.

If you don't have an ice-cream machine, the mix can be left in a bowl and placed in the freezer, making sure it is stirred every 10–15 minutes until set.

If you're in a real hurry, there are a few short-cuts you can try for any of the recipes. You can buy a good quality vanilla ice-cream and add the other flavours so it's almost home-made or replace the vanilla ice-cream base with tinned custard using 600 ml (1 pint) for the equivalent recipe; tinned custards work really well as a base for ice-creams. If it tastes a little too rich and thick, add some milk or single cream to loosen the flavour and texture.

Vanilla Ice-cream

This is the base ice-cream which you can vary in an infinite number of ways!

SERVES 4–8

300 ml (10 fl oz) double cream
300 ml (10 fl oz) milk
1 vanilla pod or a few drops of vanilla
   essence

6 egg yolks
175 g (6 oz) caster sugar

Mix together the cream and milk in a pan. Split the vanilla pod lengthways and scrape the insides into the milk and cream, then add the scraped pod. Bring to the boil.

While they are heating, beat the egg yolks and sugar together until pale and light. This can be done in a food mixer. Pour on the milk and cream, stirring all the time until well blended. Stir from time to time until the ice-cream mix has cooled. Remove the vanilla pod.

Once cooled, the mix is ready to be churned in the ice-cream maker. If you have made the full recipe, you'll need to churn it in two batches. Pour the mix into the machine and begin to turn. The ice-cream will take about 20–30 minutes and will have thickened and increased in volume. Don't leave the mix turning until completely frozen and set as this will be over-churned and slightly grainy in texture. Take out when thick and starting to freeze and then finish in the freezer. This will give you a lovely silky smooth texture.

If you don't have an ice-cream machine, simply turn the mixture into a freezer tray or bowl and freeze, turning regularly until set.

Clockwise, starting from the top right:
Vanilla Ice-cream; Toffee Ice-cream (see p.200);
Maple Syrup and Pecan Nut Ice-cream (see p.197);
Coconut Ice-cream (see p.195);
Raspberry Soft Fruit Ice-cream (see p.204);
Chocolate Ice-cream (see p.193).

Banana Ice-cream

Try this ice-cream with Chocolate Sauce (see p.216) and warm pancakes.

SERVES 4–8

1 quantity Vanilla Ice-cream (see p.190)
225 g (8 oz) peeled ripe bananas
A few drops of lemon juice

1–2 tablespoons banana liqueur
(optional)

First you need to make the vanilla ice-cream base. Once made and still warm, peel and chop the bananas and toss them in the lemon juice to help them keep their colour. Then add them to the base. This can now be blitzed in a food processor and then pushed through a sieve. Stir in the liqueur, if using. The ice-cream can now be finished in an ice-cream machine, then frozen.

Chocolate Ice-cream

This is a delicious ice-cream with lots of very adult alternatives (see p.191)!

SERVES 4–8

1 quantity Vanilla Ice-cream (see p.190), made with 100 g (4 oz) caster sugar and without the vanilla pod

175 g (6 oz) good quality plain chocolate, grated

Follow the vanilla base recipe using only 100 g (4 oz) of caster sugar. Once the milk and cream have been brought to the boil, pour on to the grated chocolate and stir. This will melt the chocolate. Taste before churning to check the chocolate flavour is strong enough. Continue with the basic recipe.

Variations

This ice-cream has many alternatives.

1 Add some rum to taste.

2 Add some Cointreau or Grand Marnier to taste.

3 Add 2–3 tablespoons of marmalade for chocolate and orange ice-cream (and maybe a little Cointreau too!).

4 Add some broken Honeycomb (see p.208) just at the end of churning.

Christmas Pudding Ice-cream

This is a great Christmas pudding alternative to surprise your guests. It eats really well on its own or as an accompaniment to a tart or flan. The other great way to use this recipe is to make it from your left-over pudding, turning it into a new dish.

For this recipe I'm using a home-made custard as the base, but here is a quick and simple alternative: if you buy a 450 g (1 lb) Christmas pudding and just chop it all up, then stir it into two tins of ready-made custard you have an instant mix for Christmas Pudding Ice-cream. It can be as simple as that!

SERVES 4–8

450 g (1 lb) Christmas pudding   1.2 litres (2 pints) Custard Sauce
                                        (see p.215)

The Christmas pudding can be used straight from the packet. All you need to do is simply cut the pudding into slices and then into small rough dice. If you are using the left-overs from Christmas lunch, then just break it down into crumble pieces. Now all you have to do is stir in the custard and mix for a minute or two. Pour some of the mix into an ice-cream machine (making sure the Christmas pudding pieces are equally distributed) and allow to turn. Once the cream has started to thicken and cream, turn the ice-cream out and finish setting in the freezer. If you overturn the ice-cream it will break down the pudding and become darker and slightly bitter in taste. Repeat the same process for the remaining mix.

To re-create the pudding theme and shape, just set the ice-cream in a pudding basin and freeze. Once turned out, you have a Christmas pudding with a difference! I also like to pour maple syrup over the top to enrich it even more.

If you don't have an ice-cream maker, pour the mix on to a tray and set in the freezer, turning from time to time until frozen. The ice-cream doesn't quite have the full volume or texture but still tastes good.

Coconut Ice-cream

This ice-cream can take on loads of combinations (see p.191). It can be coated in chocolate, almost like making your own 'taste of paradise', mixed with chopped pineapple, made into a Piña Colada pudding, or even served with Pineapple Fritters (see p.148) and Chocolate Sauce (see p.216). If you don't have a fresh coconut, just replace it with 50 g (2 oz) of desiccated coconut.

SERVES 4–8

¼ fresh coconut
175 ml (6 fl oz) double cream
250 ml (8 fl oz) milk

100 g (4 oz) caster sugar
5 egg yolks
200 ml (7 fl oz) coconut milk

Crack the coconut and peel off a quarter of the white coconut flesh. Chop the flesh finely and mix with the cream and milk. Bring to the boil. While the milk mix is coming to the boil, whisk the sugar and egg yolks together in a large bowl until pale and light. Pour over the boiling milk, then place the bowl over a pan of hot water and stir until thickened. Blitz in a blender until the coconut is shredded, then leave to cool. Add the coconut milk and churn in the ice-cream machine until beginning to freeze, then turn into a freezer container and freeze until firm.

If you don't have an ice-cream maker, pour the mix on to a tray and set in the freezer, turning from time to time until frozen.

Crème Fraîche Ice-cream

Using crème fraîche in any ice-cream really lifts the taste of other flavours. But using it as a main flavouring gives a basic vanilla ice-cream a really good bite. For every 300 ml (10 fl oz) of Vanilla Ice-cream (see p.190) you will need to add at least 150 ml (5 fl oz) of crème fraîche while the mixture is still liquid. This will give quite a strong taste. After that it's really up to you. If you want it stronger, simply start to add a spoonful at a time until you have the flavour you want. To make the flavour a little sharper, then also add 1 tablespoon of natural yoghurt to the mix.

The other alternative is to mix a tin of custard with 150 ml (5 fl oz) of crème fraîche and you have instant ice-cream mix.

Honey and Whisky Ice-cream

It is up to you how much whisky you like to add to this dessert – I use about two measures.

SERVES 4–8

1 quantity Vanilla Ice-cream (see p.190), made without caster sugar (vanilla pod optional)

350 g (12 oz) jar clear honey
Whisky to taste

This is really easy to make. Simply mix the honey with the egg yolks from the vanilla recipe and beat them together. Follow the method, adding the whisky to taste before turning.

Lemon Curd Ice-cream

This ice-cream is lovely and rich and eats beautifully as a pudding on its own or as an extra for a Steamed Lemon Sponge (see p.156). The ice-cream is superb if totally home-made, but also works very well if you substitute the fresh lemon curd for a jar of lemon curd.

Serves 4–6

1 quantity Lemon Curd (see p.208) or
1 × 350 g (12 oz) jar of lemon curd

2 large tablespoons crème fraîche
1 large tablespoon natural yoghurt

Mix the cooled lemon curd with the crème fraîche and yoghurt and churn into ice-cream. It's as simple as that!

Maple Syrup and Pecan Nut Ice-cream

You need to make the base with less sugar so that the maple syrup does not make the ice-cream too rich (see p.191).

Serves 6–8

1 quantity Vanilla Ice-cream (see p.190), using only 75 g (3 oz) of caster sugar (vanilla pod optional)

300 g (11 oz) maple syrup
50–75 g (2–3 oz) pecan nuts, chopped

Follow the recipe and method of the vanilla ice-cream using half the sugar quantity. This will allow the sweetness of the maple syrup to work without becoming over-rich. Once the vanilla base is made and cooled, add the maple syrup and begin to churn the ice-cream. The pecan nuts should only be added to the mix during the last few minutes of churning. If they are added too early, the nuts will break down and also discolour the cream.

Marmalade Ice-cream

This ice-cream is rich, tasty and wonderful! It goes really well with Steamed Orange Sponge (see p.158) or Steamed Chocolate Sponge (see p.160). It's best to buy a good quality coarse marmalade to give a strong orange taste.

SERVES 6–8

1 quantity Vanilla Ice-cream (see p.190),   1 × 350 g (12 oz) jar coarse marmalade
made without the vanilla pod

Follow the recipe for vanilla ice-cream. Stir the boiled cream and milk into the egg yolks and sugar, then add the marmalade and then continue to follow the method.

There's always time for a cup of tea.

Rice Pudding Ice-cream with Raspberry Jam Sauce

I love baked rice pudding. It was one of my favourites at home with the lovely skin on top. Creamed rice pudding is also one of my favourites, especially with raspberry jam spooned on top. Well, I thought I would come up with the opposite. Rice pudding ice-cream with warm jam sauce. It works really well and when you tell your guests they've got rice pudding and jam sauce, this will definitely surprise them. This ice-cream also works very well in a Rice Pudding Arctic Roll with Raspberry Coulis (see p.205). Remember, you can always substitute the fresh vanilla base for a tin of custard to make the recipe quicker.

SERVES 4–8

For the Rice Pudding

600 ml (1 pint) milk
15 g (½ oz) unsalted butter

40 g (1½ oz) caster sugar
50 g (2 oz) short-grain pudding rice

For the Ice-cream

600 ml (1 pint) Vanilla Ice-cream (see p.190), made with a pinch of freshly

grated nutmeg and without the vanilla pod or vanilla essence

For the Raspberry Jam Sauce

175 g (6 oz) raspberry jam

2–3 tablespoons water

Bring the milk, butter and sugar to the boil. Add the rice and bring to the simmer. Simmer and cook gently, stirring frequently, until the rice is over-cooked; this will take about 25–30 minutes. The rice has to be close to breaking/purée point to prevent it from becoming crunchy when made into ice-cream.

Once the rice pudding has cooled, mix with the vanilla base and churn in the ice-cream machine for 15–20 minutes until thickened and increased in volume. The rice pudding ice-cream can now be set in the freezer.

To make the sauce, just warm the jam and water together until they reach a thick sauce consistency. If the jam is still too thick, then add a little more water to correct the consistency. The sauce can also be pushed through a sieve to leave a smooth, clear jam sauce, ready to be poured over the creamy rich ice-cream.

Strawberry or Raspberry Ripple Ice-creams

These are lovely, home-made ripple ices that make a delicious pudding served in a Tuile Biscuit basket (see p.176) with fresh cream or Custard Sauce (see p.215). The ice-cream has a wonderful flavour with the tartness of the raspberry or strawberry to excite your tastebuds. The quantities to follow are two-thirds ice-cream to one-third fruit, so whatever amount you want, if you follow these guidelines it will always work. This ice-cream also works very well in an Arctic Roll (see p.205).

SERVES 4–8

450 ml (15 fl oz) Vanilla Ice-cream (see p.190)

150 ml (5 fl oz) Raspberry or Strawberry Coulis (see p.207)

Make the ice-cream, churn the mixture and place in a freezer container. Spoon the coulis on top and then lightly fold the coulis into the ice-cream. This will give you red streaks through the ice-cream. Set in the freezer.

Toffee Ice-cream

Here's another use for my simple toffee mix (see p.191).

SERVES 4–8

600 ml (1 pint) Vanilla Ice-cream (see p.190)

1 × 400 g (14 oz) tin of toffee (see p.164)

Follow the recipe for vanilla ice-cream, stirring in the toffee once you have made the custard. Turn the mix in an ice-cream machine.

Chocolate and Toffee Bockerglory

This has to be the ultimate in sticky puddings. The combinations are unlimited and that's the beauty of cooking, there's no limits! So rather than give you a strict recipe, I'll just give you some ideas of how it can be put together. It's best to make it in tall glasses or deep bowls.

Remember, to make this dish you don't have to go through the process of making every component. Most, if not all, of these can be found in most food stores, and you can vary the ingredients however you like. So if you want to have a try with no effort involved, use some Jamaican ginger cake diced up and mixed with chocolate or coffee sauce, top with some chocolate and vanilla ice-cream, more sauce and finish with almonds and chocolate.

To make chocolate shavings, take a bar of good, rich dark chocolate and turn it on its side, looking at the width of the bar. From top to bottom scrape along the chocolate with the edge of a palette knife. This will create shavings to sprinkle on top of your desserts.

SERVES as many as you need

Chocolate Fudge Cake (see p.168),
    chocolate sponge or Jamaican ginger
    cake
Pecan Nut Sauce (see p.168)
Chocolate Ice-cream (see p.193)
Toffee Ice-cream (see p.200)
Chocolate Sauce (see p.216)

Double cream, whipped
Flaked almonds, toasted
Chocolate shavings
Sprigs of fresh mint to decorate
Icing sugar for sprinkling
Wafer biscuits to serve

Dice the cake into 1 cm (½ in) pieces and mix them with some of the pecan nut sauce. Spoon the cake into the glasses. Next spoon some chocolate ice-cream on top and follow that with some toffee or vanilla ice-cream. Pour cold chocolate sauce on top. Cover with whipped cream and sprinkle over the toasted almonds and chocolate shavings. This pudding can now be served with a sprig of mint on top, a dusting of icing sugar, a long spoon and a biscuit. How does that sound?

Black Forest Arctic Roll

Black Forest gâteau is still a popular dessert. The flavours of chocolate, cherries and cream marry well – if the dessert is well made! With this dish I've taken all those flavours and turned them into a tasty and fun pudding. The sponge can also be used for a chocolate Swiss roll. You'll need a cylinder in which to freeze the ice-cream into shape. I use a piece of plastic piping from a hardware store, about 15 cm (6 in) long by 6 cm (2½ in) diameter. Wrap cling film securely round one end. The whole dish might sound a bit involved, but you can save time by using a ready-made ice-cream and tinned cherries if you like, so have a go!

SERVES 4–6

For the Chocolate Sponge

3 eggs
75 g (3 oz) caster sugar
50 g (2 oz) plain flour

15 g (½ oz) cornflour
25 g (1 oz) cocoa

For the Arctic Roll

175–225 g (6–8 oz) fresh cherries or
   tinned cherries
50 ml (2 fl oz) Stock Syrup (see p.217)
Kirsch (optional)

600 ml (1 pint) Vanilla Ice-cream,
   prepared and churned (see p.190)
3–4 tablespoons black cherry jam

Pre-heat the oven to 180°C/350°F/gas 4 and grease and line a Swiss roll tin.

Whisk the eggs and sugar together until pale and fluffy. Sift together the dry ingredients, then fold into the egg mix a little at a time. Spread the mix evenly in the prepared tin and bake in the pre-heated oven for 10–15 minutes. No colour is needed on this sponge, just set the mix. Allow to cool.

Stone the cherries and sit them in a pan with the syrup and a splash of kirsch, if using. Bring the cherries to the simmer and cook for 1–2 minutes. Leave to cool. Once cooled, mix half the cherries with the vanilla ice-cream. Stand the cylinder up, making sure the base has been well cling filmed. Spoon the ice-cream into the cylinder and set in the freezer.

Sieve the liquid from the remaining cherries and bring the syrup to the boil with the cherry jam. The liquid will now be a lot thicker. Mix the cherries with the syrup.

Turn the chocolate sponge off the tray but leave it still attached to the paper. Brush the sponge with some cherry jam. Remove the cling film from one end of the ice-cream and pour hot water on to the cylinder to loosen and remove the ice-cream. Sit the ice-cream on the sponge and roll until the sponge meets, creating a cylinder and cutting off any excess. Roll the whole thing in cling film and freeze for 30 minutes.

To serve, remove from the freezer and take off the cling film before cutting into portions. Each plate can be garnished with a spoon of cherries in syrup.

Variations

To add an extra garnish for a special occasion, simply shape some whipped cream and scrape a palette knife across some dark or milk chocolate to garnish with rolled pieces. Finish with sprigs of mint and lightly dust with icing sugar.

Black Forest Arctic Roll.

Knickerbockerglory

This Knickerbockerglory can be made by the same method as the Chocolate and Toffee Bockerglory. Instead of using the chocolate sponge, sandwich the Swiss roll sponge (see p.205) with raspberry jam and then cut into dice and place in the bottom of the glass. Spoon in some summer fruits mixed with a Fruit Coulis (see p.207). Next is the ice-cream. I like to use two ice-creams, starting with some Vanilla (see p.190), then adding more fruits before spooning in some Raspberry or Strawberry Ice-cream (see p.200). Finish the bockerglory with some more fruits and then whipped cream, chocolate and mint (see p.147).

It's awesome, good luck!

Soft Fruit Ice-cream

These are quick and easy to make. All you need is a sweet Fruit Purée (see p.207) and some crème fraîche. Crème fraîche is fresh cream that has been treated with a special culture which almost sours the cream and gives it a longer life. It works really well in ice-creams, giving a full flavour. Soft summer fruits, such as strawberries or raspberries (see p.191), work beautifully in this recipe, but there is no need to wait until the soft fruit season to make them. The easy alternative is simply to take a tin of almost any fruit – peaches, pears, blackberries or whatever – and purée them in their own syrup. Add some icing sugar to increase the sweetness, then add 2–3 heaped tablespoons of crème fraîche. Now you have a quick and easy ice-cream, just churn it in the machine and it's ready.

SERVES 4

1 quantity Fruit Purée (see p.207)   2–3 heaped tablespoons crème fraîche
150 ml (5 fl oz) Stock Syrup (see p.217)

Mix all ingredients together and churn in an ice-cream machine for 15–20 minutes until thick. If you don't have a machine, then spoon into a bowl and freeze, stirring every 5–10 minutes until set.

Rice Pudding Arctic Roll

This recipe is a copy of the Black Forest Arctic Roll. Simply make the rice pudding ice-cream and freeze in the plastic cylinder. Then you can create the Arctic roll with the Swiss roll sponge. Strawberry Ripple Ice-cream (see p.200) also works. I'm going to serve it with some Raspberry Coulis (see p.207).

SERVES 4–8

For the Sponge

3 eggs, separated
100 g (4 oz) caster sugar

75 g (3 oz) plain flour
25 g (1 oz) cornflour

For the Arctic Roll

Raspberry jam
Rice Pudding Ice-cream (see p.199)
Raspberry Coulis (see p.207)
Fresh raspberries (optional)

Double cream
1 sprig of fresh mint
Icing sugar, sifted

Pre-heat the oven to 180°/350°F/gas 4 and butter and line a Swiss roll tin.

Whisk the egg yolks and 75 g (3 oz) of sugar together until thick and creamy. Whisk the egg whites with the remaining sugar to a firm meringue. Sift the plain flour and cornflour together, then lightly fold into the egg yolk mix. Carefully fold in the egg white. Spread the mix into the prepared tray and cook in the pre-heated oven for 15–20 minutes. Remove from the oven and allow to cool.

Spread some raspberry jam on to the sponge, keeping the golden brown top for the outside. Remove the ice-cream from the cylinder by running the plastic under hot water for a few seconds. Sit the ice-cream on top of the sponge and roll around, cutting off any excess sponge. Roll in cling film and freeze for at least 30 minutes.

Once frozen, remove the cling film and cut into four portions. Garnish each portion with Raspberry Coulis and fresh raspberries (optional). It's also nice served with thick fresh cream, a sprig of mint and lightly dusted with icing sugar.

Fruit Sorbets

Sorbets are a light and refreshing alternative to ice-cream. They are good to have as a middle course palate cleanser or as a dessert.

You can use any soft fruits you like – strawberries, raspberries, pineapple, mango, melon – and whichever stock syrup you prefer.

SERVES 4–8

225 g (8 oz) fruit   Juice of ½ lemon
150 ml (5 fl oz) Stock Syrup (see p.217)

Simply mix the fruits with the syrup and blitz in a blender, then push through a sieve. You now have a fruit syrup. Add the lemon juice to this to help lift the flavours. Churn in an ice-cream machine for 20 minutes and freeze, or turn into a freezer tray and place in the freezer, stirring and turning every 20–30 minutes until frozen.

Variations

If you want to make an apple or pear sorbet, simply peel, core and chop the fruits, mix with the lemon juice and cook in the stock syrup until softened. Then blitz and push through a sieve and leave to cool before making into sorbet.

Chocolate Sorbet

You're going to love this recipe. It's easy to make, rich in taste and also very refreshing.

SERVES 4

25 g (1 oz) cocoa

450 ml (15 fl oz) water

150 g (5 oz) good quality plain chocolate

150 g (5 oz) caster sugar

Simmer the cocoa in the water for 5 minutes. While simmering, chop the chocolate. Pour the water and cocoa on to the chocolate and sugar and stir in. Once cool, churn in the ice-cream machine until thickened, then freeze.

Fruit Purées or Coulis

Fruit purées, or coulis, are used for many things, particularly bases for sorbets, as sweet sauces and as flavourings in mousses. The French term coulis literally means sieved and this method is used for soft fruits such as strawberries, raspberries and blackcurrants. Because of the sharpness in the flavour, the fruits may need to be mixed with icing sugar. These quantities are good guidelines; you can vary them to suit the tartness of the fruit. They go very well with ice-creams and iced parfaits.

MAKES about 225 g (8 oz)

225 g (8 oz) soft fruit

50 g (2 oz) icing sugar, sifted

A few drops of lemon juice

Blitz the fruit and sugar together in a food processer, then push through a sieve. If the flavour is still too tart, simply add more icing sugar to taste. The consistency will be of a thick sauce which can be thinned down if needed with some Stock Syrup (see p.217), or some more icing sugar blended with a little water. A few drops of lemon will help lift the flavour of the fruit.

Honeycomb

Honeycomb is, of course, the filling in a Crunchie bar. This recipe could be used to make your own, but I like to break the honeycomb into pieces and add it to a chocolate ice-cream just at the end of churning. This gives you a lovely crunchy texture in the ice-cream. It's also nice just broken and sprinkled on top of an ice-cream pudding.

To make honeycomb you need to boil the sugar, so do take care as it reaches very high temperatures. You must always make sure that you have a very clean, large pan for this recipe and also a sugar thermometer will be needed.

SERVES 4–6

2 tablespoons water	50 g (2 oz) golden syrup
225 g (8 oz) demerara sugar	15 g (½ oz) unsalted butter
225 g (8 oz) granulated sugar	1 tablespoon bicarbonate of soda

Pour the water into a saucepan, add the sugars, golden syrup and butter. Bring the mix to the boil and continue to cook to a small crack temperature. This is 138–140°C/280–284°F. The sugar mix will have a rich golden colour. Add the bicarbonate of soda; this will lift the sugar and create a light airy texture. Pour the honeycomb mix into a greased 23 × 28 cm (9 × 11 in) tray and allow to set. Once cooled and set the honeycomb is ready and can be kept in an airtight container.

Lemon Curd

Lemon curd eats very well just on toast or teacakes. I like to use it for Lemon Curd Ice-cream (see p.197) or as a sauce for steamed sponges.

This recipe is very rich with a high butter content. If you prefer, you can cut the butter down to 100 g (4 oz) and also cut down by 1 egg yolk. The lemon curd will still work without being over-rich and will have a slightly more fluid consistency. There are two alternative methods.

MAKES about 675 g (1½ lb)

225 g (8 oz) caster sugar
225 g (8 oz) unsalted butter

Finely grated zest and juice of 3 lemons
5 egg yolks

For method 1, sit the sugar, butter, lemon juice and zest in a bowl and stir over a pan of simmering water. Once the butter has melted, beat vigorously until well combined. Beat in the egg yolks and continue to cook and stir for 15–20 minutes until the curd has thickened. Pour into a clean jar and cover with waxed paper or cling film. Once cooled, seal tightly and keep in the fridge. This should keep for at least two weeks.

For method 2, whisk the sugar and egg yolks together until light and creamy. Melt the butter with the lemon zest and juice and add to the mix. Cook, stirring, in a bowl over a pan of simmering water until thickened; this will also take about 15–20 minutes.

Lemon Jelly

This is a simple home-made jelly. The lemon jelly goes very well with ice-cream. I like to serve either the Vanilla (see p.190), Lemon Curd (see p.197) or Crème Fraîche Ice-cream (see p.196) with it. This is really a good, fun dessert to offer your guests at a dinner party – jelly and ice-cream!

The recipe also works well if the lemons are replaced or mixed with limes for a different flavour.

SERVES 4

600 ml (1 pint) water
275 g (10 oz) caster sugar

Finely grated zest and juice of 5 lemons
7–8 leaves of gelatine

Warm and dissolve the sugar in the water on the stove with the lemon juice and zest. Keep on the heat for 2–3 minutes. Remove from the stove. Soak the gelatine leaves in cold water until they become soft and jelly-like. Remove the gelatine and squeeze out any excess water. Stir the gelatine into the warm, sweet lemon water until dissolved. The sweet jelly water can now be left to cool, stirring occasionally. Once cooled, the jelly can be poured into a presentation bowl and left to set in the fridge.

Home-made Blackberry Jam

In this recipe there are two alternatives for the quantity of sugar, but both work by the same method. The difference is quite simple. If equal amounts of sugar and fruit are used, more syrup is made from the sugar. Also, by using a preserving sugar containing pectin, the jam is guaranteed to set. By using half the sugar content, less syrup is made and so consequently a thicker more 'jammy' texture and not quite as sweet taste is the result. I prefer to make the jam with half of the sugar content to achieve a stronger natural taste of the fruits, although jam made in this way will only last for a maximum of two weeks.

This is a basic recipe which can be applied to most soft fruits such as raspberries, strawberries and cherries. However, sharp, firmer fruits, such as blackcurrants, will require more sugar to balance the acidity.

These berries obviously have seeds so if you prefer to make jam without them, simply strain through a sieve once.

If you intend to eat the jam within a week or two, simply allow the jam to cool, place in warmed jam jars, leave to cool, then chill. The sugar and pectin are both natural preservatives so the jam will keep perfectly fresh.

If you want to store the jams for longer, you'll need to sterilize them. Sterilize the jars first by covering them with cold water in a large pan, then bringing the water to the boil. Leave to boil for 10–15 minutes, then remove and dry. The glass should be warm before adding the hot jam to prevent the jar from shattering. Once the jars are filled, covered and sealed, you can sterilize them further by sitting the jars on a wire rack or cloth in a large pan and almost covering with water. Bring the water to the boil, then repeat the process. Store the jam in a cool, dark place, or chill it; it will last almost indefinitely.

MAKES about 900 g (2 lb)

900 g (2 lb) blackberries   Juice of 1 lemon
450 g (1 lb) or 900 g (2 lb) sugar with
    pectin

Carefully rinse the blackberries, making sure you do not damage the fruits. Warm the sugar in a large, heavy-based pan over a low heat; this will take 1–2 minutes. Add the fruits and the sugar will begin to dissolve. Once some liquid is forming, turn up the heat and bring to the boil, stirring gently. Stir in the lemon juice. As the mix is heating, some froth and impurities will begin to rise to the top. This froth should be skimmed off. Once boiling rapidly, continue to cook for about 6–7 minutes. The jam should have reached the temperature of 105°C/220°F. With the pectin in the sugar this will be at setting point. If you don't have a sugar thermometer, simply sit a spoonful of mix on a saucer and set in the fridge. Once cold and touched, the jam should have a jellied, wrinkled texture and is now ready to pour into the jars and cover with waxed paper. Allow to cool before closing the lids. The jam should be kept in a dark, cool place or chilled for extra life.

Shortcrust and Sweet Crust Pastry

This recipe really is short! In ingredients and in texture.

This quantity is really the minimum amount to make for a good texture. The beauty of this pastry is that it freezes so well to be used later.

MAKES about 400 g (14 oz)

175 g (6 oz) unsalted butter, chopped   4 tablespoons cold water
240 g (8½ oz) plain flour

Rub the butter into the flour until a crumble effect is achieved. Add the water and fold in very lightly until the pastry is only just beginning to form and bind. Press the pastry between two sheets of cling film. The pastry will have a marbled look; this indicates just how short the pastry is going to be.

Variations

This pastry works very well with the Fillet of Mackerel with Caramelized Onions and Sweet Peppers (see p.26) or as a savoury or sweet flan base. To make sweet pastry, simply add 50 g (2 oz) of sifted icing sugar to the flour.

Puff Pastry

This recipe is useful for all kinds of desserts and for savoury pies as well. It's very satisfying to make your own pastry, but you can resort to the chill cabinet of your supermarket if you are short of time.

MAKES about 450 g (1 lb)

225 g (8 oz) unsalted butter
225 g (8 oz) strong plain flour
A pinch of salt

150 ml (5 fl oz) cold water
A few drops of lemon juice

Cut off 50 g (2 oz) of the butter, melt it then leave it to cool. The remaining block should be left out to soften. Sift the flour and salt together into a large bowl and make a well in the centre. Pour the water, lemon juice and cooled, melted butter into the well in the flour and gently fold in the flour to make a pliable dough. Wrap in cling film and allow to rest in the fridge for 20 minutes.

On a lightly floured board, roll out the pastry from four sides, leaving a lump in the centre. The dough should look like a crossroads. The remaining block of butter should have softened to a similar texture to the dough; it should be easy to roll without melting but not so hard that it will break the pastry.

Sit the butter on the centre lump of the dough (A) and fold over each pastry flap (B). Pat the pastry into a 30 × 15 cm (12 × 6 in) rectangle and leave to rest in the fridge for 10–15 minutes.

A   B   C   60 cm (24 in)   D   E

15 cm (6 in)

Roll out the pastry lengthways to make it double in length to about 60 cm (24 in) but the same width (C). Fold in both ends to the centre (D) and then fold once more (E). This is called a double turn and should be completed a further three times, each time rolling out the same length and then finishing with a double turn. Always roll with the folded edge on the left, and always leave to rest for 20–30 minutes in the fridge before each turn. The pastry should now be rested for at least 30 minutes in the fridge before using.

This puff pastry is perfect for the savoury tarts (see p.120). To make the pastry cases, butter and flour your chosen moulds: 25 cm (10 in) ring or six 10 cm (4 in) rings. Roll the pastry out thinly and line the moulds, leaving any excess turned over the sides of the rings. Sit the cases on a baking sheet and rest in the fridge for 10–15 minutes. Line with greaseproof paper and baking beans or rice. Bake in a pre-heated oven at 200°C/400°F/gas 6 for 15–20 minutes until the pastry is baked and golden. Remove the paper and beans, then use a sharp knife to trim off any excess pastry around the tart cases, leaving the cases in the pastry rings.

Almond Paste or Frangipane

This almond paste is the recipe which is used to make Bakewell Tart, that old favourite nursery pudding. The mixture freezes well, or you can make it in smaller amounts, just maintaining the same proportions.

SERVES 4–8

225 g (8 oz) unsalted butter, cold
225 g (8 oz) caster sugar
175 g (6 oz) ground almonds

50 g (2 oz) plain flour
4 eggs

Cream together the butter and sugar until almost white. Mix together the ground almonds and flour. Add one egg at a time to the butter and sugar mixture, sprinkling a handful of ground almonds and flour at the same time. This helps the butter and sugar cream to accept the eggs. Once all the eggs have been added, just continue to fold in the remaining almond and flour mixture.

Cook as directed in the recipes.

Banana and Toffee Cream Pancakes

Here's a great alternative for Shrove Tuesday! Of course, the pancakes can also be used in many other puddings, especially when served with ice-creams. How does warm pancakes with vanilla ice-cream and hot jam sauce sound?

SERVES 4–6

4 bananas
1 quantity Toffee Cream (see p.165)
Maple syrup (optional)

Icing sugar, sifted
A few sprigs of fresh mint

For the Pancakes

100 g (4 oz) plain flour
A pinch of salt
1 egg

300 ml (10 fl oz) milk
25 g (1 oz) unsalted butter, melted
Vegetable oil

Sift the flour and salt together. Beat the egg into the milk and whisk into the flour. Add the melted butter. The pancake mix is now ready. Pre-heat a 25 cm (10 in) pancake pan and trickle some vegetable oil into the pan, making sure the oil has very lightly covered the pan. Add a thin layer of pancake mix to the pan. Cook for 15–20 seconds until golden, then flip over and cook for a further 10–15 seconds on the other side. The pancake is now ready. Repeat the same process until all the mix is finished.

Peel the bananas and cut diagonally into thick slices. Sit the pancake on the plate and fold in half, keeping the semi-circular side facing you. Overlap the banana slices on one quarter of the pancake and spoon some toffee cream on top. Fold the other half of pancake over the cream, leaving a triangular-shaped pudding on the plate. Sprinkle with maple syrup, if using, and dust icing sugar around the plate. Garnish with a sprig of mint.

Variations

Try dusting the sliced bananas with icing sugar and glazing them under the grill until the sugar has caramelized, then use them in the pancakes.

Anglaise (Fresh Custard) Sauces

This recipe is for a fresh custard or anglaise sauce, which can act as a base for so many different flavours. You must only ever serve it warm, not boiled, as this will scramble the egg yolks in the cream mix. The fresh vanilla is optional and can be omitted when using other flavours. To have the flavour of vanilla always at hand, keep a vanilla pod in your jar of caster sugar; the aroma from the pod will impregnate the sugar.

MAKES 750 ml (1¼ pints)

8 egg yolks
75 g (3 oz) caster sugar
1 vanilla pod, split (optional)

300 ml (10 fl oz) milk
300 ml (10 fl oz) double cream

Beat the egg yolks and sugar together in a bowl until well blended. Split and scrape the insides of the vanilla pod, if using, into the milk and cream and bring to the boil. Sit the bowl over a pan of hot water and whisk the cream into the egg mix. As the egg yolks warm, the cream will thicken to create a custard. Keep stirring until it coats the back of a spoon. Remove the bowl from the heat. The custard can now be served warm or stirred occasionally until it cools. Serve warm or cold.

Variations

For Lemon Custard Sauce, add the pared rind of 2 lemons, not the pith, to the milk and cream when heating, then leave it in the mix throughout the cooking process. Once the custard has thickened, add the juice of one lemon and taste. If the lemon flavour is not strong enough, simply add more lemon juice to taste. Strain the custard through a sieve.

For Orange Custard Sauce, add the pared rind of 2 oranges to the milk and cream when heating, then cook as for the basic recipe. Orange juice will not be used in this recipe. To lift the flavour of the sauce, try adding a few drops of Cointreau or Grand Marnier.

For Rum Custard Sauce, add some rum to taste at the end of cooking the vanilla custard. This goes very well with Pineapple Fritters (see p.148). Desiccated coconut could also be added to this recipe during the cooking process and/or coconut milk added at the end.

Coffee Custard Sauce can be made by replacing the vanilla pod with 2 teaspoons of good fresh ground coffee and cook as for the vanilla base recipe. Once the coffee custard has completely cooled just strain through a sieve to remove any excess granules.

Chocolate Sauce

This chocolate sauce is lovely and rich in flavour and texture. It eats really well either hot or cold and goes with so many different puddings. Chocolate must be very carefully treated. If overheated, the chocolate will become split and grainy. Not every commercial chocolate works in cooking, but I have always found Bournville to be quite a safe bet.

SERVES 4–8

200 g (7 oz) good quality plain chocolate, finely chopped
25 g (1 oz) unsalted butter, chilled and diced

150 ml (5 fl oz) milk
2 tablespoons double cream
25 g (1 oz) caster sugar

Mix together the chocolate and butter. Boil the milk, cream and sugar and pour on to the chocolate mix. Stir the mixture until completely melted, but do not allow it to re-boil. The chocolate sauce is now ready. Serve warm or cold – the cooler the temperature, the thicker the sauce.

Stock Syrups

These syrups have many uses. They are a great base for sorbets, for poaching, and for steeping fruits. Any spirits or liqueurs can be added; even teabags or fresh tea can be added for sorbets or ice-creams. I'm going to give two recipes. The first is very basic and the second is almost a dish on its own and packed with flavour. Both keep almost indefinitely if chilled. The fruit stock syrup is good to use in a fresh fruit salad and can also have mint added to take on another flavour.

For Simple Stock Syrup

600 ml (1 pint) water

350 g (12 oz) caster sugar

For Fruit Stock Syrup

600 ml (1 pint) water

350 g (12 oz) caster sugar

Pared zest and juice of 2 lemons

Pared zest and juice of 2 oranges

½ cinnamon stick

1 vanilla pod

Whichever syrup you are making, bring all the ingredients to the simmer, stirring to dissolve the sugar, then remove from the heat and allow to cool and infuse.

If you prefer a thicker, sweeter syrup, add an extra 100 g (4 oz) of caster sugar. If you are making the fruit stock syrup, it's best to leave the syrup with all ingredients included until needed, and then just drain off.

Stocks, Sauces and Basic Recipes

T his chapter will give you all the basics you need for your stock and sauce making – plus a little more. Making stocks is a time-consuming occupation, but the results are worth every minute. A good stock can have the clarity of a consommé and when reduced, the shine will get even deeper and the taste even better.

ABOVE *Preparing Salsa Dressing (see p.243).*
LEFT *A selection of ingredients needed to make the dressings.*

If you don't have time to make your own stocks, I've included some alternatives that are available from most supermarkets – all of them have been tried and tested.

There are also some extras here that I picked up on my travels around Britain, such as the Irish Soda Bread.

In this section I have included some miscellaneous dishes. These are recipes that don't really need to be mixed with any particular dish in the rest of the book but are really good to eat so I decided to include them. There's the home-made Worcestershire sauce, lovely sprinkled on a steak or used to lift a sauce, Bone Marrow Dumplings, a great addition to any stew or soup, and my favourite Peanut Sauce, which reminds me of when I lived in Amsterdam years ago and was always eating chicken saté sticks with a hot peanut sauce to dip them in. The flavour is hot and spicy, so at your next barbecue have a go!

Fish Stock

To make a good fish stock, you'll need a friendly fishmonger. Turbot and sole bones produce the best stock, giving a good, full taste and clear jelly-like finish. The stock is good for poaching fish and for making fish soups and sauces. (For information on ready-made alternatives, see p.226).

MAKES about 2 litres (3½ pints)

1 large onion, sliced
1 leek, sliced
2 celery sticks, sliced
50 g (2 oz) unsalted butter
A few fresh parsley stalks

1 bay leaf
6 black peppercorns
900 g (2 lb) turbot or sole bones, washed
300 ml (10 fl oz) dry white wine
2.25 litres (4 pints) water

Sweat the vegetables in the butter without colouring. Add the parsley stalks, bay leaf and peppercorns. Chop the fish bones, making sure there are no blood clots left on them. Add them to the vegetables and continue to cook for a few minutes. Add the wine and boil to reduce until almost dry. Add the water and bring to a simmer. Allow to simmer for 20 minutes, then strain through a sieve. The stock is now ready to use, or to store for a few days in the fridge.

Chicken Stock

Chicken stock is one of our most important bases. It's used for most soups and many cream sauces. It's also very simple to make. I'm sure your local butcher will help you out with some chicken bones. If not, then cook a boiling fowl with vegetables in water and you will have a tasty stock and the bird to eat as well. You'll need a large stock pot, about 8.5 litre (15 pint) capacity, but if you don't have one you can easily reduce the quantities. (For information on ready-made alternatives see p.226).

MAKES 2.25 litres (4 pints)

2 onions, chopped
2 celery sticks, chopped
2 leeks, chopped
25 g (1 oz) unsalted butter
1 garlic clove, crushed

1 bay leaf
1 sprig of fresh thyme
A few black peppercorns
1.8 kg (4 lb) chicken carcasses, chopped
3.4 litres (6 pints) water

In a large stock pot, lightly soften the vegetables in the butter without colouring. Add the garlic, bay leaf, thyme, peppercorns and chopped carcasses. Cover with the cold water and bring to the simmer, skimming all the time. Allow the stock to simmer for 2–3 hours. Strain through a sieve. The stock is now ready to use and will keep well chilled or frozen.

Vegetable Stock

A very similar recipe for vegetable stock is included in the original Rhodes Around Britain *book. This recipe gives a different result. I have increased the quantity of carrots to give a sweeter taste to the stock. It can also be cooked to various stages leaving it at almost full capacity for risottos or vegetable stews, or reducing while cooking for butter sauces.*

MAKES about 900 ml (1½ pints)

350 g (12 oz) carrots
4 celery sticks
1 large onion
1 leek
25 g (1 oz) unsalted butter

1 bay leaf
1 sprig of fresh thyme
1.2 litres (2 pints) water
Salt and freshly ground black pepper

Roughly chop all the vegetables into 1 cm (½ in) dice. Melt the butter in a pan and add the vegetables. Cook on a low heat with the bay leaf and thyme for 10–12 minutes until softening. Add the water and bring to the simmer. Continue to simmer for about 20–30 minutes until the stock has reduced to about 900 ml (1½ pints). Strain through a sieve. The stock is now ready to use or can be stored for a few days in the fridge.

Veal or Beef Stock or *Jus*

This stock is a base to a lot of cooking, and really holds the essence of a good dish. Reading this recipe may well make you want to think twice about it, but it is worth making and so satisfying once made. It will give you great sauces and, of course, will store well in your freezer, so go on – have a go! It is best started in the morning which will allow the stock to cook throughout the day. Ask your butcher for a few beef or veal trimmings to make the stock.

If this really is too much, then a lot of good gravy bases can be found but do use them carefully, not making them too thick and strong. (For information on ready-made alternatives see p.226).

MAKES about 5 litres (9 pints) stock or 900 ml (1½ pints) *jus*

3 onions, halved
2-3 tablespoons water
2.25 kg (5 lb) veal or beef bones
225 g (8 oz) veal or beef trimmings
225 g (8 oz) carrots, coarsely chopped
3 celery sticks, coarsely chopped

1 leek, chopped
3-4 tomatoes, chopped
1 garlic clove, halved
1 bay leaf
1 sprig of fresh thyme

Pre-heat the oven to 110°C/225°F/gas ½.

Lay the onion halves flat in a roasting tray with the water. Place in the very cool oven and allow to caramelize slowly until they have totally softened and coloured. This process will take 1–2 hours. The sugars in the onions will slowly cook and give a wonderful taste. Put the onions on one side.

Increase the oven temperature to 200°C/400°F/gas 6. Place all the bones and trimmings in a roasting tray and roast for about 30 minutes until well coloured. Roast the chopped carrots and celery in another roasting tray for about 20 minutes until lightly coloured.

When ready, add the bones, trimmings and vegetables to the onions in the pot along with the leeks, tomatoes, garlic, bay leaf and thyme. Fill the pot with cold water – you'll need about 5 litres (9 pints). Bring the stock to the simmer and skim off any impurities. Allow to cook for 6–8 hours, and with this you will achieve the maximum taste.

When ready, drain and discard the bones and vegetables. This is now your veal stock and you can cool it and freeze it in convenient quantities.

Alternatively, you can make a *jus* from the stock. Allow the liquid to boil and reduce down to about 900 ml (1½ pints), skimming occasionally. The stock should be thick and of a sauce consistency. Make sure that you taste all the time during reduction. If the sauce tastes right but is not thick enough, thicken it lightly with cornflour mixed in water. (Of course, I do hope that won't be necessary!) You now have a veal *jus*, a classic sauce.

Onion Gravy

Serve this classic gravy to accompany sauces or liver dishes.

SERVES 4

8 onions, thinly sliced
2 tablespoons water

600 ml (1 pint) Veal *Jus* (see p.224) or bought alternative (see p.226)

Place the onions in a pan with the water and cook very slowly, stirring all the time. The sugar from the onions will slowly caramelize and become dark golden brown and sweet-tasting. The process will take about 2 hours. Add the veal *jus* and simmer for a further 30 minutes. The gravy will be even richer in taste and colour with a lovely, shiny finish.

Alternative Stocks and Sauces

Making fresh stocks at home is not always possible, so I've been out doing some homework on stocks and sauces in search of some good commercial alternatives to make the cooking of some of my dishes a little easier.

Fish and Chicken Stocks

Alternatives to these can be found in the chill cabinet of most Sainsbury's and other quality supermarkets. They are sold in plastic tubs each containing about 284 ml (about 9-10 fl oz). The beauty of these is they taste great, they have good colour and jelly texture, and they are sold as stocks ready to use. They really are the best I've found, but if you can't get hold of them there are also some good quality stock cubes.

Beef and Veal *Jus*

In the basic recipe, these start out as stocks and then for use in other recipes they are reduced to a sauce consistency. I've found a sauce which will cut out all of this, and is an instant *jus* to use as a base sauce in many of the recipes asking for veal or beef *jus*. Madeira Wine Gravy or White Wine Gravy are both made by Crosse & Blackwell in their Bonne Cuisine range, and should be available in just about every supermarket or good grocery shop. The Madeira flavour gives it good body and, when made, it has a lovely glossy finish. My only advice is to mix it with 600 ml (1 pint) of water instead of 300 ml (10 fl oz). This way, when slow-braising or stewing, there's room for reduction and it won't become too thick.

Other Sauces and Ingredients

Another sauce which I found very good is in the same range as the Madeira Wine Gravy: the hollandaise sauce. If you are unsure about making hollandaise, give this bought version a try; it's so easy.

There's only one other small suggestion. If you don't have any chillies, use the chilli sauce made by Maggi. It's sold in bottles and can be added slowly to taste.

As for dried pastas and ready-made pastry, all varieties can easily be found in local shops. If you're lucky enough to have a good delicatessen nearby, then perhaps buy your pasta there; it's often made on the premises.

I hope these few suggestions will help. It's always good to have a go at making your own stocks, sauces, jus *and pasta, but cooking has to be practical and for regular use the products mentioned above will help tremendously. I certainly think they will make life for you an awful lot easier.*

Tasting is an essential part of preparing any dish.

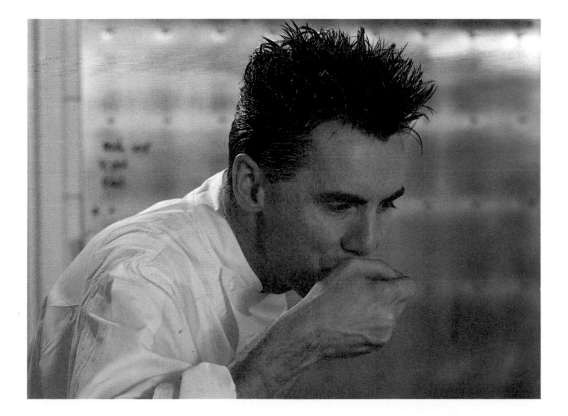

Vegetable Butter Sauce

This is a simple sauce which is easiest to make if you have an electric hand blender.

SERVES 4

150 ml (5 fl oz) reduced Vegetable Stock (see p.223)

50–75 g (2–3 oz) unsalted butter at room temperature

Salt and freshly ground white pepper

Pour the vegetable stock into a small pan and add 50 g (2 oz) of the butter. Bring to the simmer, whisking all the time. Season with salt and pepper. Whisk vigorously or use the hand blender and you should have a light creamy consistency. If the sauce seems a little too thin, then simply add the remaining butter and blend once more. The sauce is now ready.

Lemon Butter Sauce

This is one of the simplest possible sauces which has a silky texture and just enough to complement cod and salmon dishes in particular.

SERVES 4–6

225 g (8 oz) unsalted butter

Juice of 1 lemon

50 ml (2 fl oz) Chicken Stock (see p.222) or Vegetable Stock (see p.223)

Salt and freshly ground white pepper

Chop the butter into 1 cm (½ in) pieces and put it into a pan with the lemon juice and stock. Bring to a simmer, whisking all the time. Do not allow the sauce to boil or the butter will separate. If it is too thick, add more stock. If you like a sharper taste, add more lemon juice. Season with salt and pepper and serve immediately. To give a creamier texture, simply blitz the sauce with an electric hand blender.

Fennel Butter Sauce

This is a good sauce for fish. The aniseed flavour of fennel is helped by the addition of star anise in the cooking liquor. To increase the flavour for a fish dish, use some Fish Stock (see p.221) in the reduction for the sauce. However, you'll find that fennel creates a good stock and when reduced by three-quarters should be strong enough on its own.

Serves 4

2 fennel bulbs
900 ml (1½ pints) water
Juice of 1 lemon

1–2 star anise
Salt
50–75 g (2–3 oz) unsalted butter

Trim the root and top stalks from the fennel. Place in boiling water with the lemon juice, star anise and a pinch of salt. Return to the boil, cover the fennel with a butter paper or greaseproof and simmer until tender; this will take about 20–30 minutes. When ready, a sharp knife will just be able to reach the centre of the bulb.

Remove the fennel bulbs, then boil and reduce the cooking liquor down to about 150–300 ml (5–10 fl oz) to give a good, strong taste. Dice the fennel into 5 mm (¼ in) pieces. The liquor can now be finished with the butter, just whisking it in to create a fennel butter sauce. Remove the star anise. Blitz the sauce with a hand blender to give a more creamy texture. Add the fennel and warm through. Check and adjust the seasoning.

Variations

Chopped chives, tarragon or mint could be added to this sauce at the last minute to give it another flavour.

Red Wine Sauce

This sauce tastes good with almost any meat – chicken, beef, pork, veal – and even eats well with baked fish.

MAKES about 1.2 litres (2 pints)

4 shallots, chopped	225 g (8 oz) beef skirt or beef trimmings
1 large carrot, chopped	(optional)
2 celery sticks, chopped	1 tablespoon olive oil (optional)
25 g (1 oz) unsalted butter	1 bottle red wine
1 garlic clove, crushed	1.2 litres (2 pints) Veal *Jus* (see p.224) or
1 bay leaf	bought alternative (see p.226)
1 sprig of fresh thyme	Salt and freshly ground white pepper

In a large pan, cook the chopped vegetables in a little butter with the garlic and herbs, allowing them to colour. In a frying-pan, fry the meat, if used, in the oil, colouring on all sides, then add the meat to the vegetables. Pour the red wine into the frying-pan to release any flavours from the trimmings. Scrape and stir, then pour the wine on to the meat and vegetables and boil to reduce until almost dry.

Add the veal *jus* and bring to the simmer, skim off any impurities, then simmer the sauce gently for 30 minutes. Pass through a sieve, squeezing all the juices from the vegetables and meat. Check for seasoning and you now have a rich, glistening red wine sauce.

Quick Red Wine Sauce

At work I always make fresh stocks, gravies and sauces, but when you're at home it's not often or ever possible. But there is always an alternative. Whenever making packet sauces it's best to add half again or even double the quantity of water given in the recipe to give a better consistency. Bonne Cuisine Madeira Wine Gravy is a good one to use. To make the sauce even simpler, you can leave out the shallots, bay leaf and peppercorns.

MAKES about 1.2 litres (2 pints)

600 ml (1 pint) red wine
2 shallots, sliced
1 bay leaf

A few black peppercorns
1 packet instant gravy made up with
900 ml (1½ pints) water

To make this red wine sauce, bring the wine to the boil with the shallots, bay leaf and peppercorns, then boil until reduced by three-quarters, leaving about 150 ml (5 fl oz) of strong red wine. Add the gravy and cook for a few minutes. Strain before serving.

Tomato Coulis

This is a very useful basic for all sorts of recipes.

MAKES about 900 ml (1½ pints)

1 large onion, chopped
2 celery sticks, chopped
1 large carrot, chopped
1 garlic clove, crushed
A few fresh basil or tarragon leaves or a
  pinch of dried tarragon
1 sprig of fresh thyme or a pinch of
  dried thyme
2 tablespoons olive oil

50 g (2 oz) unsalted butter
150 ml (5 fl oz) dry white wine
450 g (1 lb) tomatoes, chopped
300 ml (10 fl oz) Chicken Stock (see
  p.222) or Vegetable Stock (see p.223)
1 tablespoon tomato purée
Salt and freshly ground white pepper
A few drops of Spicing Essence (see
  p.233) (optional)

Cook the chopped onion, celery and carrot with the garlic and herbs in the olive oil and butter for a few minutes until softened. Add the white wine and boil to reduce until almost dry. Add the tomatoes and cook for a few minutes, then add the stock and tomato purée, bring to the simmer, cover with a lid and continue to cook for 20 minutes. Liquidize the sauce, then push it through a sieve to give a smooth sauce consistency. If the sauce is a little thick, add more stock to reach the right consistency. Season to taste with salt and pepper. The coulis is now ready. To make the sauce more spicy, add a few drops of spicing essence at a time, if using, whisking and tasting until you have the flavour you want.

Variations

You can also use this recipe to make a red pepper coulis. Just replace 350 g (12 oz) of the tomatoes with an equal weight of seeded red peppers, then follow the same procedure.

Spicing Essence

I think this little trick comes from Escoffier's days; it is often used for spicing up a sauce or other dish. It was also occasionally used to mask the flavours of a meat that wasn't quite right! Well, I'm glad to say that I use it purely for enhancing flavours, and it works its magic particularly with Tomato Coulis (see p.232).

MAKES about 150 ml (5 fl oz)

50 g (2 oz) demerara sugar | 150 ml (5 fl oz) malt vinegar

Simply dissolve the sugar in the vinegar, then boil for a few minutes until reduced to a syrup. It is now ready to use, and only a few drops are needed to spice your sauces. After that, it can be kept in an airtight jar in the fridge for as long as you like.

Tomato Dressing or Sauce

This tomato dressing can also be a thick fresh tomato sauce. When tomatoes are cooking, they create a lot of excess water. This sauce is cooked until almost all the water has evaporated, leaving you with almost a fresh tomato purée. To make the sauce into a dressing, loosen with Basic Vinaigrette (see p.241) or olive oil to taste.

SERVES 4

15 g (½ oz) unsalted butter
1 tablespoon olive oil
½ onion, finely chopped
1 small garlic clove, crushed
1 glass white wine

450 g (1 lb) ripe tomatoes, skinned and
    seeded
1 teaspoon tomato purée
Salt and freshly ground black pepper

Melt the butter with the olive oil in a warm pan until the butter begins to bubble. Add the onion and garlic and cook for a few minutes until the onions have softened. Pour the white wine over the onions and bring to the boil. Continue to boil until the wine has reduced and is almost dry.

While this is reducing, chop the tomatoes to a coarse pulp. Add the tomatoes and tomato purée to the pan and bring to the simmer. While the tomatoes are cooking, a lot of water will be created, so allow this to evaporate. Season with salt and pepper and the sauce is ready.

Spicy Tomato Sauce

This sauce goes so well with seafood of all types. It's almost like eating a loose, spicy tomato chutney. Once made, it can be kept chilled for up to two weeks.

MAKES about 450 g (1 lb)

85 ml (3 fl oz) olive oil
3 shallots or 2 onions, finely chopped
2 garlic cloves, crushed
A few fresh basil, thyme and tarragon leaves
900 g (2 lb) tomatoes, skinned and seeded

2 tablespoons red wine vinegar
1 teaspoon caster sugar
Salt
2–3 drops of Tabasco sauce

Warm the olive oil in a pan and add the chopped shallots or onions, the garlic and herbs. It's best to have the herbs in sprigs as these can then be easily removed at the end of cooking. Allow the shallots and herbs to cook gently for 4–5 minutes until tender.

Cut the tomato flesh into 5 mm (¼ in) dice and add to the shallots. Have the pan on a very low heat, just on a light simmer, and cook for about 45 minutes. The sauce may cook a little quicker or take a little longer – this will really depend on the water content of the tomatoes. After 45 minutes, add the wine vinegar and sugar and cook for a further 15 minutes. The tomatoes should have taken on an almost lumpy sauce texture; if the sauce is very thick, simply fold in a little more olive oil. Allow to cool until just warm, then season with salt and Tabasco.

Pesto Sauce

Pesto sauce can be bought in most supermarkets and food stores, but here is a simple version to make yourself. No Parmesan will be needed for this sauce.

SERVES 4

50 g (2 oz) pinenuts
150 ml (5 fl oz) olive oil
1 small garlic clove

1 large bunch of basil
Salt and freshly ground black pepper

Simply colour the nuts lightly in the olive oil, then allow to cool. Add the crushed garlic clove, basil, a pinch of salt and pepper and blend to a purée. This is now ready and can be kept for 2–3 days in the fridge.

Hollandaise Sauce

This is a quick way of making a French classic.

MAKES about 250 ml (8 fl oz)

225 g (8 oz) unsalted butter
2 egg yolks
1 tablespoon warm water

Juice of ½ lemon
Salt and cayenne pepper or freshly
  ground white pepper

Melt the butter in a pan, then leave it to cool slightly so that it is just warm when added to the sauce; if it is too hot, the sauce will curdle. The butter will have separated, so you will only be adding the butter oil to the sauce. This is clarified butter.

Add the egg yolks to the water in a bowl and whisk over a pan of hot water until cooked and thickened. Remove from the heat and add the clarified butter, whisking until the sauce is thick. Add the lemon juice and season with salt and cayenne or white pepper.

Worcestershire Sauce

I enjoy finding, trying and hopefully developing recipes like this. I looked through a lot of old cookery books to find this so that I could have a go at matching the famous bottle we all know and use. Well, it's not quite the same, and you can't really match that distinctive taste, but it's fun and interesting to make, especially when you have to wait a few weeks for the result!

The Worcestershire sauce recipe must be 160 years old. The recipe was found and given to the makers in India. They soon discovered how popular the sauce was and I don't think they ever looked back.

MAKES 900 ml (1½ pints)

600 ml (1 pint) malt vinegar	A pinch of cayenne
150 ml (5 fl oz) walnut or mushroom ketchup	A pinch of ground cinnamon
	1 garlic clove, crushed
2 tablespoons anchovy essence	A pinch of freshly grated nutmeg
2 shallots or 1 onion, finely chopped	A pinch of ground cardamom
3 tablespoons soy sauce	A pinch of salt

There are a few ways of putting this recipe together.

The first is simply to mix all the ingredients and keep in an airtight bottle or container for 2–3 weeks, making sure the bottle is shaken every day.

Another way is to mix all the liquid ingredients with the onion and garlic, bring to the boil and simmer for 30 minutes before adding the spices and salt. Bottle and cool, make airtight and keep for two weeks, shaking every day.

The mix can also be made without the herbs, just mixing the liquids and onion. This will still need to be left and shaken every day for 2–3 weeks.

After the marinating period, strain the sauce before use.

Peanut Sauce

This is the sauce that you find in Thai restaurants served with chicken or pork satay. It's a good sauce to go with barbecued chicken pieces or wings, such as my recipe on page 51. You can follow the recipe with lemon and paprika, marinate simply in lime juice, or just plain grill the chicken. You can lift the flavours in the peanut sauce with a dash of lime juice, too.

SERVES 4

225 g (8 oz) crunchy peanut butter
3 garlic cloves, crushed
15 fresh coriander leaves
50 ml (2 fl oz) soy sauce

2 tablespoons Japanese sake
¼–½ teaspoon chilli oil
120 ml (4 fl oz) coconut milk
Water

In a food processor, blend the peanut butter with the garlic and coriander. In a separate jug, mix the soy sauce, sake, chilli oil and coconut milk. With the motor running, pour the mixture slowly into the processor until all the liquid has blended in. The sauce should be thick but not set like peanut butter. If the sauce is too thick, just loosen it by adding a tablespoon of water at a time. The sauce can be served warmed or kept chilled for 2–3 days.

Cranberry *Jus* or Gravy

The flavour of this sauce can be helped by taking a good handful of vegetable mirepoix *(roughly chopped carrots, shallots or onions, celery and leeks) and cooking them with 2 bay leaves and a sprig of fresh thyme for a few minutes before adding the red wine. The sauce will then need to be sieved before adding the cranberry sauce.*

SERVES 4–8

2 glasses red wine
600 ml (1 pint) Veal *Jus* (see p.224) or
   alternative (see p.226)

2 large tablespoons Cranberry Sauce
   (see p.239)

Boil the red wine until reduced by two-thirds. Add the veal *jus* or alternative and bring the sauce to the simmer. Add the cranberry sauce and continue to simmer gently for 10–15 minutes. Stir in the cranberry sauce until well blended.

Variations

To make a quick cranberry-flavoured sauce just take 600 ml (1 pint) of *jus* alternative (see p.226) and add 2 tablespoons of bought or home-made cranberry jelly. More can be added to adjust the taste to your liking.

Cranberry Sauce with Orange

The obvious main ingredient here is, of course, the cranberries. Cranberry sauce can be made with just cranberries, sugar and a little water, but I replace the water with orange juice, and spice it with a little port; a combination that has become a classic. I also like to add a little chopped shallot to help the savoury taste of the dish.

This sauce eats very well with roast turkey, pork or game and with any of the bubble and squeak variations. It's also good to serve with cold meats and pies.

SERVES 4

450 g (1 lb) fresh cranberries
100 g (4 oz) caster sugar
Juice of 2 large oranges

½ teaspoon very finely chopped shallots
1 glass of port

Simply place all the ingredients in a pan and bring to a simmer. Cook gently for 10–15 minutes until the cranberries are just beginning to break.

Vinegars and Oils

Malt vinegar is probably the best known, especially for sprinkling on your fish and chips! Malt vinegar is made from malted barley (as, of course, is whisky!), and gets its colour from caramel. The strongest of vinegars, it is used mostly for pickling, and I've often used it in chutney recipes where it helps to achieve the right acidity for the ingredients. Don't use it in basic dressings as its strength is just too much for salads.

Red and white wine vinegars are the ones to use for most general dressings and purposes. Red wine vinegar is the best. Wine vinegars are allowed to mature slowly in barrels until the vinegars have turned the alcohol into acetic acid. They can be made more swiftly by heating, but this tends to destroy some of the flavours.

Balsamic vinegar must be the most-used vinegar in modern cookery, which doesn't surprise me as it really is astounding. There are many cheap copies on the market which aren't worth buying. Real balsamic vinegar is made from Trebbiano grapes and should be a minimum of five years old to have any true flavour. The older it gets, the better and stronger it tastes but, of course, the more expensive it is to buy. Twelve-year-old balsamic is a great medium and although it's pricey, you need very little because of its immense flavour. Some balsamics can be as old as forty years, but this is very rare and you'll probably have to wait another forty years to try one!

Oils

The oils that I generally use are extra-virgin olive oil and ground-nut (peanut) oil.

*Ground-nut is a very basic oil which is used in France (*huile à l'arachide*) as a base in most dressings and in frying. It's very similar to sunflower oil and has quite a bland flavour. In basic dressings I mix it with olive oil, which prevents the dressing from becoming too overpowering. It is also cheaper to make and works well on all simple salads.*

Virgin olive oil is an oil from the first pressing which is totally pure, without any heating or chemical processing. The 'extra' in front applies to its low acidity grade. Extra-virgin oil has 1 per cent acidity, which is the lowest and the best.

Basic Vinaigrette

This basic recipe is very convenient. Once made, it can sit in your fridge and be used at any time and for any dish you might fancy. The vinegar just gives a very slight sweetness to the taste.

MAKES 600 ml (1 pint)

300 ml (10 fl oz) extra-virgin olive oil
(French or Italian)
300 ml (10 fl oz) ground-nut oil
25 ml (1 fl oz) balsamic vinegar
1 bunch of fresh basil
½ bunch of fresh tarragon

3–4 sprigs of fresh thyme
12 black peppercorns, lightly crushed
3 shallots, finely chopped
2 garlic cloves, crushed
1 bay leaf
1 teaspoon coarse sea salt

Warm the olive and ground-nut oils together. Place all the remaining ingredients into a 750 ml (1¼ pint) bottle. Pour the oil into the bottle and close with a cork or screw top. For the best results, leave to marinate for a week, which will allow the flavours to enhance the oils. To help the dressing along, shake the bottle once a day. Taste for seasoning before use.

Red Wine Vinaigrette

This is a basic recipe to which you can add your favourite herbs. The best to use, unchopped, are basil, tarragon or thyme. When you are going to use the dressing just add some chopped fresh chives, basil, thyme or tarragon to finish the dressing.

MAKES about 600 ml (1 pint)

4 shallots or 1 large onion, finely
    chopped
2 garlic cloves, crushed
300 ml (10 fl oz) red wine

300 ml (10 fl oz) red wine vinegar
2 teaspoons Dijon mustard
600 ml (1 pint) olive oil
Salt and freshly ground black pepper

Mix the shallots or onion with the garlic in a pan and add the red wine. Bring to the boil, then boil to reduce until almost dry. Add the red wine vinegar and boil to reduce by three-quarters. Remove the pan from the heat.

While the shallots are still warm, add the Dijon mustard and blend in with the olive oil. Season with salt and pepper. The dressing can now be left to cool and then bottled. Chilled, it keeps for several weeks.

Mayonnaise

Home-made mayonnaise is so much tastier than bought mayonnaise. Use it with potatoes in a salad, or as a dressing for sandwiches.

MAKES about 600 ml (1 pint)

3 egg yolks
1 tablespoon malt, white wine or
    balsamic vinegar
A pinch of English or Dijon mustard

Salt and freshly ground white pepper
300 ml (10 fl oz) olive oil
1 teaspoon hot water
A few drops of lemon juice (optional)

Whisk the egg yolks, vinegar, mustard and seasonings together, then slowly add the olive oil, whisking continuously. When all the oil has been added, finish with the hot water and correct the seasoning. A few drops of lemon juice can be added to enhance the taste.

Vierge Dressing

This dressing has a very different flavour and lends itself best to fish dishes. I was first inspired to make it whilst staying at La Côte St Jacques in Joigny, France, in the mid 1980s when it was served with a red mullet dish. That restaurant now has three Michelin stars.

MAKES 600 ml (1 pint)

600 ml (1 pint) extra-virgin olive oil
(French or Italian)
15 g (½ oz) coriander seeds, crushed
1 bunch of fresh tarragon

12 black peppercorns, crushed
4 shallots, chopped
2 garlic cloves, crushed
A pinch of sea salt

Warm the olive oil with the coriander seeds. Place the remaining ingredients in a 600 ml (1 pint) screw-top jar and pour the oil and coriander on top. Screw on the lid and leave to marinate for 1 week, shaking the bottle daily.

Salsa Dressing

Salsa is a Mexican relish that has so many variations. It's really a fresh sweet and sour chutney, come sauce, come dressing. Another ingredient is chillies, so not only is it sweet and sour but hot, too! This recipe goes well with hot or cold fish, meats, chicken or you can even use it as a relish for a hamburger. The most classic version is Salsa Verde, a green chutney with garlic, parsley, mint, mustard, capers, green chillies, oil and vinegar. There are also red salsas and fruit salsas and more, but this we'll just call 'Salsa Dressing'!

SERVES 4

2 red onions, finely chopped
2 green peppers, seeded and diced
2 green chillies, seeded and finely diced
1 garlic clove, finely chopped
1 tablespoon olive oil

Juice of 1–2 limes
8 plum or salad tomatoes, skinned,
seeded and diced
Salt

Mix together the diced red onions, green peppers, chillies and garlic. Add the olive oil and the juice of 1 lime. Add the tomato flesh and stir in well to slightly break down the tomato flesh. Adjust the seasoning with a good pinch of salt.

The salsa should have a good balance of flavours. More lime juice maybe needed to lift the other tastes. The salsa is now ready and can be kept in the fridge for a few days.

Cucumber Pickle

This pickle goes very well with salads. It can be served with pork pies, corned beef or just with cold meats. But I like to serve it with fish, in particular salmon. We've all heard of smoked salmon and cucumber sandwiches, a classic combination. This pickle eats very well with simple poached salmon, but I particularly like it with Seared Peppered Salmon (p.32).

Serves 4

4 cucumbers, peeled and de-seeded
1½ teaspoons salt
150 ml (5 fl oz) ground-nut oil
1 teaspoon chilli oil
1 large garlic clove, crushed

1 fresh red chilli, finely chopped
2 tablespoons soy sauce
25 g (1 oz) caster sugar
2 tablespoons white wine vinegar
½ bunch of spring onions, thinly sliced

Grate the cucumbers on a basic cheese grater. Mix the salt with the cucumber, place in a colander and allow to drain for 20 minutes. This will take out any excess water.

Warm the ground-nut and chilli oils with the crushed garlic and finely chopped red chilli for a few minutes. Add the soy sauce, sugar and white wine vinegar and bring to the simmer. Lightly dry off the cucumber. Mix the spring onions with the cucumber, then add the mixture to the simmering oil and increase the heat, stirring for 30 seconds. Remove from the heat and tip the pickle on to a deep tray or into a large cold saucepan to cool as quickly as possible. Place in an airtight jar.

Bone Marrow Dumplings

These dumplings can be eaten as a savoury dish and go particularly well with pan-fried diced bacon, button onions and button mushrooms in a red wine sauce. They are used mostly as an accompaniment in beef stews and casseroles but I also use them with a grilled steak in red wine sauce. Just one good dumpling a portion is enough, and the beauty of using this recipe is that it keeps for three or four days if chilled. So if you want to lift just a simple, ordinary steak then have a go at this recipe.

SERVES 4

100 g (4 oz) fresh bone marrow
100 g (4 oz) white breadcrumbs
2 tablespoons double cream
3–4 egg yolks
1 heaped tablespoon chopped fresh
    parsley

A pinch of freshly grated nutmeg
Salt and freshly ground black pepper
Chicken Stock (see p.222) or water

Break the bone marrow down in a food processor, then add the breadcrumbs. Add the cream and 3 yolks with the chopped parsley. Add the remaining yolk if necessary to make a stiff mixture. Season with nutmeg, salt and pepper and chill for 1 hour before cooking to help set the mix.

Bring a pan of stock or water to the boil. The mix can be either shaped into ovals between 2 tablespoons or simply rolled into balls and dropped into simmering stock. The dumplings should be ready in 10–15 minutes. You can then add them to a stew or braised dish.

Variations

Try using other herbs instead of the parsley; thyme or sage taste particularly good.

Soda Bread

This is a recipe I tried in Ireland – another easy recipe with great results. The first time I ate soda bread, it was filled with bacon and fried egg with a big mug of tea for breakfast – it was lovely. So if you want to have a go at making your own bread for your next 'full Irish/English', follow this recipe.

If you can find traditional Irish self-raising soda bread flour, all you need to add is the salt and buttermilk, but this recipe will work just as well.

Serves 4

350 g (12 oz) plain flour
1 level tablespoon bicarbonate of soda

A good pinch of salt
300 ml (10 fl oz) buttermilk

Pre-heat the oven to 190°C/375°F/gas 5.

Sift the flour, bicarbonate of soda and salt together and make a well in the centre. Pour in the buttermilk and mix gently to form a dough. Knead until smooth without overworking. Lightly dust the work surface with flour and roll out the dough to a circle about 2 cm (¾ in) thick. Cut the circle into quarters. Place on a baking sheet and bake in the pre-heated oven for 30–40 minutes until golden brown and hollow-sounding when tapped.

To cool and keep crispy, stand the bread on a wire rack. If you prefer a softer bread, wrap in a cloth to cool.

Variations

You can cook the bread on a griddle or frying-pan. Heat the pan over a moderate heat. To test the temperature, sprinkle a little flour on the pan; it should turn slightly off-white. Sit the bread into the pan and cook for 12–15 minutes on each side.

Soda Bread.

Beremeal Bannocks

Another recipe from my Scottish friend, this traditionally uses beremeal, which is an ancient northern barley. If you can't get hold of it, use oatmeal or wholemeal flour. I had a go at making these while staying in Scotland. They are easy and fun to make and eat superbly.

SERVES 4–6

100 g (4 oz) plain flour
1 teaspoon salt
2 heaped teaspoons bicarbonate of soda
1 heaped teaspoon cream of tartar

350 g (12 oz) beremeal or oatmeal
50 g (2 oz) unsalted butter
300–600 ml (½–1 pint) buttermilk

Sift the flour with the salt, bicarbonate of soda and cream of tartar. Add the beremeal or oatmeal. Rub in the butter, then gradually add the buttermilk, mixing to form a soft dough. You may not need all the buttermilk; it will depend on the meal you are using.

Warm a frying-pan or griddle. Shape the mix with a rolling pin or push and shape it by hand into a circle 3 cm (1¼ in) deep; or you might find it easier to shape it into smaller loaves. Cook the bannocks directly on the griddle or in the pan over a medium heat for 2–3 minutes each side. Serve at once.

Pasta Dough

This pasta dough can be used for lasagne, fettucine, ravioli and many more pasta dishes. You can make it by hand or in a food processor. It also freezes very well.

MAKES 450 g (1 lb) to SERVE 4

250 g (9 oz) fine semolina or plain flour   2 eggs
A pinch of salt   3 egg yolks
½ teaspoon olive oil

Mix the semolina or flour with the salt and olive oil and mix well for 1 minute. Add the eggs and egg yolks and stir well until it becomes a dough. Knead the dough for 1–3 minutes until it has a smooth texture. Wrap it in cling film and chill for 30 minutes to rest.

The pasta is now ready to use. It can be rolled, cut and cooked straight away, or cut and left to dry and used later. If dried, the pasta will always take a little longer to cook.

More Ideas

I hope this book has given you lots of ideas and alternatives to a range of quite basic recipes. I could probably go on and on throwing ideas at you, hoping that you'll all have a go at at least one, but I have to stop somewhere. Just before I finish, though, I've got a few more for you to have a look at and think about.

Potted Salmon (see p.24) can quite easily be changed to potted shrimps. Just cook the butter with the shallots and herbs, then remove from the heat and add peeled shrimps or prawns and spoon into the moulds.

Banana Ice-cream (see p.192) can be really lifted by adding 2 tablespoons of natural yoghurt and 3 tablespoons of toffee (page 164). A brilliant ice-cream.

The crispy shrimp used in a skate dish (see p.76) can be used in a warm salad with lots of crunchy shrimps sprinkled over the top.

The lager batter (see p.72) can be used to deep-fry almost anything: vegetables, meat balls, sausage, fish.

Try a good Barnsley lamb chop (double chop) grilled with Hollandaise Sauce (see p.235) flavoured with chopped mint and served with home-made crisps (see p.22).

Calves' liver, cut into 2.5 cm (1 in) slices, can be grilled to medium, then sliced and served with Champ (see p.134) or Dijon Mustard Mashed Potatoes (see p.91).

All the herbs I use in the book are fresh. If you can't get them, then use dried herbs tied in muslin cloth or buy the tea-bag bouquet garni.

The potatoes used in the cod dish (see p.68) can be turned into a complete starter. Just mix them with slices of red and green peppers lightly cooked in olive oil with garlic, basil, tarragon and tomatoes. Sit a warm poached egg on top of each portion and your starter is ready.

Another good duck breast dish is to score and grill the breast, keeping the skin crispy, and serve it with home-made chips and a maltaise sauce. This is Hollandaise Sauce (see p.235) with a reduced blood orange juice. Straight orange juice can be used, reducing down until very strong. Add it to the hollandaise and you have an orange sauce. Serve this with the duck breast and you have a modern canard à l'orange.

Parsnips are so versatile. Once you've tried them roasted or puréed, try frying cooked parsnips in batter, like the beetroot on page 138

Here's one of my favourite alternatives. If you're making one of the risottos and have some left over, spread it into a dish or tray 2.5 cm (1 in) deep and allow it to set in the fridge. Once set, the risotto can be cut out with round pastry cutters (like fish cakes) or rolled into balls and dusted with flour. There are now several ways of cooking them:

shallow-fry in butter until golden brown;

roll in egg and breadcrumbs and deep-fry until golden;

dip in savoury pancake mix and shallow-fry until golden on both sides.

Any of these methods will give you golden risotto cakes with creamy risotto inside. These eat well as a separate starter, with a fish or meat main course or even small ones made as canapés.

A good alternative for the Mushroom Risotto (see p.57) is to turn it into a breakfast risotto. Crispy pieces of bacon can be added or sprinkled over the black pudding and then a poached or fried egg placed on top.

Here's an extra idea for the duck breast dish on page 86: just replace the parsnip with neeps and tatties.

So that's it, I've had to stop. My whole feeling about cooking is never to be afraid of any dish or ingredient. If you believe in it, then try it.

Until the next time ...

Index

Page numbers in *italic* refer to the illustrations